The Quick Reference Guide *to the* Catholic Bible

Mary Ann Getty-Sullivan

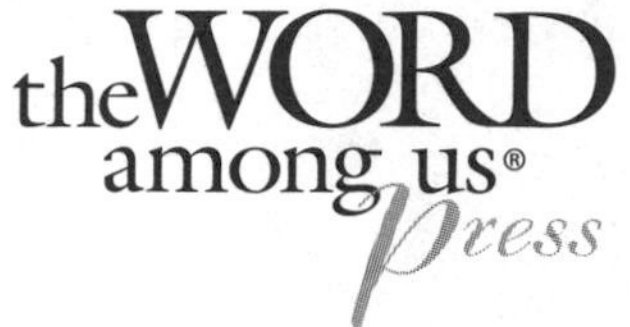

Published by The Word Among Us Press
7115 Guilford Road
Frederick, Maryland 21704
www.wau.org

18 17 16 15 14 1 2 3 4 5

ISBN: 978-1-59325-258-8
eISBN: 978-1-59325-459-9

Cover design by Koechel Peterson & Associates

Made and printed in the United States of America

Library of Congress Control Number: 2014937405

Contents

Introduction to the Bible

When Philip asked the Ethiopian if he understood the Scriptures he was reading, the Ethiopian replied with this question: "How can I, unless someone guides me?" (Acts 8:31). At one time or another, we have all looked to guides to help us, whether we are planning a trip, visiting a site, or delving into some new project. The inspiration behind this guide to reading the Bible comes from the common human experience of building on what we already know to gain new insight and wisdom for living. We rely on the collective wisdom of many authorities—scholars, teachers, researchers, pastors—to help us understand a little more about the Bible. This guide attempts to make some of that learning accessible to all.

For something so familiar as the Bible, there are many oddities connected with reading it. It is not your ordinary best seller. One doesn't necessarily read it from start to finish. There is the matter of translation. There are various books in the Bible rather than just chapters of one book. And the sequence is not necessarily logical or historical. The very binding of these particular books as one and the order in which the books appear are a matter not only of discussion but of dispute. When it comes to the Bible, we know that there are literally thousands of years that can either separate us from our sources or unite us as believers in the endeavor of understanding our common spiritual heritage.

The Bible: One though Many

The word "bible" means "book," but it can also mean "library" or "a collection of books." Actually, there are two collections of books in the Christian Bible, an Old Testament and a New Testament. The Old Testament consists of books recognized by Jews and Christians as God's revelation. The New Testament was written by followers of Jesus who believed that he was the long-awaited Messiah. The term "testament" means "covenant," and the Bible is understood by believers as an expression of God's covenant with them.

The Scriptures contain *revelation*: they reveal God to us and also show us more about ourselves. The Scriptures were inspired by and given to us by God rather than being a product of our imagination. Whereas some civilizations (the Greeks, for example) sought wisdom in nature and concluded that the probability of the existence of a higher power was very strong, the Jews (and later Christians) were less impressed with the possibility of demonstrating or "proving" the existence of God as a logical human conclusion. Rather, for Jews, God is unknowable to us unless he reveals himself to us. For Christians, God is seen and known through the revelation of God's Son, Jesus, the Incarnate Word. Believers would agree with the Greeks that human beings seek truth, unity, and beauty. Believers assert that these are not found as a result of human effort, however, but are given as gifts to us from God through the Son and the Spirit.

The Uniqueness of the Bible

It has been said that the Scriptures record God's love affair with the world. The Bible is an unfolding story that continues as we attempt to grasp its meaning in our lives and share our lives with others. But the Bible is not just any story—for believers, the Bible has special qualities that distinguish it from all other literature. Three of these qualities are *inspiration, inerrancy,* and *canonicity.*

Inspiration in this context means that God is the source of the Bible's authority. This quality is supported by a verse from 2 Timothy: "All scripture is inspired by God" (3:16). The implications of this assertion are continually being clarified by scholars and other authorities. But a basic tenet of "inspiration" is that the Scriptures have unique authority in the church and are reliable as a guide for righteousness and salvation for its members.

Closely linked to inspiration is the quality of *inerrancy.* The Bible contains no errors with respect to the purpose for which the various writings were intended. Skeptics enjoy pointing out that errors of science and of history can, in fact, be found in the Bible. One of the most famous examples is that Joshua is said to have prayed for the sun to "stand still" as if it circled around the earth; he wanted daylight to be extended so that a battle could be won that same day (Joshua 10:12-13). There are anachronisms and unfinished sentences in the Bible. Sometimes there are two versions of the same story, called "doublets." Such idiosyncrasies have led some people to challenge the church's traditional teaching on the Bible's inerrancy. But the church has insisted that the meaning of inerrancy is restricted to the purpose for which the Bible was intended. Inerrancy means that the Scriptures are reliable as a guide for salvation for all who believe.

The Bible is also *canonical*; that is, its books are part of a "canon," or standard, for believers. The term "canon" originally meant a "reed," but it came to mean a standard of measurement, like a yardstick or measuring tape. In other words, these particular books that are identified as inspired and inerrant also qualify as a standard for faith and, at the same time, are part of a larger whole. The term "canon" also refers to the list of books contained in the Bible. Taken together, each book is part of the "canon" of faith and is reliable as a measuring stick of the faith of the church and its members. For example, murder is wrong. Even though there are examples of war and killing and violence in the Bible, the impact of sayings such as "Love your neighbor as yourself" (Leviticus 19:18; Matthew 5:43; 19:19; 22:39; Mark 12:31; Romans 13:9; Galatians 5:14; James 2:8), "Do to others as you would have them do to you" (Matthew 7:12; Luke 6:31), and other precepts of Jesus' Sermon on the Mount (Matthew 5–7) is overwhelming. No one can really justify bad behavior on the basis of individual passages in the Bible but must take the whole canon of the Scriptures into consideration in order to understand them as a measure of righteousness and as a means of salvation.

Choosing a Translation

Even the simple question of choosing a translation of the Bible to read and study can be a daunting task, especially today with so many options. At the time of the Protestant Reformation, the question of making copies of the Bible available to common people was not only debated but sometimes cause for fierce persecution. Some worried that the Bible could be dangerous if people were left to their own devices of imagination or opinion. And opinions, starting with what the "correct" translation of the Bible into the vernacular is, differ greatly. It is good to remember too that every word of a translation is a matter of choice, a decision on the part of the translators about the best way to convey the meaning of the original Hebrew or Greek. Even the tone and punctuation are a matter of an educated choice in many instances. Also, some translations are quite literal, while others try to capture the symbolic sense of the text and produce a translation that is more fluid and poetic to the contemporary ear while still attempting to remain true to the original.

This is not really a new problem. Most of the Old Testament books were written in Hebrew. But after Alexander the Great (356–323 BC), Greek became the universal language, and many Jews did not even speak—much less read—Hebrew fluently. Approximately two hundred years before Jesus, the Old Testament Scriptures were translated from Hebrew to Greek, a translation that came to be known as the Septuagint. Despite reluctance among Jews who feared that this translation would lack the authority of the Hebrew, the Septuagint (LXX) came to be more popular than the Hebrew text. The Christian writers of the New Testament, in most cases, seem to have used the LXX when they referred to the Jewish Scriptures.

How the Bible Was Written

The Bible was composed over a period of about two thousand years, containing stories from the time of Abraham and Sarah to around the end of the first century AD. Many people or groups of people contributed to it. With respect to the Old Testament books, there was a long period of oral tradition when stories of the creation of the world, the patriarchs and the exodus, the judges, and the first kings were handed down through families, clans, and tribes for generations. People did not recount these events in a detached, objective way but interpreted them through the prism of their strong faith that the God of Israel was the creator, the Lord of history, the judge of human hearts, and the initiator of the covenant that defined and motivated Israel. Similarly, in the time of Christ and immediately afterward, it seems not to have occurred to eyewitnesses to write accounts of Jesus' life and death in order to leave behind an objective, factual record. Rather, it was only with the second generation of Christians—believers like Paul and Mark who had probably never even met the earthly Jesus and were more interested in preaching than in history—that the books of the New Testament began to take shape. History and faith combined to form the Scriptures, just as they both contribute today to determining their meaning for us.

After hundreds of years of oral tradition, around the time of David stories of the patriarchs and kings began to be written down. But still, the form of our Scriptures underwent many more years of shaping and editing. Historical events, such as the division of the empire into North and South and the fifty-year exile of Israelites in Babylon, prompted prophets and other sages of Israel to compose works glorifying the foundation of Israel's greatness—the covenants, the temple, and the unity of the people were all rooted in faith in Yahweh. The writing and editing process for the Old Testament books took about eight hundred years. A similar phenomenon, but covering a much shorter time span, happened as the New Testament began to be written. Paul, for example, the first Christian author, wrote letters mostly dating from the fifties AD that focused more on the meaning of the death of Jesus than on events that had happened in Jesus' life or on the things that Jesus had said twenty years earlier, in the thirties. It wasn't until Mark's writing in the sixties that the Gospel as narrative theology came to be a form of Christian literature. Some of the New Testament works were written only very late in the first century or early in the second century AD.

Before reaching the form of the Bible that we read today, most, if not all, of the books underwent much editing. Some of this process extended over many years, and many hands were involved. For example, the Torah, or Law, is attributed to Moses. But most scholars agree that the five books of the Pentateuch only began to be written down almost four hundred years *after* Moses. And the material in Genesis about the patriarchs extends back some five hundred years or so *before* Moses. Furthermore, since we hear of Moses' death and burial in the final chapters of Deuteronomy, how could he have written it? Actually, there seems to have been a long period of oral tradition that preceded the first attempts to consolidate stories, laws, legends, and poems into the epic story of God's covenant with Israel and to write it down. Scholars have identified many levels of editing in the books of the Torah, beginning during the time of David and continuing until after the Babylonian Exile. In like manner, many of the other books of the Bible were composed of contributions of many people over many years until they took on their final form.

The Canonical Process

The books of the Bible were not the only compositions about the people, places, and events of the times; other works were written and used by believers. Eventually Jews and, later, Christians would come to identify certain works as sacred. Jews arranged these into three groups, referred to with the acronym *Tanak* or TNK for the first letter of their names in Hebrew: *Torah* (the Law); *Nevi'im* (the prophets); and *Ketubim* (the writings). It was not until near the end of the first century AD that the Jews recognized the need to establish the canon of the Scriptures.

The order as well as the number of books in the Catholic Old Testament differs from that established in the Jewish canon. In the Catholic Old Testament, the writings are inserted between the Law and the prophets. The number of Books included in the canon was affected by subdividing some works that originated as a single scroll. The Books of Samuel, Kings and Chronicles are examples of this. The Catholic Old Testament canon also includes some books not found in the Jewish Scriptures. The disputed books were generally later works, written just a few hundred years before Christ, mostly in Greek, the universal language of the time. They appeared in the Septuagint, the Greek translation of the Jewish Scriptures. There are seven books included in the Catholic canon of the Old Testament that do not appear in the Jewish or Protestant Scriptures: Tobit, Judith, 1 and 2 Maccabees, Wisdom, Sirach, and Baruch. The Catholic canon of the Old Testament also includes additional passages for the Books of Daniel and Esther. These disputed works are called "deuterocanonical" by Catholics and "apocryphal" (in the sense of noncanonical) by Protestants.

At the time of the Reformation, Catholics determined that the Vulgate, that is, St. Jerome's Latin translation of the Catholic Scriptures, was the authoritative translation. The Vulgate was based on the Septuagint. Protestants, on the other hand, used the Hebrew canon as the basis for translations of the Bible into the vernacular, that is, the common language of the people of a particular region. One of the oldest translations into English is the famous King James Version (translated in AD 1611), a very literal (word-for-word) translation and the literary ancestor of many of the Protestant Bibles in use today in the English-speaking world.

The canon of the New Testament Scriptures is the same for Catholics and Protestants. Although there were other gospels and letters written under the names of the apostles and other early Christian leaders, some of these had fallen into disuse by the end of the second century. The canon of the New Testament was "fixed" or "closed" by about the fourth century but was only officially defined by the Council of Trent in the sixteenth century. Trent focused on three criteria in particular for establishing the Catholic canon:

1. *Apostolic origin*. The work, such as a Gospel or letter, was thought to have originated in the age of the apostles and attributed to them, even if it was actually written down later by a disciple or group of disciples.
2. *The rule of faith*. The work must be judged to be consistent with the teachings of Jesus and his disciples so that believers could rely on it as a standard of faith.
3. *The consensus of the church*. The work was cited and referred to in patristic writings (e.g., Origen and Eusebius) as an indication that it was recognized for its authority and was well-known and circulated in the early church.

How We Interpret the Bible as Catholics

For Catholics, the Bible is one of the most important factors in forming our individual and collective consciences. The Bible is a significant part of the basis for the church's instruction on issues of faith and morals. Catholics, especially since Vatican II, have eagerly pursued biblical study as an avenue to ecumenism as part of our common heritage with other people of faith and as a guide to the ways in which we can contribute to bettering our world. The Bible informs our celebration of the sacraments. The Scriptures shape our liturgy, our prayer as a community, and teach us to pray as people of faith. The Bible contributes to the foundation of our preaching, our positions on social issues, our educational projects, and our entire ministry. Catholics have long been known for their respect for authority, especially to the Tradition of the church. Catholics interpret the Scriptures in the light of this Tradition. We therefore recognize the role of the community of faith in forming and shaping our individual interpretation of the Scriptures. But this dimension does not at all take away from our responsibility as committed Christians to learn as much as we can about the Scriptures, to allow it to form our own critical thinking, and to grow in praying the Scriptures and living out the implications of its message in our lives.

Great Themes of the Bible

Although there are seventy-three books in the Bible, certain themes unify the Scriptures. It is difficult to reduce these themes to only a few, but we will try to identify some of the most important ones.

- **There is one God who is the Creator and Redeemer,** who is both transcendent (almighty, omnipotent, all-knowing) and immanent (personal, caring, accessible to all who have faith). The history of the covenants reveals to us a God who wills a relationship with human beings and who is faithful even when people are not. Jesus came as a human being to teach us the ways of God. All of the previous means of coming to know God pale in comparison to the Incarnate Word of God, Jesus Christ.

- **Human life is blessed by the Creator with dignity and authority.** All creation is good and is intended by God for the good of humankind. Since life is sacred, human beings partner with God in the responsibility to respect, preserve, and maintain not only physical life but the life of the spirit as well.

- **Human beings are sinful and require God's grace** to live well, to do good, to help others, and to help better the world. The story of creation reveals order in God's design for the world. Human beings sinned and disrupted this God-ordained order, and all creation has been harmed by their disobedience. Theologians later called this "original sin." The story of the covenants reveals a humanity that repeatedly sins and a God who faithfully comes to their rescue. The Bible illustrates time and again that when people turn back to God, they are forgiven and restored. God showers humanity with gifts; in return, we are called to offer our prayers of adoration, petition, repentance, and thanksgiving as expressions of our faith, our trust, our gratitude, and our reliance on God.

- **God is the Lord of history** who invites us to everlasting life. Most of the stories in the Bible have a historical basis, but our interest in them goes far beyond simple curiosity about the past. Stories such as the exodus function as a paradigm illustrating our personal spiritual journey to God and life with God forever. Elements of this paradigm include slavery, liberation, and celebration. The Bible teaches us that just as God loves us into being, God rescues us from sin, forgives us, reconciles us to himself, and restores us to new life. The Bible uses multiple terms for God's mercy and grace, speaking of our "redemption," our "justification," and our "salvation." Time and again we are shown that God comes to our aid, healing us and restoring us to wholeness, thus enabling us to become the creation we were meant to be.

- **We are called as individuals and as a community** to life in this world and after death. The Bible urges us to be filled with faith, hope, and love. We see in the lives of the holy men and women whose stories are recorded in the books of the Bible our calling to share our own experience, strength, and hope with others and to encourage ourselves and others on the journey to God, which we believe gives meaning to human life. And we believe that, above all, this life on earth is more than it seems—it is only the beginning of life. We are called to the fullness of life we can find only in God.

The Challenge to Study the Bible

The Second Vatican Council's *Verbum Dei* (Declaration on Revelation), published toward the end of the council in 1965, challenges Catholics to immerse themselves in the Scriptures and to discover as much as they possibly can about how the Scriptures came to be and all that is involved in understanding them. As you read this guide, for example, you will realize how important it is to have at least some understanding of what was going on in the world when Israel decided that she wanted to become a monarchy or when Judah was taken into slavery and exile in Babylon. The historical context helps us understand what issues the biblical historians or the prophets were addressing. Similarly, the literary context is very important. Just as it is imperative to know whether you are reading a novel or a history book, so it is essential to have the basic understanding of what kind of literature a certain book of the Bible is—whether it is poetry, such as in the Book of Psalms, or collected wisdom, as is found in the Book of Proverbs, or the beginnings of Christian preaching about Jesus, which we find in Paul's letters or in the Gospel of Mark. We are very fortunate today to have so much help in interpreting the Bible. Since the early nineteenth century, biblical scholarship has advanced our understanding of the literary and historical background of the biblical books, and these findings have been made accessible to all readers through many tools for study, such as commentaries, biblical theology introductions, monographs dealing with specific topics, and so forth. Additionally, Bible study groups, both big and small, ongoing and seasonal, have proliferated and are invitations to Catholics to grow in their knowledge of Scripture and their faith.

A Brief Timeline of Biblical Events

- **Prehistory:** The collective memory of the people prior to Abraham's call is expressed in the stories found in Genesis 1–11, having been passed down as part of Israel's collective memory through centuries by oral tradition until they were written down in the period of the monarchy and later edited.

- **The Time of the Patriarchs (ca. 2000–1800 BC):** The call of Abraham (see Genesis 12) marks the historical beginning of Israel's history. The stories of Abraham and Sarah, Isaac and Rebecca, Jacob and Rachel, and Joseph form the foundation of the covenant story found in Genesis 12–50.

- **Moses, the Exodus, and the Law (ca. 1300 BC):** God's people were enslaved in Egypt until Moses was called to lead them to freedom. The people wandered in the desert for forty years and finally arrived at Jericho; their entrance into the land had been promised to Abraham as part of their inheritance due to the covenant. This is the story found in Exodus, Leviticus, Numbers, and Deuteronomy.

- **The Tribal Confederacy (ca. 1260–1060 BC):** Joshua led the people into the land previously occupied by their ancestors from the time of Abraham. As the people settled in, they organized themselves by tribe and were governed by judges and priests. Stories of this period are found in books such as Joshua, Judges, Ruth, Tobit, and Judith.

- **The United Monarchy (1060–922 BC):** This was a short but very creative period that witnessed the ordination of just three kings: Saul, David, and Solomon. It is ambiguous as to whether the kings were successful, and the biblical writers reflected the divine reluctance to allow the people to have the monarchy they wanted so that they could be a nation "like other nations" (1 Samuel 8:20). The prophets assumed a very important role in interpreting God's will for the people; as times and circumstances changed, the people needed help to understand how the Law applied in new situations. Under David's leadership, the epic story of Israel began to be written down. The biblical books that reflect this period include 1 and 2 Samuel, 1 Kings, Psalms, Proverbs, and the Wisdom of Solomon, although these last three works were actually centuries in the making.

- **The Divided Kingdom: Israel (921–722 BC) and Judah (921–587 BC):** After the death of Solomon, the kingdom was divided (around 921 BC) into Israel to the north, with its capital in Samaria, and Judah to the south, with its capital in Jerusalem. The Northern Kingdom of Israel fell to the armies of Assyria in 722. Books reflecting life in Israel during these times include 2 Kings, Amos, and Hosea. Judah survived for another 135 years after the fall of Israel. The prophets tried to get the weakened kings of Judah to return to Yahweh and live according to the terms of the covenant. First Isaiah (chapters 1–39) and Jeremiah were powerful voices of the times, but they were largely unsuccessful in converting the kings and people. Other prophets of this period of Judah's history include Micah, Nahum, Zephaniah, and Habakkuk.

- **The Exile in Babylon (587–539 BC):** The Babylonians represented a frightening and powerful enemy, and their humiliation of Judah was complete when they not only destroyed Jerusalem and the temple built by Solomon but took all the people back to Babylon, forcing them into slavery. The people mourned the loss of their freedom to worship the God of the covenant. The Books of Lamentations and Baruch are connected to Jeremiah and reflect the troubles of these times. During this time of crisis, a new form of literature developed in which the people's longing for rescue, freedom of faith, and a chance to return to their land and to their religious roots could be expressed. In their enslaved situation, this new literary form, which came to be known as "apocalyptic," was necessarily communicated in a code that only believers could interpret. Books reflecting this period include Ezekiel, who is sometimes called the father of Jewish apocalypticism, and Second Isaiah (chapters 40–55).

- **The Exiles' Return and Efforts to Rebuild the Temple (539–400 BC):** Babylon was conquered by the Persians in 539 BC, and Cyrus issued a proclamation to free the people and allow them to return to Judah. After more than a generation in Babylon, the people return to the land, filled with determination to reform and rebuild the temple and to reassert their religious independence and identity. 1 and 2 Chronicles, Ezra, Nehemiah, Third Isaiah (chapters 56–66), Haggai, most of Zechariah, Malachi, Obadiah, Joel, and perhaps Jonah are from this period.

- **Hellenism and the Maccabean Revolt (336–164 BC):** Alexander the Great conquered the Mediterranean region between 336 and 323 BC and attempted to unify all its diverse nations under the Greek culture and language. But when he died at a young age, there was no one among his lieutenants who was able to assume his leadership role and influence. Tensions were especially marked between the Egyptian (Ptolemy) and Syrian (Seleucid) forces. Israel was caught in the middle. Already under the influence of Greek rule and culture, Israel struggled to maintain its own national and religious identity. Finally, after Seleucid King Antiochus IV Epiphanes attacked and defiled the temple and pillaged its treasury, the Jews revolted under the leadership of the Maccabees. They rededicated the temple, which became a major symbol of their independence. The Books of 1 and 2 Maccabees, Esther, and Daniel reflect this period. Much of the wisdom literature, including Job, Ecclesiastes, the Song of Songs, and Sirach, were also composed and edited around this time and reflect thinking influenced by Hellenism. This period marked the end of the composition of the books of the Old Testament.

- **The Roman Empire (63 BC–AD 312):** The Roman general Pompey led his triumphant forces into Palestine in 63 BC as part of Rome's successful bid to take over the Western world. Rome later installed Herod the Great (37–4 BC), whose political ambitions for Rome's approval were much stronger than his religious ties to Judaism as king of Palestine. To ingratiate himself with his own people who held him in suspicion, Herod began to rebuild the temple around 14 BC on a much larger and grander scale than Solomon had foreseen, although it was still unfinished when it was destroyed, along with all of Jerusalem, by the Romans in AD 70. The stage was set for the birth of Jesus. The Gospels of Matthew and Luke tell us that Jesus was born during Herod's reign, thus insinuating the turmoil and political unrest of the times. Eventually, after Herod's death, Rome appointed its own procurators for the southern region of Judea; Pontius Pilate, under whom Jesus was executed, was one of these. Paul's and Mark's writings were probably composed in the years just prior to the destruction of the temple. The remainder of the New Testament comes from the latter part of the first century and the beginning of the second century.

A Look Ahead

We are companions on a wonderful journey exploring the wonders of the Bible. To mark various stages of our exploration, introductions are offered to each major section of the Scriptures, such as the Law, the prophets, the Gospels, and the letters. Useful terms for each section are provided with these introductions. This guide follows the order of books as they are presented in the Bible. In a section entitled "At a Glance," issues related to each book's composition are summarized briefly. The structure, content, and major themes of each book are presented, as well as the consensus about the human author. Of course, it is not possible to understand a book unless we know what kind of literature it is, so a short section on relevant literary forms accompanies the commentary on each book. This is followed by a section on key passages, meant to remind the reader of the book's most famous references. (Since this guide was designed to be concise, the key passages—as well as the themes listed—are not meant to be all-inclusive.) A final section entitled "Food for Thought" is intended to show how each biblical book stimulates reflection on some of life's most inspiring, puzzling, challenging, encouraging, and meaningful experiences.

Mary Ann Getty-Sullivan

Introduction to the Old Testament

The Hebrew Scriptures are a collection of writings that tell the story of the covenant between God and Israel. These writings or books were composed over the course of several centuries, from the tenth to the second centuries before Christ. Eventually the collection became known among Christians as the Old Testament, a title of honor implying that the roots of faith are found there. These pre-Christian writings spell out what it means to believe in the promise of a Messiah.

The Old Testament has three major parts: the Pentateuch (also known as the Torah, or Law), the writings, and the prophets. The Pentateuch contains the first five books of the Bible and tells the story of creation and the election of Israel as heirs to the promises God made first to Abraham and then to all of his descendants. The "prophets" include three major prophets: Isaiah, Jeremiah, and Ezekiel; related works such as Lamentations and Baruch; and twelve minor prophets, so-called not because they are less important but because their books are much shorter than the major prophets. All the remaining works of the Bible are included as the "writings," a rich tapestry of various kinds of literature and teachings related to how the people of God can live in a manner worthy of their election and calling. In the Catholic Bible, the writings are inserted between the Pentateuch and the prophets. By placing the prophets last in the collection and just before the Gospels, the Catholic Bible underscores the essential unity of the Scriptures and the continuity of divinely inspired prophecies about the Messiah and their fulfillment in Jesus.

The forty-six books in the order that they appear in the Catholic canon of the Old Testament are divided into the following categories:

—Books of the Old Testament—

THE PENTATEUCH (i.e., the Torah, or Law):

Genesis
Exodus
Leviticus
Numbers
Deuteronomy

THE WRITINGS

The Historical Books

Joshua
Judges
Ruth
1 and 2 Samuel
1 and 2 Kings
1 and 2 Chronicles
Ezra
Nehemiah
Tobit
Judith
Esther
1 and 2 Maccabees

Wisdom Literature

Job
Psalms
Proverbs
Ecclesiastes
Song of Songs
Wisdom
Sirach

THE PROPHETS

Isaiah
Jeremiah
Lamentations
Baruch
Ezekiel
Daniel
Hosea
Joel
Amos
Obadiah
Jonah
Micah
Nahum
Habakkuk
Zephaniah
Haggai
Zechariah
Malachi

Introduction to the Pentateuch

Humans long to communicate, to understand and be understood, to love and be loved, to reach out beyond their own individual boundaries and limitations. People began by communicating orally; but soon they added writing, first in pictures and then in words that formed pictures in their minds. One of the oldest and most popular forms of communication is through stories that first were told orally and later written down as a form of preserving them for future generations. The Bible is evidence of how effective storytelling can be. From Moses to Jesus, from David to the Evangelists, stories are one of the most popular, cherished, and memorable ways of getting a point or two across to others. Children of all ages love them and beg for them. The Bible fulfills that desire.

People have always looked for ways to express the bonds that identify them and tie them to one another. Often we do this by creating written documents that form and nourish us as a people and that act as a standard for our continued development. In American history, for example, we revere the Declaration of Independence, the Constitution of the United States, and the Gettysburg Address. In light of such documents, we examine our history, our conscience, our traditions, our laws, and our behavior. If this is true for us as a proud nation, it is all the more true for people of faith who claim to be the chosen people of God. So Israel, a people that defined themselves as the "people of God," look to the Torah (a word that means "instruction") as an expression of their identity, as a basis for law, as a standard for appropriate liturgical celebration, and as the way to form their consciences and inspire their behavior. Although these books are sometimes referred to as "the Law," their content is much more varied and rich than simple legal ordinances or prohibitions. In addition to law, there are narratives or stories, poetry, genealogy, rituals or liturgical texts, historical indicators, and many other types of literature within the Pentateuch. All together, these help to express the covenant through which believers celebrate their belief and their commitment to God.

Useful Terms to Know

Anthropomorphic means "humanlike." In one of the oldest traditions of the Pentateuch, God is called *Yahweh* and is featured as being "like" humans in the sense that God is personal, interactive, and approachable. This tradition undoubtedly reflects the idea from Genesis that humans are made in the image and likeness of God rather than the other way around.

Deuteronomy means "second law" and also refers to a reiteration of the law understood as God's instruction to Moses. In the Book of Deuteronomy, Moses does not present this as a collection of laws, prohibitions, or ordinances, but as a unified expression of the people's covenant with God.

Exodus: Meaning "the way out" or "departure," it tells of the migration of the chosen people from Egypt. For them, this was a liberation from the misery of slavery, and it was a result of God's initiative in calling Moses to lead the people out and instructing them on what to do and how to live.

Genesis means "beginning." The title is taken from the first words of the book: "In the beginning" (1:1).

Leviticus: The English title is the Latin translation of the Septuagint name (*Leuitikon*). This book, which served as a liturgical guide for the priests from the tribe of Levi, consists almost entirely of laws and rubrics. The priests were to teach the Israelites how to make themselves a people set apart by holiness as a sign of their special covenantal relationship with God.

Monotheism: Belief in *one* God. There may be various names (Yahweh, Almighty One, Lord) and images for God (almighty and majestic or personal and approachable), but there is only one God.

Numbers: The English title is derived from the Greek title, *Arithmoi,* and apparently refers to the census of the Hebrews that is featured near the beginning and the end of the book, as well as other numerical data that is given in this book. But the title is somewhat misleading in that there is considerably more than "numbers" given here. The work has extensive narrative, poetry, and legal materials. The Hebrew title of the book, which means "in the desert," seems more appropriate.

Oral Tradition: Stories circulated orally long before they were written down. Israel's oral traditions combined such genres as religious myths, legends, genealogies, and narratives with a historical basis and the people's belief in a single God; this God is not only the creator of the universe but also a caring, personal God who initiates a relationship with human beings built on promise and trust.

Patriarchs and Matriarchs: Israel's history began with God's promises to Abraham and Sarah of descendants and land. The story of Genesis unfolds through Isaac and Rebecca, Jacob and Rachel, and Joseph.

The Pentateuch (also known as "the Law") refers to the five scrolls that compose the Torah, or "instruction," of God. The five scrolls contain the first five books of the Bible, which are Genesis, Exodus, Leviticus, Numbers, and Deuteronomy.

YHWH: The name for God revealed to Moses in the encounter with the burning bush (see Exodus 3:14). Through this name, God is revealed as immanent—as accessible and close to the people, a caring and personal God who hears the cry of the people and responds by liberating them.

Genesis

In tracing a family tree, people tend to identify their beginnings with important ancestors who functioned as leaders and visionaries. Memories of such people serve as a unifying and inspiring source of strength, pride, and identity for all. Such were Abraham and Sarah and their family, whose story begins with God's call to Abraham (see Genesis 12). But the biblical writers realized that before God called Abraham, God had created the world and all that is in it. They also knew that God's purpose for creation was larger and more inclusive than the covenant made with Abraham. For believers, it was an easy step from God's selection of Israel, represented in the call to Abraham, to God's plan for the creation of the world. They tacked onto the story of the patriarchs and matriarchs an introduction showing God's care in creating a world of order and wonder out of chaos (see Genesis 1–11).

In doing so, the biblical writers combined several traditions that feature God as majestic and transcendent but also immanent and approachable. They attributed the reversal of the proper order of creation, the source of suffering, and even death to human sin and disobedience. Yet even while asserting this, they expressed hope in God's promise of ultimate salvation for all generations. God promises to "put enmity" between the offspring of the serpent, a symbol of evil, and that of the woman, representing all humanity, adding that humankind "will strike [the serpent's] head," that is, evil's source of life (Genesis 3:15).

In the first section of Genesis (chapters 1–11), characters such as Adam and Eve, Cain and Abel, the builders of the tower of Babel, and Noah are portrayed not so much as individuals as generalized descriptions of people who make choices and then reap the consequences of those choices. The all-knowing, loving, and personal God who created the universe establishes a relationship with human beings. But humanity tends toward sin in the forms of disobedience, pride, envy, and greed. Humankind suffers from sin and continually needs God's intervention.

Chapters 12–50 of Genesis contain the story of one such divine intervention in the form of God's call to Abraham; together with his wife, Sarah, and nephew, Lot, they begin the journey to a land promised to them by God. These chapters go on to trace the story of the patriarchs and matriarchs through four generations. Some parts of the story become stylized and are reused in the telling of the stories of their children and their wives. So, for example, the call, trouble, and rescue by God, the passing on of the blessing to the heir, and the continuation of the protection of God down through the ages become repeated elements of the story of successive generations. The story proceeds from Abraham and Sarah, Isaac and Rebecca, Jacob and Rachel, and finally ends with the death of Joseph, beloved son of Jacob and Rachel, whom God protected even when his brothers sold him into slavery.

At a Glance

Who: After a series of primordial stories about creation and the first humans, Genesis turns to the stories of the patriarchs, from Abraham to Joseph, describing their call from God and their responses to it.

What: Genesis shows the interpersonal relationship God establishes with the world since the creation of the first human beings, and especially with the Israelites, beginning with Abraham.

When: The first eleven chapters are not meant to be historical but tell of the origins of the world. Historical data can be seen in the call of Abraham, who may have lived sometime between 2000 and 1800 BC.

Where: Creation's beginning is located in a Garden in Eden, watered by the Tigris and Euphrates Rivers, which are in present-day Iraq. This is more of a symbolic than an actual geographical location. Abraham lived in "Ur of the Chaldeans" (Genesis 11:28), or Babylonia, and migrated to Palestine following a command of God.

Why: To unify the Israelites into one people with a common commitment to the covenant and common goals when the kingdom under David and Solomon was established.

Structure and Content

1–2: Origin of the world. These two chapters provide distinct accounts of the creation of the world and humankind. In both accounts, humans are given dominion over creation and are creation's pinnacle.

3: Origin of sin. Man and woman are prideful and disobey God's command not to eat of the fruit of the tree of knowledge. There are then devastating long-term consequences for all humans, as sin and death have now entered the world.

4–11: Multiplication of sins of the human race. Cain kills his brother, Abel, out of jealousy and is doomed to wander the earth. Sin multiplies through successive generations, so much so that God sends a flood to cleanse the earth and then renews his covenant with creation.

12–50: Origins of the patriarchs. God calls Abraham (then called Abram) out of the land of the Chaldeans and tells him that he will be the father of a great multitude. Genesis continues with stories of Isaac, Jacob, and Joseph, focusing on their settlement in Palestine and ultimately their sojourn in Egypt.

Major Themes

- **The God of our fathers and mothers is also the God of creation.** Proceeding from a belief that all of creation is good, the writers conceived of a world where everything is under the direction of God, including the sun, water, the earth, human beings, and animals.

- **The origin of evil stems from the disobedience of human beings.** God created good, not evil. Human will and action are at the root of evil. Yet as soon as humans sin, God promises redemption and salvation.

- **A promise or covenant** begins with God's initiative and prompts the obedience and faith of Abraham, who is the father of Israel. God's call to Abraham is the starting point of the story of the Jewish people.

Authorship

Traditionally, Genesis is ascribed to Moses. But modern scholarship has identified layers of traditions that were passed down orally and combined over a relatively long period of time. The oldest written source, known as the Yahwist (J), may date from the end of David's reign (ca. 950 BC), when national sentiment was very strong. David wanted to promote the monarchy and unify the people around their common heritage. Another fundamental source from around the ninth century before Christ is called the Elohist (E), which derives from the divine name "Elohim," and stresses the majestic, transcendent characteristics of God. The Deuteronomistic (D) editing of the Pentateuch comes from the seventh century BC and focuses on the reciprocal responsibilities of God and Israel for the fulfillment of the terms of the covenant. The Priestly (P) tradition is associated with the Babylonian Exile and was composed sometime around the sixth and fifth centuries BC, with its final composition happening perhaps as late as 400 BC. These four sources can each be identified by what details their authors or editors chose to include or the name that they used to refer to God, as is the case with the Yahwist and the Elohist. The Old Testament that we have today thus went through many inspired revisions over the course of several centuries.

Literary Forms

Farewell Address: A leader, in his final days, gathers his heirs (his sons or disciples) and tells them of his impending death. He reviews the legacy he is leaving them, including the values that have inspired his life, and he challenges them to continue to follow these. Perhaps he warns of the suffering, conflicts, and obstacles they will face. He promises eventual success if they are faithful, seals his words with tears and gestures of affection, and leaves them. Examples of this genre in Genesis are found in chapters 49 and 50 with the accounts of the deaths of Jacob and Joseph. A similar pattern is found in farewell speeches of later biblical figures, including Moses, Joshua, Jesus, and Paul.

Hero-Centered Stories, Historically Based Stories, and Legends: These are found in Genesis 12–50 and focus on ancestors who were the patriarchs and matriarchs of all the people. Remembering and embracing these common ancestors were ways of unifying the people.

Origin Stories: These are contained in the first part of Genesis (chapters 1–11) and are prehistorical. These stories reflect the people's monotheistic faith rather than factual history or science.

Key Passages

1:1-2:25: Two stories of creation.

12:1-3: The call of Abram and God's promise to make of him a great nation.

Food for Thought

The Book of Genesis, like other books in the Scriptures, is important less for its scientific or historical implications or accuracy than for its meaning for believers as part of the teaching about salvation. The stories of creation, for example, focus on the goodness of God and on creation as an expression of God's goodness. The stories of the patriarchs and matriarchs illustrate how God continues to care for and protect humankind. God is pictured as intervening in history whenever the people, because of their sin, get into a greater jam than they can handle.

Christian believers base many of their fundamental hopes on the portrait obtained in Genesis, including views of the sanctity of marriage, the beauty of human sexuality, and the sacredness of life. Christian teaching on the problem of original sin shows how humankind has been wounded by disobedience and rebellion against God from the beginning. Yet Genesis also opens us to the belief that ultimately, God will save us. Genesis shows us how God has entrusted us to be stewards of our world as well as heirs to the promises to Abraham. Genesis challenges us to respond to our call from God with generous faith, abundant hope, and unconditional love.

Exodus

Many people, perhaps most, can identify an experience of liberation and grace as part of the story of their relationship with God. Such an experience is sometimes so momentous and so defining that it is seen afterward as a birth, a new beginning—the actual start of life and a vision of purpose for life. The Israelites claim just such an experience in their exodus from Egypt where they had experienced slavery, hardship beyond imagination, and liberation, because God was faithful to the covenant even though they had not been.

The Book of Exodus begins with a description of the plight of the people in Egypt, who are too overwhelmed by slavery to even form a prayer to God. A short transition from the ending of Genesis identifies the tribes of Israelites, named for Jacob's sons, who had come to Egypt when Joseph was the pharaoh's trusted steward. In the first chapter, the number seventy, a reference to the number of Israelites who had come to Egypt seeking food and security, is contrasted with the number of their descendants, so great that it threatens the Egyptians, who seek to limit them by subjecting them to cruel slavery and even killing their infants. In chapter 2, Moses emerges, as if from nowhere, to become an instrument of God's liberation.

Exodus inaugurates the epic story of God's choice of Moses to lead the people out of Egypt to the Promised Land. The people begin to practice the Law and to learn the ways of YHWH. After a series of plagues in Egypt, the people succeed in crossing the Red Sea and come to rest in the desert at Mount Sinai. There, Moses has an encounter with God and receives the stone tablets engraved with the Ten Commandments. The people accept these and many other prohibitions and ordinances as part of their covenant with God. As Exodus ends, the people remain at the foot of Mount Sinai, awaiting further word that they should continue their journey.

At a Glance

Who: The people were at first called "Hebrews," a name that suggested their status as refugees in a foreign land. They later became known as the Israelites, the people of God.

What: The account of liberation from slavery for the people of the covenant, led by Moses out of Egypt to the Promised Land.

When: The events of the story took place in the thirteenth century before Christ, around 1250 BC.

Where: Exodus traced the journey of the Israelites from Egypt to Mount Sinai, where they pitched camp and were given the stone tablets with the Ten Commandments, as well as many other laws designed to transform them from a motley crew of refugees to a people living in covenant with God, and then as they wandered in the desert until they reached the Jordan River.

Why: To preserve the traditions about the way the people had been liberated from slavery by God and to remember the terms of the covenant.

Structure and Content

1:1–15:21: The Egyptians enslave the Israelites, afraid of their exponential growth. God calls Moses to lead them out of Egypt and then sends ten plagues, the tenth of which is the death of the firstborn of every Egyptian family. Finally, Pharaoh grants permission to the Israelites to leave.

15:22–18:27: The people leave Egypt and walk across the Red Sea after Moses parts the waters. Miriam, Moses' sister, leads the people in a hymn that praises God for hearing their cries and freeing them from slavery. They finally arrive at Mount Sinai, where they encamp.

19–40: There is a great theophany at Mount Sinai, where God appears as lightning and clouds, accompanied by thunder and the sound of trumpets blaring. God then gives the Israelites the Ten Commandments.

Major Themes

- **God responds to the people's intense suffering** and delivers them from slavery.

- Remembering the promise to Abraham, **God makes a covenant with Israel.**

- **God guides the people** wandering in the desert.

Authorship

According to tradition, Moses is the author of Exodus. But like the rest of the Pentateuch, Exodus was composed over centuries, from the end of David's reign until after the exile.

Literary Forms

Call Narrative: The call of God and commissioning of a person, followed by an objection, reassurance by God, and a sign. For instance, God speaks to Moses in the burning bush and commissions him to lead the people out of Egypt (Exodus 3:1-4, 10). Moses objects and God reassures him, giving him a sign (3:11-12). The call of Gideon (Judges 6:11-17), Isaiah (6:1-11), Jeremiah (1:4-9), and Jesus' mother, Mary (Luke 1:26-38), are examples of this pattern being repeated.

Covenant: Legal material resembling a treaty and ratification. By agreement, God and Israel pledge to hold themselves mutually accountable for keeping the covenant; God promises to protect and guide Israel, who will, through obeying the Law, be faithful to God alone. This agreement is sealed in the manner of legal treaties, with blessings and curses (see Exodus 19–24).

Legend: A story of extraordinary events believed to have a historical basis that is handed down orally for generations. Moses, for example, is larger than life. His reputation and popularity grew until he was perceived as probably the most important figure of the Pentateuch, if not the whole of the Old Testament.

Key Passages

3:1-20: Moses' call and the theophany of the burning bush.

3:13-14: The name of God, YHWH, is revealed to Moses.

13:21-22: The cloud by day and the pillar of fire by night are signs of God's presence with Israel as the people journey in the wilderness.

16:1–17:7: God feeds the people in the desert with manna and quail and gives them water from a rock.

20:1-17: The oldest version of the Ten Commandments in the Old Testament (see Deuteronomy 5:6-21 for a later version).

Food for Thought

In Hebrew, the terms *dabar* (word) and *midbar* (desert) are related. Israel hears the word of God in the desert and responds. Later, the prophets likened the time of the people's wandering in the desert to the special intimacy between a parent and infant (see Hosea 11:1-7) or as the honeymoon period of their relationship with God (see Jeremiah 2:2-3; 3:4). It became for the prophets the ideal time of Israel's reliance on God and God's repeated demonstrations of fidelity to the people of the covenant.

The exodus was far more than a historical event. Allusions to the exodus appear throughout the Old and New Testaments, evidence of its great importance to the Jewish people as well as to Christians. Annual celebration of this event is central to Jewish and Christian liturgical life. Jews and Christians also understand the exodus as a basic paradigm for their relationship with God. The pattern seen in the Book of Exodus of bondage, liberation, and commitment to the covenant is seen as one of the most common and fundamental experiences of our spiritual lives as believers. The water from the rock and the manna in the desert are symbols used by the church for the Sacraments of Baptism and the Eucharist. We can see this symbolism already used by the Evangelists and St. Paul in their understanding of the miracles Jesus performed and especially of the Lord's Supper and its meaning for the church (see John 6:30-35, 48-51; 1 Corinthians 10:1-4).

Leviticus

Our family recently participated in the Sacrament of the Anointing of the Sick for my brother, who was dying. The anointing and the prayers reminded us again of the sacredness of human life, including, of course, the body. Such an awareness permeates the Book of Leviticus, which pays close attention to the rituals and laws governing the ordinary lives of the chosen people. According to Leviticus, the Israelites were to affirm their special relationship with God in everything they did—in what they ate and in how they prepared the meals, in how they offered their prayer and sacrifices, in how they married and had sexual relations, in how they dressed, and in how they asked for and received forgiveness. Often repeated in Leviticus is what was to be their motivation for keeping the Law; God says, "I am the LORD your God; . . . be holy, for I am holy" (11:44,45; 19:2; 20:7, 26). Theirs was an everyday holiness that included, of course, the body and all human behavior. The Book of Leviticus might seem to some of us today to be only a long list of laws, but for the Israelites, it provided wisdom for a good and, therefore, a happy life. Without divine guidance, our lives would be wasted on meaningless, self-absorbed pursuits. But the Torah shows us that every action or endeavor can be inspired and motivated by the fundamental willingness to be a person of the covenant.

At a Glance

Who: A continuation of the sojourn of the people in the desert.

What: Laws and rituals centered on the command that the people were to remain holy; part of the ongoing description of the instruction by Moses for how the people were to demonstrate the holiness that should result from their covenant relationship with God.

When: The people were in the desert for forty years, beginning just after the call of Moses around 1250 BC.

Where: Moses is described as having encountered God in the tent of meeting while the Israelites wandered in the desert; there, he received all the laws, ordinances, and prohibitions found in Leviticus (see Exodus 20:24, Leviticus 1:1; Numbers 1:1).

Why: To preserve the tradition of holiness based on living the covenant and to affirm the Israelites' belief that every action of their lives ought to reflect their desire to live according to the instruction of God.

Structure and Content

1–10: Sacrifice and the priests. The Israelites designate times, places, and the manner of sacrifice, which they see as a specific kind of prayer that invites God to respond to them; these prayers are for expressing petitions, such as the need for forgiveness, thanksgiving, reparation for sin, and adoration of the one, living, and true God. The priests, as mediators between God and his people, certify the offerings and, in the case of some, partake of their benefits.

11–15: Legal purity. In this section, Leviticus contains laws regarding diet. Foods were classified as either "clean" (the Hebrew word is *kosher*) or "unclean." The purpose of these laws is to recognize that God is the source of all blessings and to preserve the people as set apart or holy even in the everyday act of eating.

16–26: Here Leviticus covers the liturgical year from spring to fall. There are three pilgrimage feasts: the spring Feast of Unleavened Bread (Passover); a Feast of First Fruits celebrated fifty days plus one after Passover; and the fall or harvest Feast of Tabernacles. Leviticus also describes *Yom Kippur* (Day of Atonement), regulation of the Sabbath observance, the sabbatical year, and the jubilee year.

27–34: Redemption of offerings. This final section is an appendix containing laws from later times. Some persons and things are offered to God and, as God's property, should be "redeemed," or "bought back." In honor of the Passover event, for example, the firstborn sons are dedicated to God.

Major Themes

- **Human life,** down to the smallest details, is precious in God's sight.

- **Humans beings can live every aspect of their lives** as an offering to God in thanksgiving.

Authorship

According to tradition, Moses is the author of Leviticus. But like the rest of the Pentateuch, Leviticus was composed over centuries, from the end of David's reign to after the exile. Concerns of the priests for holiness and ritual purity are particularly evident in Leviticus.

Literary Form

Laws: Leviticus is composed almost entirely of legal prescriptions, with very little narrative.

Key Passages

25:1-22: Ordinances regarding the sabbatical year and prescriptions for the jubilee year which was to be celebrated every fifty years.

Food for Thought

Leviticus is important for us today, not so much because of the letter of the law, but because of the purpose of all the laws it contains. Leviticus helps us understand that all life is sacred because it is part of our covenant with God. There are so many contemporary issues that might be addressed more wisely if viewed in the context that Leviticus is meant to convey, namely, the holiness of the people as God's chosen ones, whose every action is a reflection of the covenant. How would we approach and solve some of our most pressing social issues today—for example, abortion, capital punishment, war, stewardship of the world's resources, reduction of waste, and careless consumerism—if we were preoccupied with mirroring to the world our covenant relationship with God?

Numbers

Editing often leaves its own mark on a work. An excellent example of this is the editorial work of the so-called Priestly tradition that contributed much to the formation of the Pentateuch in its present form. This is especially true of the Book of Numbers, which contains a preponderance of Priestly material. This tradition was interested in numbers, census genealogy, obedience to the Law, and the reliability of God's faithfulness to the people, no matter how dismal their situation seemed. About five hundred years before Christ, the Priestly authors reworked and reordered previous traditions, emphasizing themes that they held most important, such as the demand for the people's faithful response to the covenant. The footprint of the Priestly editors can also be seen in their emphasis on God's blessing in increasing their numbers and on the consistency of God's presence with them, traceable back through all the generations to the patriarchs.

At a Glance

Who: The chosen people, whom Moses organized according to tribe, clan, and family, in order to take a census. They had grown from an original group of seventy people to the large nation the Egyptians enslaved so as to limit their power.

What: Combining composition of census and genealogical material, fables, and accounts of the continuation of the exodus story, Numbers gives an account of about forty years in the desert, from the encampment at Sinai to the arrival of the people at the threshold of the Promised Land.

When: The thirteenth century before Christ, when Moses led the Israelites.

Where: Numbers 1:1–10:11 depicts the Israelites at the foot of Mount Sinai, organized according to family groups based on the twelve tribes. The presence of God with them was symbolized by the cloud over them by day and the fire by night (9:15). The rest of the book tells of the wandering of the people in the desert as they made their way to "the plains of Moab by the Jordan at Jericho" (36:13).

Why: To accent personal commitment to Yahweh as a result of the exodus experience.

Structure and Content

1:1–10:10: Organizing the community and preparing for departure from Sinai. This involves a census of the community, the ritual purity of the camp, and preparation for departure from Sinai.

10:11–21:35: The march through the desert from Sinai to Moab. As they proceed toward the Promised Land, the people grow restless and weary, and some of them revolt, including Moses' sister, Miriam, and his brother, Aaron. God sends serpents that bite many of the people, who then die. Moses mounts a bronze serpent on a pole, and all who gaze on it recover.

22–36: Preparation for entry into the land. A second census is taken, and it is found that the whole generation of people who had left Egypt has died, and a new generation has grown up in the desert, ready to inherit the land that God had promised to their ancestors.

Major Themes

- **Holiness is manifest** in the dedicated life of the people who became numerous, victorious, and prosperous in the desert.
- **The Priestly writers emphasize the importance of rituals and purity** and the roles of the priests and Levites in leading the people.
- **God responds to the people's constant complaints** with escalating demonstrations of power through Moses' and Aaron's intercession.

Authorship

According to tradition, Moses is the author. But like the rest of the Pentateuch, Numbers is actually the product of several centuries and was finally edited by the Priestly tradition in the postexilic period (after the return of the people around 539 BC).

Literary Forms

Census Numbers and Genealogies: The descendants of each tribe are identified; for example, 3:1-51 enumerates all of the Levites to document their heritage as members of the priestly tribe.

Fables: Such fictitious tales, told to teach moral lessons, are common in Numbers, such as the story of Balaam and his talking donkey (22:22-35), the red heifer and the water of purification (19:1-22), and the fiery serpents (21:4-9).

Oracles: Messages from God, like the ones found in the prophetic books, also appear here; for example, Balaam is a non-Israelite prophet who is asked to curse the Israelites but can only bless them because that is the message he receives from God (23:7; 24:25).

Key Passages

6:22-27: Priestly blessing upon the Israelites.

14:1-10; 16:1-17:26: The revolt of the people in the desert (see Paul's reference in 1 Corinthians 10:10).

20:1-13: God provides water from a rock for the people at Meribah (see Paul's reference in 1 Corinthians 10:4).

21:5-9: After being bitten by poisonous serpents, those who gaze on a bronze serpent mounted on a pole are healed. Jesus used this image in referring to himself as the "Son of Man" who is "lifted up" (John 3:14).

22:2–24:25: The Balaam oracles; these prophecies are referenced in 2 Peter 2:15-16.

31: "Holy war" description evident in the battle against the Midianites.

Food for Thought

The grumbling and disbelief of the people are obstacles. They keep looking back and even start to believe that they were better off in Egypt. How soon they forget the misery that caused God to take pity on them and rescue them! After forty years, that is, a whole generation of wandering in the desert, they return again to the God who saves them. They become ready to enter the land that God has promised them. The people are stubborn in their sin, but God is constant in mercy. Their experience becomes an example for the New Testament authors to draw on; Paul makes the point that "these things happened to them to serve as an example, and they were written down to instruct us" (1 Corinthians 10:11). In Romans, Paul adds, "For whatever was written in former days was written for our instruction, so that by steadfastness and by the encouragement of the scriptures we might have hope" (15:4).

Significantly, we see that God's expectations of the Israelites are greater than when they were first fleeing Egypt. The Book of Numbers shows us that faith is cumulative, that each day we are given the opportunity to choose either to grow in trust or regress into rebelliousness, ingratitude, and selfish ambition. Our memory needs to be fixed on all that God has accomplished, not only for us, but also through us until now. When we remember our blessings, we nurture gratitude in our hearts, and we grow in confidence that the same God who has given us life and sustains us will continue to be with us.

Deuteronomy

People often repeat rituals as a means of celebration. For example, we blow out candles on birthdays, we sing the national anthem before baseball games, and we attend Mass weekly and grow accustomed to the rhythm of the readings, songs, preaching, and celebration of the Eucharist. Repetition is one way of expressing reverence, allegiance, and honor. The Book of Deuteronomy probably grew out of the people's liturgical celebration of the exodus as the central event of their lives as individuals and as a community. In the Book of Deuteronomy, there is a lot of repetition of material already found in the previous four books of the Pentateuch. It is as if the people never tired of celebrating their covenant with God.

The title *deuteronomion*, probably from the Septuagint translation of the Hebrew Scriptures, is a Greek term meaning "second law." It may also be based on Deuteronomy 17:18, where the Hebrew text says that the king must write for himself a "copy" of the law, obviously meaning the same law, not a second or different one. The Book of Deuteronomy uses the name "Horeb" as the name of the mountain on which God gave the Ten Commandments to Moses, rather than "Sinai" (Deuteronomy 1:2; 5:2; 9:8), and includes an edited recap of the Decalogue (5:6-21). It also contains the two ways (30:15-20), or choices, of life and blessing or death and curses by which Moses challenged the assembled people to be faithful to the covenant.

At a Glance

Who: "The words that Moses spoke" (1:1) are remembered and celebrated by the community and probably only put in written form as one of the later traditions of the Pentateuch.

What: In eloquent speeches, Moses is pictured as challenging the people to be faithful to the covenant.

When: Toward the end of the thirteenth century BC; as the people of Israel made their way to the Promised Land, they occasionally assembled and renewed their commitment to God and to obeying the commandments.

Where: Near the Jordan River, just before the people left the desert and moved into the Promised Land.

Why: To recall the people to faithfulness to the covenant.

Structure and Content

1–4: Moses addresses the people and gives them a review of their history, beginning with the command from God to leave the land of Egypt. Moses exhorts the people repeatedly to remember the covenant and be faithful to it.

5–11: Moses' second address to the people, summoning them to hear and obey all of the laws and ordinances as their response to the covenant. The address begins with a reiteration of the Decalogue (5:6-21; cf. Exodus 20:2-17) and includes the *Shema Israel* (6:4-5), a summary of the command to "love the LORD your God with all your heart, and with all your soul, and with all your might."

12–26: Exposition of the Law. Moses reiterates how to properly worship God and follow the commandments, instructing the people in how to avoid adopting any idolatrous practices from the people they will come into contact with in the Promised Land.

27–34: Moses' farewell discourse. He sets before the people the choice between life, or following God and the commandments, or death, which is falling prey once again to idolatry. Moses gives a final blessing to the people and then dies on Mount Nebo, which overlooks the Promised Land.

Major Themes

- **God and Israel are mutually bound to one another** in a treaty expressed in the form of a covenant. God's blessing upon the people is conditional on their fidelity to the Law.

- **True worship, social justice, and repentance** are signs of belonging to the covenant people.

Authorship

According to tradition, Deuteronomy contains the words and speeches of Moses. But modern scholarship shows that it was probably the product of several sources, edited by the so-called Deuteronomic historian who represents the view that the people are in a covenant with God, which governs their lives.

Literary Form

Moses' Speeches: Moses' authority is featured in his addresses to the people, to challenge them to return to faithfulness to the God of the covenant.

Key Passages

6:4-9: The *Shema Israel* (Hear, O Israel) is Israel's call to worship God alone. This challenge of Moses came to be used as the distinctive prayer recited daily by pious Jews.

30:15-20: The two ways that invite Israel to choose between life, which is the worship of the one true and living God, or death, which is sin.

Food for Thought

Deuteronomy consistently stresses that the covenant is the basis of the Law that governs all of Israel's life and actions. Like a pious Israelite, we might frequently examine ourselves on how our own actions, prayers, aspirations, and hopes are reflections of our covenant with God. Moses is pictured in Deuteronomy as speaking to the assembled people and setting before them a choice between life, living and dedicating themselves to God, or sin, going astray to follow false gods. Moses concludes his speech, urging the people, "I have set before you life and death, blessings and curses. Choose life so that you and your descendants may live, loving the LORD your God," (Deuteronomy 30:19-20). We find ourselves still faced with this same decision. Which do we choose?

Introduction to the Historical Books

A very creative college professor made me fall in love with history. In his class, history came alive. I wondered if he had personally met all those people whose lives and contributions he sketched in our minds, so vivid were his descriptions of them. It was with the same enthusiasm that I began to probe this next category of the Bible: the historical books. Here we are introduced and captivated by figures such as Samson, whose strength was in his hair; Ruth, whose virtue was loyalty; David, who soothed King Saul with his music before Saul turned on him in jealousy; the mother of the seven sons who encouraged them, one by one, to be courageous even in the face of death before they, and finally she herself, were killed. Israel's history is personified here, from Joshua at the end of the thirteenth century BC to the Maccabees of the second century before Christ.

The historical books have been known by several different designations. Jewish tradition considered a number of these books following the Pentateuch as belonging with the prophets; they also distinguished between the "former prophets" (Joshua through 2 Kings) and the "latter prophets" (Isaiah to Malachi). Christians assigned the name "historical books" to the writings known to the Jews as the "former prophets." Some other works were then also included in this historical category. "Historical" in this context does not coincide with our contemporary view of factual or objective history. Rather, this is "theological history," giving an account of Israel's covenant relationship with God from the occupation of the land under the leadership of Joshua to the great tragedy of the fifty-year exile known as the Babylonian Captivity (587–539 BC).

The works known to us as the historical books include

Joshua
Judges
Ruth
1 and 2 Samuel
1 and 2 Kings
1 and 2 Chronicles
Ezra
Nehemiah
Tobit
Judith
Esther
1 and 2 Maccabees

Within the category of the historical books, there are further subdivisions that may be considered as distinct units. So, for example, 1 and 2 Samuel and 1 and 2 Kings tell of the rise of the monarchy, especially under David and Solomon, and then its steady decline until the division into two separate kingdoms of the North (Israel) and the South (Judah). 1 and 2 Chronicles are meant to be read along with Ezra and Nehemiah. It is also within this category of historical books that Catholic Bibles exhibit a unique trait that make them different from the Jewish or Protestant canon of Scripture. Catholics accept the Books of Tobit, Judith, and 1 and 2 Maccabees as part of the canon or list of inspired books of the Bible, whereas these books are considered "apocryphal" in Jewish and Protestant Scripture. In the Catholic Bible, there are also additional passages in the books of Esther and Daniel not found in the Jewish and Protestant Scriptures.

Useful Terms to Know

Babylonian Captivity or Exile (587–539 BC): This was a very significant event in Israel's history, a time of great suffering but also a time of renewal of the covenant and of hope. The people experienced the hardship of life without a national identity, the land, and the temple. During the exile, we see the development of apocalyptic literature that promises a new and better life after the exile. Longing for this new life was eventually expressed as belief in the resurrection and in an afterlife representing an end of suffering, the destruction of evil, and the vindication of faith in God.

The Ban: The destruction of all enemies and, with them, all the booty of war, including animals and all valuables. The explanation for this is so that there will not be any temptation to wage war for the enrichment it might bring. The ban is one of the primary conditions for permission to wage a "holy war" (see Joshua 6:17-18; 10:39-40; 1 Samuel 15:4-23).

Books of Kings: The Greek translation of the Hebrew Scriptures (i.e., the Septuagint or LXX) called 1 and 2 Samuel and 1 and 2 Kings the "Books of Kingdoms." St. Jerome called them simply "Books of Kings." 1 and 2 Samuel were originally a single scroll but were divided into two by those responsible for the LXX. 1 Samuel takes its name from its leading character who plays the triple roles of priest, judge and prophet. 2 Samuel tells the story of David's reign. The story of Solomon dominates the book now called 1 Kings. Successive kings after Solomon are the subject of the remaining book, now known as 2 Kings.

Cult: Referring to all that is related to worship, cult is a very important aspect of the monotheistic religion of Israel. Cult embraces prayer, sacrifice, and ritual purity–everything usually considered the domain and special responsibility of the priests. Whereas the theology of the Books of Samuel and Kings stresses prophecy, 1 and 2 Chronicles, Ezra, and Nehemiah emphasize the increased role of the scribes, priests, and Levites as leaders of the Jewish people.

Deuteronomist or Deuteronomic Historian: The perspective of the narrative recorded in the Books of Joshua through 2 Kings; characteristic also of the Book of Deuteronomy. In 1 and 2 Samuel and 1 and 2 Kings, the Deuteronomist traces the continuity of Israel's history from the end of the period of the Judges through the reigns of Saul, David and Solomon, and their royal successors. The Deuteronomist judges the kings on how well they upheld and represented God's law. David and his son, Solomon, are examples of kings who did well.

Fall of Jericho: An oasis, Jericho represented the "land flowing with milk and honey" (Exodus 3:8, 17; 13:5; 33:3; Numbers 16:14; Deuteronomy 11:9) promised to the chosen people by God. But the inhabitants of the land refused to allow the Israelites, returning from their long sojourn in Egypt, to enter. The walls of the city "fell down flat" (Joshua 6:20) with the blowing of trumpets by the priests and the shouts of all the people.

Judges: Military leaders who answered a call from God to deliver the people, usually from their enemies, but at times also from other Israelite tribes. For example, peace among the people was threatened by such pagan tribes as the Philistines, the Moabites, and the Ammonites. Each time, a leader called a *shofet* appears (a term loosely translated "judge"), who then conquers the enemy, and restores peace. The judges acted as agents of God, sent to end the cycle of rebellion and punishment and to reestablish the peace of the covenant. The periodic upheaval that characterized the time of the judges prompted the people to call for a more unified government presided over by a king.

Just or Holy War: The Book of Joshua illustrates the dilemma about the morality of warfare that continues to challenge us today. After Joshua, the Israelites justified war and even the killing of innocents under certain conditions, including a divine mandate to possess the land, a defensive war in response to that mandate, the religious dedication of the combatants to ensure that the war was as brief as possible, and the ban to ensure that there was no booty to be gained through warfare.

Levirate Marriage: To protect the family, the basic unit of Israelite society, and women who were widowed without male heirs, the Law provided for the brother of a deceased man to have intercourse with the widow in order to produce an heir for the deceased (see Deuteronomy 25:5-10). The Book of Ruth illustrates how the levirate privilege provided a means for the care of childless widows.

Moab/Moabite: The name of a region and a people who lived to the east of the Dead Sea. They were considered pagans or Gentiles by the Israelites. Ruth was a Moabite who adopted the people and way of life of her mother-in-law, Naomi (see the Book of Ruth).

The Nazirite Vow: Consecration for a certain mission, signified by growing one's hair from the time of dedication by vow; the sincerity of one's commitment was then ascertained by the length of the person's hair (see Numbers 6:2-8). This is illustrated in the famous story of Samson (Judges 13–16). His power was not literally in his hair but in his mission to defeat the Philistines. After succumbing to the seductions of Delilah and giving away his secret, Samson rededicated himself and was again empowered by God.

Paraleipomena: A Greek word referring to "things omitted or passed over," it is the name used in the Septuagint for 1 and 2 Chronicles, Ezra, and Nehemiah, which originally formed a single scroll. These writings exhibit the same basic characteristics of style and ideas that emphasize the importance of cult, prayer, and ritual purity. St. Jerome gave these books the names we use today, calling them a "chronicle of divine history."

Prophet: A prophet is a mediator, someone chosen by God to speak to the people on God's behalf. A prophet remains outside of institutional leadership but speaks to the leadership about God's will and to God about the people's response. With the rise of the monarchy, the prophet came to prominence as an adviser and conscience of the kings.

Samaria/Samaritans: After the death of Solomon, the Deuteronomist notes that his son Rehoboam could not rally the nation behind him. As a consequence, Jeroboam was named king over the Northern Kingdom of Israel and established the capital at Samaria. Tension between Samaria and Jerusalem, the capital of the Southern Kingdom of Judah, continued for many centuries. The Samaritans claimed to be legitimate descendants from the tribes of Ephraim and Manasseh, although Ezra and Nehemiah portray them as imposters, people resettled by the Assyrians. The Samaritans' offer to help in the restoration of the temple is seen as interference by the Judeans, according to Ezra (see Ezra 4–6).

Tribal Confederacy: This phrase refers to the loose association of the twelve tribes during the period of the judges, that is, the time between the death of Joshua and the rise of the monarchy.

Joshua

As times and circumstances change, so did the needs of the people. When Moses died before entering the Promised Land, the people must have been bewildered and discouraged. What now? Joshua emerged as a leader, but his role was very different from that of Moses. Joshua was a warrior. The people were entering the Promised Land, while those who had already occupied it were intent on preventing them from coming in. As the people adjusted to a new form of leadership from Moses, the lawgiver, to Joshua, the warrior, they also adjusted to a new image of God as one going before them into battle, protecting them and confounding the enemy. The Book of Joshua takes the relationship of God and the people to another level of meaning.

At a Glance

Who: Joshua, Moses' successor, leads the people into the Promised Land.

What: The occupation of the land and resettlement according to tribes descended from the sons of Jacob after their sojourn in Egypt.

When: The events recounted here are from the twelfth century BC, as the people entered the land under Joshua's leadership.

Where: The land of Canaan; the regions are then named according to the tribes that settled there.

Why: To encourage unity among the people and faithfulness to the covenant.

Structure and Content

1–12: Conquest of the land of Canaan. Joshua is confident that God is guiding him in his mission. Three times in the first chapter, God encourages him, saying, "Be firm and steadfast" (1:6, 7, 9). Chapters 3–12 recount the military battles Joshua and the Israelites wage with all of the peoples that already inhabit the land.

13–22: Division of the land. The Israelites are ready to settle in the land after conquering the fortified city of Jericho as well as other less significant towns. With Joshua and Eleazar, son of Aaron, overseeing the allotment, the land is divided among twelve tribes; each region receives its name from the tribe that inherits it. Members of the tribe of Levi, who serve as priests for all the Israelites, inhabit significant cities spread across the land. This assures the presence of priests among all the tribes.

23–24: Joshua's farewell address. Joshua addresses the people, speaking in God's name. He reviews what God has done for them, making good on the promises made to Abraham, Isaac, and Jacob, delivering the people from Egypt, destroying their enemies, and establishing them safely in the land. Joshua admonishes the people to "choose this day" (24:15) to serve God completely and reject false gods. The people, in response, promise to be faithful to its terms as they renew their covenant with the God of Israel. Joshua erects an altar at Shechem, warning that it will serve as a witness against the people if they are unfaithful. The death of Joshua.

Major Themes

- **God continues to be present** with the people and their leaders, even after the death of Moses.
- **The conquest of the land** is an essential link in the chain of transmission of the Torah from Moses.
- **Yahweh has given Israel the land,** but to maintain possession of it, Israel has to obey God's Torah.

Authorship

The Book of Joshua is a product of the seventh century BC (the reign of Josiah), which was revised in the exilic period in the light of the events of 587 (i.e., when the Babylonian Exile began).

Literary Forms

Deuteronomic History: Narrative grounded in the history of the covenant between God and Israel.

Legend: A story of extraordinary events believed to have a historical basis, such as the stories that surround the figures of Joshua and Rahab. Such stories were handed down for generations by word of mouth.

Key Passages

2: Rahab, the prostitute who is later named by Matthew as one of the ancestors of Jesus, assists the spies in Jericho.

6: The battle for Jericho. All the inhabitants, with the exception of Rahab and all who were in her house, are put under the ban and slain.

10:12-13: Joshua prays for the sun and the moon to stand still until the Israelites defeat the Amorites.

23–24: Joshua's farewell address.

Food for Thought

The time of Joshua, when the people were beginning to retake possession of the land, represents both a time of simplicity in the dedication of the people to the God of all the tribes and also the temptation of the people to move away from the single-minded devotion they had shown in the desert when they were forced to rely on God for food, water, and guidance. The exodus would remain a symbol of a honeymoon period when the people were faithful even in the midst of stark dependence on their leaders, who mediated God's will and word for them. Joshua represents a transition between Moses and the far more complicated (and dangerous) time of the monarchy.

Judges

After the time of Joshua, the tribes settled in the land and governed themselves under the leadership of judges, who were not legal experts but warriors. Judges emerged in times of crisis as people chosen by God to lead the Israelites back to the ways of the covenant. In the Book of Judges, the Deuteronomic historian illustrates once again the importance of the people's reliance on God. When they were rebellious and disobedient, they suffered at the hands of pagan neighbors like the Philistines and Midianites. When they repented and turned to the Lord, Yahweh sent judges who rescued them, often through battles. The Book of Judges tells the story of twelve of these charismatic leaders, who each seems to have held authority over a particular tribe rather than over all the tribes. Accounts of some of the judges are developed and detailed. More often, the reference is quite short with very little information given. The most famous of the judges are Deborah, Gideon, Jephthah, and Samson.

At a Glance

Who: The leaders during the interim period between Joshua, who led the people into the land, and the monarchy under David and Solomon and their successors.

What: A record of the time of the loose federation of tribes as the people settled in the land according to their tribes, based on the sons of Jacob.

When: The period between the thirteenth and eleventh centuries before Christ.

Where: The land was allotted to ten tribes assigned to the more fertile North and two tribes (Judah and Benjamin) to the South in the land previously known as Canaan.

Why: To support and promote the ideals of obedience, faithfulness, and tribal cohesion as characteristic of the period of the judges.

Structure and Content

1:1–3:6: The prologue describes the land and the tribes after Joshua's death. There is an overlap between the first three chapters of Judges and the end of the Book of Joshua. Joshua's death leaves a void of leadership, which is filled by the judges until the time when a king is chosen for Israel.

3:7–16:31: Stories of the judges. This section of the book recounts the stories of twelve who serve as judges during the time between Joshua and David. These are charismatic leaders who are recognized as instruments of God's will in times of crisis against foreign enemies. Some judges are only mentioned briefly, and others' stories are well developed and well-known. In the order of their appearance, the twelve judges are Othniel, Ehud, Shamgar, Deborah, Gideon, Tola, Jair, Jephthah, Ibzan, Elon, Abdon, and Samson.

17–21: The epilogue recounts the settling of the disputes between the tribes of Dan and Benjamin.

Major Themes

- **God protects** the people through judges and priests.
- **Heeding their leaders** is all Israel needs to do to prosper.

Authorship

Along with several other historical books, Judges is thought to have been composed around the seventh or sixth centuries before Christ and revised in the years after the exile to reflect the emphases of the Deuteronomic historian, especially trust in God and faithfulness to the covenant.

Literary Forms

Fable: A fable is a fictitious story meant to teach a moral lesson. The characters are usually animals, as in the example of Balaam's talking donkey in Numbers 22:22-35, or they may be vegetation. Such is the case in Judges 9:7-15, one of the best examples of a fable in the Bible. This fable illustrates the dangers of giving someone, such as a king, unlimited power.

Canticle of Deborah and Barak: Considered to be one of the oldest parts of the Bible, this song was probably part of liturgical celebrations praising God for rescuing the people from their enemies. It was preserved in Israel's oral memory and passed on through the liturgy until it was finally put in writing and contextualized by the story of Deborah and Barak (see Judges 5).

Key Passages

4:4–5:31: Barak, the commander of the Israelite army, needs the help of Deborah, a judge and prophet, and Jael, an Israelite woman, to conquer the Canaanites.

6:7–8:27: God's choice of the timid, reluctant, and youthful Gideon is clear evidence that God's power and mission, rather than human talent, are the basis of Israel's strength.

11:29-40: Jephthah's vow and the death of his daughter.

16:4-22: Samson's betrayal at the hands of Delilah, a Philistine.

Food for Thought

The judges, together with the priests, governed the people as they settled in the land according to their tribes. The judges represented God's ongoing care and faithfulness to the people of the covenant. The judges led the people with examples of faithful allegiance to and trust in God despite everything, including overwhelming opposition, temptations, fear, and great hardship.

Ruth

The Book of Ruth reflects on aspects of life during the tribal period and highlights the precarious situation of widows without sons, personified by Naomi, Orpah, and Ruth. The threat of famine, the foreign land of Moab, and death compound the problems of the widows in this story and heighten their destitution. Perhaps it seems strange that stories of these three women would be included in the Scriptures. However, their predicament after the deaths of their husbands exemplifies the need for God's protection and the potential inclusion of all people in the covenant first made with Israel. They need to depend on and trust in God, their only source of hope. The devotion that Ruth, a Moabite woman, shows to Naomi, her Jewish mother-in-law, is evidence of her true status as one of the people of God and makes her worthy to be a revered ancestor of the most beloved king, David. Her popularity is undiminished throughout Old Testament times, which helps explain why Matthew makes reference to Ruth, along with four other women in his genealogy of Jesus' ancestors (1:1-17).

At a Glance

Who: Naomi, a Jewish woman, was widowed and childless when her husband and two sons died. Her daughter-in-law, Ruth, a Moabite woman, eventually became the great-grandmother of King David.

What: Ruth's devotion to her mother-in-law is the centerpiece of this popular story.

When: Reflects the "time of the judges" (1:1), i.e., about 1200–1020 BC.

Where: Following the deaths of their husbands, Ruth followed her mother-in law, Naomi, from Moab to her ancestral home in Bethlehem.

Why: To illustrate the universal scope of salvation; it also exemplifies filial devotion as well as faith and its rewards, even as shown by a stranger.

Structure and Content

1: The predicament of Naomi and her daughters-in-law, Orpah and Ruth, is explained: Naomi, her husband, and their two sons move to Moab because there is a famine in Judah. Once there, Naomi's husband dies, leaving her a widow, and several years later, her two sons die as well. She then decides to return to Judah. Orpah stays in Moab, but Ruth makes a moving declaration of loyalty to her and goes with her to Judah.

2–4: Ruth and Naomi settle in Bethlehem, and Ruth meets Boaz, one of Naomi's kinsmen. He marries her, and Ruth and Boaz provide the foundation of the family that will produce a king (David) and change the course of Israel's history.

Major Themes

- **Conversion was an issue very much alive after the exile,** as well as the question "Who shall be included among the people of the covenant?" Ruth provides a partial answer, however ironic: although a foreigner, she is more faithful than most, even when it seems like she has no hope.
- **Dependence on and trust in God are essential.** Ruth also manifests the inseparability of faith in God and care for God's people.
- **Out of faithfulness comes new life**; despite all manner of suffering, there is hope.

Authorship

This book has an anonymous, or unknown, writer. Hypotheses about why Ruth was written are linked to theories regarding when it was written. Ruth is listed in the Hebrew Bible among the "writings," an arrangement suggesting a later date. On the other hand, in the LXX (and in most Christian versions of the Bible), Ruth is placed between Judges and 1 Samuel, a sequence that suggests an early dating. A compromise envisions an early story that was later edited and embellished.

Literary Form

Historical Fiction: This is a story of the filial piety of a woman, set in history, beloved for her connection to David (and later, Jesus), and useful to both Jews and Gentiles.

Key Passages

1:8-18: Three times Naomi tells her two daughters-in-law, "Go back." Ruth's failure to obey is an expression of her persistent faithfulness.

1:16-17: Ruth's pledge to remain with her mother-in-law is well-known as an expression of filial devotion.

4:14-15: Women come to Naomi with a blessing when Ruth becomes pregnant and bears Obed; they say that "Ruth is more to you than seven sons," which is high praise indeed. Seven is the perfect number and also represents infinity.

Food for Thought

The Book of Ruth affirms the possibility of a non-Israelite becoming a model of a true Israelite. Ruth reappears in the genealogy of Jesus according to Matthew to emphasize this possibility. Boaz redeems Ruth, we learn in chapter 4. The fact that redemption is a financial term that involves money and other indicators of wealth, such as land and inheritance, makes this a difficult concept to accept with regard to the value of women or as a concept used in relation to God. The Book of Ruth seems to suggest that women have no value in themselves and that their worth is measured by their husbands or male heirs. Yet Ruth's devotion and faith, in view of cultural limitations, reverse the judgment of her times. Although she seems to be dependent on male relatives, she actually becomes famous for her steadfast devotion to a woman, her mother-in-law. Ruth is an example of the limitations of cultural norms and the transcendence of God's forms of justice. Finally, she is praised as worth more than many men, negating the criteria of her culture and pointing to a completely new paradigm for evaluating people.

The Book of Ruth describes a fidelity or loyalty born of covenant bonding. Naomi prays for her daughters-in-law who have acted faithfully with regard to the dead and toward her (1:8-9). Naomi later praises God, who likewise shows covenant fidelity regarding the living and dead. Boaz asks God's blessings on Ruth because of the depth of her covenant fidelity, not only in caring for Naomi, but also by seeking Boaz, her dead husband's nearest relative.

1 and 2 Samuel

1 Samuel traces the transition from the time of the tribal rule overseen by the judges and the priests to the beginning of the monarchy with the selection of Saul as the first king of Israel. The time of the kings was fraught with a number of problems, many of which the people brought on themselves with their desire for a king.

When the people persist in their demand to have a king, God relents. The prophet outlines some of the responsibilities of a king that will distinguish him from the rulers of their pagan neighbors. For example, the king of Israel must be an advocate and protector of the widows and orphans, who are symbols of the poor and dependent, those who have no rights. The king would be chosen by God and act on God's behalf. He was to be an example to the people of living according to the Torah.

1 and 2 Samuel consist of originally independent narratives centering around the prophets Samuel and Nathan and the kings Saul, David, and Solomon. We also notice the Deuteronomist's theological emphasis on the succession of the first kings of Israel in accordance with God's choice and blessing, as well as the importance and authority of the prophets running as a continuous narrative through these books.

At a Glance

Who: The first kings of Israel, Saul and David, and the prophets Samuel and Nathan.

What: A theological history imbued with the thinking of the Deuteronomic historian during the establishment of the monarchy and the unified kingdom.

When: Around 1050–960 BC.

Where: Centered in the southern part of Israel, in Bethlehem and Jerusalem.

Why: To tell the epic story of Israel and the establishment of the monarchy, featuring David as a great king because of his loyalty to Yahweh.

Structure and Content

1 Samuel 1–7: Transition from tribal confederacy to monarchy, from the last of the judges to the first king. The book begins with the story of Eli, the last of the priests who advised the judges, and the apprenticeship of Samuel, the prophet chosen by God to anoint Saul as the first king of Israel. This section tells the story of Eli, of Hannah, mother of Samuel, and of Samuel.

1 Samuel 8:1–2 Samuel 2:7: The beginning of the monarchy. The people persist in their demand for a king, despite Samuel's warnings that this is not God's will for them. Samuel cautions that with a king will come armies and wars, taxes, and the conscription of their children and resources into the service of the king. Nevertheless, God chooses Saul as the first king. David is then anointed and succeeds Saul. This section also recounts David's reign, his adulterous affair with Bathsheba, and his repentance.

2 Samuel 2:8–24:25: The book ends with more details from the reign of David and appendices, including stories of David's sons, Absalom and Solomon.

Major Themes

- **God is faithful** and makes a covenant with David and his son despite their sin.
- **With David is the beginning of an expectation of a Messiah** (i.e., one who is anointed) who would be a king, that is, a political as well as a spiritual leader.

Authorship

The underlying blocks of narratives concerning Samuel and Saul and Nathan and David are ancient. They are rooted in the times of these first kings and reflect their great popularity. These blocks were finally put into a continuous narrative under the influence of the prophets, most likely those associated with the figure of Elisha. The final editing may have been done as late as the seventh and into the sixth century BC.

Literary Form

Legends Based on Historical Persons: Examples of this tendency to idealize certain leaders and turn them into characters of mythic proportions include Samuel, Saul, and David. Thus, even Samuel's birth is something of a miracle; Saul is the tallest and most handsome of men; and the youth, David, slays the giant, Goliath, with a slingshot and a stone. Later, David would conquer many enemies, far greater a number than Saul had done before him.

Key Passages

1 Samuel 1:1–2:36: Hannah's prayer and the birth of Samuel; the last of the judges.

2 Samuel 12:1-12: The prophet Nathan gives a parable of two men, one poor and one rich, to indict David's adulterous relationship with Bathsheba and call him to repentance.

2 Samuel 22:2-51: A hymn of David praising God.

2 Samuel 23:1-7: David's last words reaffirm his faith in God.

Food for Thought

In the telling of its national story, Israel acknowledges that God is the Lord of history, that divine providence protects and governs them, and that God continues to act faithfully, no matter what. The story of David emerges as the story of every man and every woman. It is a story of God's election and love shown before and despite human sinfulness and failings. The prophets work with the kings, acting as their conscience when power seduces them and also reassuring them of God's faithfulness even after they sin and especially after they repent. The kings are identified as "great" by the Deuteronomic historian insofar as they live according to the covenant. 1 and 2 Samuel illustrate God's mercy and forgiveness, Saul's illness of the heart in not remembering that he was ordained to exemplify God's own authority among the people, and David's superiority because he did remember who he was through God's grace.

No king ever measured up to the expectations surrounding David, not even David himself. But David represented Israel's hope that one day God would send a Messiah who would govern the people with justice. This view of a Messiah-king like David was always nurtured throughout Israel's history. It was particularly strong when Israel experienced the cruel effects of oppressive governments like Rome and the hardships of times such as when Jesus was born.

1 AND 2 KINGS

Like 1 and 2 Samuel, 1 and 2 Kings were originally a single scroll but were divided early on. The two books trace the period from the death of David to the fall of Jerusalem and the beginning of the Babylonian Captivity in 587 BC. The story of 1 Kings chronicles the reign of Solomon, son of David, who built the temple; the temple held great prominence in 1 Kings but became a symbol of division after Solomon's death. His rebellious sons were unable to maintain unity, and the kingdom was divided into two parts. 2 Kings traces this division of the single kingdom into Israel to the north and Judah to the south. Israel was eventually overthrown, and Judah's people were taken into exile. The story of the succession of the kings is interrupted with an account of two great prophets, Elijah and Elisha. A cycle of Elijah stories is recounted in 1 Kings 17–22, whereas the prophetic career of Elisha dominates 2 Kings.

The point of view here continues to be that of the Deuteronomist, who evaluated the reigns of the various kings according to whether or not they were faithful to the covenant as expressed in God's Law. Those who were deemed righteous prospered. Those who were unfaithful suffered, and the people suffered along with them. In a sense, 1 and 2 Kings record the Deuteronomist's final chapter. The story that began with Moses and Joshua and seemed so full of promise ends in tragedy. While God's side of the covenant was fulfilled in the glorious reign of David, his successors and the people consistently sinned and were unfaithful.

The purpose of the Deuteronomist's "history" is to explain how God's people could have been taken into exile, since God is faithful. The explanation is that the people themselves are responsible for their own suffering, since they were unfaithful. The leaders as well as the people of both kingdoms have sinned, especially by trusting on powers other than Yahweh.

At a Glance

Who: The story of the reign of Solomon, David's son and successor, and of his successors in the North and the South.

What: A theological history of the time of Solomon and the split of the kingdom in two through the end of the Northern Kingdom of Israel and the exile of the people of Judah in the South.

When: Covers the period from Solomon (960–922 BC) to the beginning of the exile in 587 BC.

Where: The Northern and Southern Kingdoms of Israel and Judah, respectively.

Why: To rekindle the religious and national spirit of the people.

Structure and Content

1 Kings 1–2: David's death and Solomon's succession. When David is advanced in years, a man named Adonijah appoints himself David's successor; the prophet Nathan and David's wife, Bathsheba, hear of Adonijah's "coronation ceremony" and inform David of this new event. David then has Nathan and Zadok, a priest, anoint his son Solomon as his successor. David dies shortly thereafter.

1 Kings 3–11: The reign of Solomon. Although not as great or beloved as his father, Solomon is devoted to God and to the covenant; these characteristics help explain his political and economic success. Chapters 3–11 portray Solomon as virtuous and wise, intent on building the temple that would serve as an appropriate expression of worship of God. At the same time, there is a shift in Solomon's allegiance as he turns from love of the Lord to concerns about maintaining his own wealth and fame, a shift the Deuteronomist equates with idolatry.

1 Kings 12–16: The early days of two kingdoms, Judah and Israel. Jeroboam, the first king of Israel, builds two calves of gold and proclaims them the god of Israel. He places one at the northernmost border and the other at the border to the south.

1 Kings 17–2 Kings 9: Cycle of stories of two great prophets, Elijah and Elisha. Elijah is the great prophet who alienates King Ahab of Israel and especially his wife, Jezebel, who has imported her pagan gods and influenced the king to lead the people astray. Elisha is called to succeed Elijah as prophet. Both Elijah and Elisha perform many mighty works, such as the multiplication of loaves, the curing of a man with leprosy, and even the raising of a young man from the dead. These acts show that God works through them.

2 Kings 10–17: An abridged history of the two kingdoms until the fall of the North (Israel) in 722–721 BC. Kings are judged on the basis of their fidelity or, more frequently, their infidelity to Yahweh. Many of them have very short reigns, as they do "what [is] evil in the sight of the LORD" (14:24).

2 Kings 18–25: These final chapters record the decline and defeat of Judah, symbolized by the destruction of Jerusalem and the exile of the captive people in Babylon in 587 BC. However, there is still hope since the covenant with David continues as was promised in 2 Samuel 7; the promise of David's never-ending reign will be fulfilled through the Messiah (see Matthew 1:1).

Major Themes

- **The prophets bring God's message of hope** and a call to repentance for a people suffering the consequences of their many sins.
- **Jerusalem and the temple** finally become symbols of hope and restoration.
- **God's covenant with David is a model of every other covenant.** God initiates it and remains faithful even when David sins.
- **Likewise, David remains the ideal of a good king** and the example all successive rulers ought to emulate. Despite his great sin, David trusted in God. He repented and received the promise of an everlasting dynasty.
- **Most kings, including his son Solomon, fail to follow David's example.** Jeroboam becomes the example of all that is wrong with Israel, since he leads the North to idolatry, which was considered particularly loathsome.

Authorship

These books are attributed primarily to the Deuteronomic historian, a designation that no doubt means a group of people, rather than a single individual, who was interested in the renewal of the covenant. The Deuteronomist evaluated Israel's history and leaders in terms of their fidelity to the covenant.

Literary Forms

Tales: In 1 Kings, many stories are told to illustrate the depth of Solomon's wisdom; see, for example, 1 Kings 3:16-27, in which Solomon is asked to decide between two women, both of whom claim to be the mother a small child.

Miracle Stories: Many astonishing events occur during the lives of Elijah and Elisha, such as Elijah ascending to heaven and Elisha purifying water (2 Kings 2).

Official Records/Archives: Some parts of 1 and 2 Kings explain the infrastructure that Saul, David, and Solomon created to administer the kingdom; see 1 Kings 4:7-19 for one example.

Key Passages

1 Kings 2:1-10: David's farewell discourse.

1 Kings 3:4-28: Solomon's prayer for wisdom and an example par excellence of his wisdom.

1 Kings 10:1-29: The Queen of Sheba visits Solomon and is impressed with his wisdom and his wealth.

1 Kings 19:1-18: Elijah's flight to Horeb, where he finds God in a still, small voice.

Food for Thought

From the time of David, the expectation of a Messiah who would be one like David persisted. Jesus' birth in Bethlehem, the witness of the sick who appealed to him for healing, and the "hosannas" of the crowds as he entered Jerusalem are all part of the Gospels' presentation of Jesus as the "Son of David." David provides a good example of the meaning of the covenant. God does not abandon David as a result of his sin. David repents, is forgiven, and is much stronger as a result of his experience of mercy and healing.

1 and 2 Chronicles

As a child, I puzzled over one of the requirements of a worthy reception of the Sacrament of Penance, namely, the meaning of "a firm purpose of amendment." I could understand that to be truly sorry for something, I would have to make an effort to stop doing it. But how? My reaction might have echoed the sentiments of the exiles from Babylon, returning, after fifty years, to the land of their ancestors. They were firmly resolved that their forced exile would never happen again, that they would not repeat the mistakes of the past. But how? The Books of 1 and 2 Chronicles, Ezra, and Nehemiah record how they meant to keep that resolution and truly become God's holy people.

1 and 2 Chronicles originally formed one scroll with the Books of Ezra and Nehemiah. They were composed after the exile and meant to describe a new way of life without dependence on a king or even national identity or freedom. They are essentially a rewriting of Israel's history under the monarchies from the perspective of the priests after the exile. Unlike the Books of Samuel and Kings and many of the prophets, these works seldom point to politics as the explanation for events but show how divine action is at work in the world to save and to punish.

Chronicles insists that Israel's importance is not political but religious and emphasizes the unity of the people as the holy people of God. The anonymous author, known as "the Chronicler" (probably a group of scribes rather than an individual), recapitulates the history of Israel from the reign of Saul to the edict of the Persian King Cyrus, who permitted the people to return to Jerusalem after the exile.

At a Glance

Who: The returning exiles, led by Ezra, a priest and scribe, and Nehemiah, the governor of Judah after the exile, reinterpreted their own history, especially the time from the beginning of the monarchy, in the light of the suffering they had experienced while exiled in Babylon.

What: A recap of Israel's history, emphasizing faithfulness as the appropriate worship of God.

When: The events described date from the eleventh through the seventh centuries before Christ.

Where: Judah, after the return of the people from exile.

Why: To renew the religious cult in Israel; if Israel was to have any future at all, it would be as God's holy people, faithful to the Law and to temple worship.

Structure and Content

1 Chronicles 1–9: Genealogies from Adam to Saul. 1 Chronicles heightens the importance of David by eliminating the narrative of Israel's story from Adam (creation) to the reign of Saul, as if this is all a prelude to the great king, David.

1 Chronicles 10–29: David's reign. God's covenant with David is continuous with the Mosaic covenant. Even though subsequent kings do not live up to the terms of the covenant, God's promise to David is reliable and trustworthy. 1 Chronicles omits or mitigates some of David's sins and describes him as a holy, dedicated, and righteous leader who prays often (for example, he composed the psalms); who lays out the plans for the Jerusalem temple (a claim that contradicts the judgment of the Books of Samuel and Kings); and who establishes the Levites' service in the temple.

2 Chronicles 1–9: Solomon's reign. Although Solomon is also held in high esteem, no one can compare to his father, David. As soon as he is inaugurated as king, Solomon builds a most magnificent temple where the ark of the covenant is enthroned; commerce and urban renewal testify to Solomon's great success until his death.

2 Chronicles 10–27: The kingdom is divided after the death of Solomon; 2 Chronicles tells of the kings of Judah, most of them sinning grievously.

2 Chronicles 28–36: The reforms of Hezekiah and Josiah. Ultimately, God uses even foreign kings such as Cyrus of Persia to finally liberate the people from captivity and to proclaim their freedom to return to the land and rebuild the temple.

Major Themes

- **David is the example par excellence of a devout and righteous leader** who ought to be imitated. David's achievements are less in the political and more in the religious realm.

- **The people's and especially the leaders' neglect of the cult** that identifies them as a holy people results in particularly bad consequences.

Authorship

Traditionally, since 1 and 2 Chronicles formed a single work with Ezra and Nehemiah, Ezra himself was thought to be the author, or "Chronicler." Taking older sources into account, 1 and 2 Chronicles were probably composed later, around 400 BC, to reinforce the future of Israel as God's holy people.

Literary Form

Annals: As befits their name, 1 and 2 Chronicles contain many records of events, which together with several sermons and genealogies, all form a history rewritten from the perspective of the central importance of cultic ritual as an expression of reverence for God's word.

Key Passages

1 Chronicles 10:13-14: The Chronicler denounces Saul for his unfaithfulness to God and declares that this is the reason David would ascend the throne.

2 Chronicles 36:22-23: The decree of Cyrus liberating the captives in Babylon and allowing them to return home to rebuild the temple. Cyrus' decree became something of a blueprint for Jesus' farewell address in Matthew (cf. Matthew 28:16-20).

Food for Thought

The influence of the beginning of 1 Chronicles (the genealogies) and the end of 2 Chronicles (Cyrus' proclamation of freedom for the people to return to the land and rebuild the temple) can be seen in the Gospel of Matthew, which used a similar framework. Matthew begins his Gospel with the genealogy of Jesus (1:1-17) and concludes with Jesus' mandate to his apostles to make disciples of all nations and his promise to remain with them always (28:18-20).

The author of Chronicles shows an intense concern for God's revealed word, celebrated in liturgy appropriate to and expressive of our faith: that from the beginning, we are created to worship Yahweh in every aspect of our lives. The God of Adam, of the patriarchs, and of David, Solomon, Samuel, and the other prophets is the God we worship.

EZRA

Ezra and Nehemiah originally formed a single unit referred to as "Ezra." Around the third century AD, Christians separated the two into distinct books based on their protagonists. They are similar in theological perspective, vocabulary, and time frame. They are so closely linked with the outlook and goals of 1 and 2 Chronicles that their anonymous author is known as "the Chronicler" and is often identified as Ezra, although most believe that more than one hand contributed to this collection of writings. In fact, Ezra begins with a recapitulation of the conclusion of 2 Chronicles with the decree of Cyrus and the return of the people to Jerusalem after fifty years of exile and captivity in Babylon. In the Hebrew Bible, 2 Chronicles is placed after Nehemiah, perhaps suggesting that 2 Chronicles was the last book to be received into the Hebrew canon.

"Ezra" is taken from the Hebrew word meaning "to help," and appears in chapter 7 of this book that bears his name. There, Ezra is described as a scribe, well versed in the Law of Moses, who came up from Babylon to Jerusalem. Because "Ezra had set his heart to study the law of the LORD," the favoring hand of God was on him (7:10). In the Books of Ezra and Nehemiah, we see the rise in the importance of various groups connected with the temple and the dedicated study of the Law, groups that will be very significant in the Gospels. These groups include the priests, Levites, and scribes. Although the priesthood was a complicated matter in Old Testament history, the role of the priests was significantly strengthened from the time of Ezra and the return of the exiles as the temple was rebuilt and its liturgy was revived; the Book of Ezra sheds light on this development.

At a Glance

Who: Ezra is a religious leader described as a scribe and later as a prophet.

What: Leaders want to teach the people how to live in the Promised Land even without national identity and prestige. Their worship would form their bond, and they would be distinguished from other people by their practice of the Torah.

When: Depending on which Artaxerxes is referred to (Ezra 7:1; Nehemiah 2:1), these works may depict events from the late sixth century or, more likely, from the late fifth or early fourth centuries BC.

Where: Postexilic Judah.

Why: To teach the proper practice of the Torah as the exiles returned to Jerusalem and rebuilt the temple.

Structure and Content

1–6: The first exiles return to Judah. The reconstruction of the temple is built into the story of the return. Cyrus' decree gives permission for the people to return for the purpose of rebuilding the house of the Lord (cf. 2 Chronicles 36:23; Ezra 1:2-4). The returning people bring with them the temple vessels that Nebuchadnezzar, the Babylonian king, had confiscated when he subdued Jerusalem and took the people captive. Jewish efforts to rebuild the temple are at first frustrated by Samaritans, but the prophets Haggai and Zachariah urge the people to complete the reconstruction (Ezra 5). Darius, the new Persian king, upholds the old decree of Cyrus and adds that the rebuilding effort will be subsidized with Persian funds (6).

7–10: Ezra and his reform. This section is a kind of memoir, which includes genealogical lists that help to establish Ezra's priestly credentials and trace his lineage back to Aaron, brother of Moses and father of the priests.

Major Themes

- **David was the ideal king,** and all the successive kings would have done well to imitate his example. When most did not, their reigns were judged negatively, and the people suffered.

- **The temple, its rituals, and prayer** are most important.

- **Mixed marriages are banned** as a threat to the purity of the people.

- **Feasts were reestablished** and celebrated as part of the effort of reunification.

Authorship

The book is ascribed to Ezra in the years following the return of the people from exile but may have been composed much later, perhaps even as late as three centuries before Christ.

Literary Forms

Annals: Ezra records his journey out of exile back to Jerusalem as well as how the temple is rebuilt and worship is restored in Jerusalem.

Decrees: Solemn proclamations from the Persian rulers Cyrus, Darius, and Artaxerxes affirm the freedom of the people to return to their land, to rebuild the temple with help from the Persians, and to worship their God (see 1:1-4; 6:1-12; 7:11-26).

Genealogies: Lists of the returned exiles are incorporated as it becomes increasingly important for the people to trace their heritage back to the age of the patriarchs (see 2:1-67; 8:1-14).

Key Passage

7:6-15: Ezra acknowledges the people's sin and God's faithfulness. Ezra leads the people in prayer for God's mercy.

Food for Thought

The importance of priests and scribes that we see in the Gospels comes from this period of the people's history. Israel no longer experiences political greatness but must distinguish itself as the holy people of God. David, Jerusalem, and the temple are important in their function of leading the people to God. Ezra and Nehemiah recognize that the people's sense of identity depends upon their purity as people committed to the Law. In this light, we can better understand the significance of Herod's later attempts to curry favor with his own people by building a magnificent temple to rival the glory of the one built by Solomon.

The ability to trace one's ancestry back beyond the period of the exile to the patriarchs becomes important at this time as well. Matthew's genealogy of Jesus is meant to show Jesus as a direct descendant of Abraham and David. Paul similarly insists that he is a "Hebrew born of Hebrews" (Philippians 3:5), suggesting that his lineage goes back to Moses.

Nehemiah

Nehemiah seemed to have been something of a whiner. He kept asking God the equivalent of "Do you see this? Do you realize what I am going through for you?" Nehemiah was building the walls around the temple and Jerusalem, and his opponents kept taunting him to come down from the wall and fight with them. It can be amusing to see how often Nehemiah displays bursts of emotion, frustration, and even a little hubris; he asks repeatedly if God is aware of his dedication to the project of rebuilding the temple and looks for credit for his achievements and even for taking abuse from his opponents. But through it all, Nehemiah is single-minded in his dedication to reestablishing the people as belonging to God. Nehemiah may be the patron of the insecure and petulant, but he is also an example for all ages of one who devotes his considerable talents to the service of God and the community.

This book is a continuation of the story from Ezra, told from the complementary perspective of a dedicated layman, Nehemiah, who actually carried out the program envisioned by Ezra. Ezra and Nehemiah shared a common understanding that the temple was a potent and indispensable symbol needed to reestablish the identity of the people as God's people. The walls of Jerusalem and, more important, of the temple were finally finished by the Feast of Booths, or Sukkot. According to the Torah, this harvest feast is one of celebration for all God's blessings. In a kind of interlude of Nehemiah's memoirs, Ezra dramatically appears in chapter 8 and reads the Torah to the assembled people. Then he urges them to celebrate the Feast of Booths, after which they confess their sins and, under the leadership of the priests and Levites, make a pact to live as God's holy people.

Besides Ezra, two others are significant in the telling of Nehemiah's story. King Darius is the Persian king who, in about 520 BC, reiterated the original decree of Cyrus from around 539 BC, which permitted the Jews to return to their native land and rebuild their temple (see Ezra 4:24; 6:1-12). Not only that, but Darius agreed to pay for the restoration of the temple. Zerubbabel was the leader of the returning exiles charged with the responsibility for rebuilding the temple (3:2-8; 5:2). As a descendant of David, he is included in Jesus' genealogy (Matthew 1:12-13; Luke 3:27).

At a Glance

Who: Nehemiah was a political leader, the governor of Judah in the early days of the people's return from exile. Nehemiah and Ezra had authority to rebuild the temple and teach the people the Torah.
What: The rededication of the people and the temple to God and to the Torah.
When: Set about a century after the return of the people from exile, around 439 BC.
Where: Jerusalem.
Why: To establish the returning exiles as God's people.

Structure and Content

1–7: Memoirs of Nehemiah about rebuilding Jerusalem's walls, a symbol of pride, strength, and identity. Nehemiah requests permission to return to the land of his ancestors to rebuild the walls of Jerusalem and not only receives permission but also funding and an escort. Nehemiah organizes the people to work on portions of the walls surrounding Jerusalem near their own homes, a shrewd strategy that reinforces the idea that in protecting the city, they are protecting themselves. The rebuilders and Nehemiah himself suffer many obstacles; the Samaritans threaten violence, and Nehemiah receives death threats. The workers, in fact, keep not only their tools but also their weapons nearby.

8–10: Ezra's covenant renewal ceremony. Finishing the wall coincides with the Feast of Sukkot, and Ezra, the priest, is called upon to read the Book of the Law before the assembly of all the people, some of whom had never heard of many of the instructions in the Law. At first, many weep to think that they do not know the Law, but their sorrow soon turns to joy. The people revive the celebration of the Feast of Booths and erect tents and dwell in them for the duration of the feast.

11–13: Nehemiah's memoirs continue. The book concludes with personal reflections balanced with official-sounding resolutions to some practical problems. Families are chosen by lot to reside in Jerusalem to assure its ongoing protection, defense, and population. The priests and Levites and other liturgical officials, so important to the temple, are reconstituted and dedicated, as the people identify themselves evermore with their religious symbols. Nehemiah reinforces a number of religious reforms, which are all intended to underscore the purity and integrity of Jewish observance and its freedom from foreign contaminating influences.

Major Themes

- **The people's religious identity is inseparable from their political aspirations,** especially their hopes for peace and prosperity.

- **Prayer sustains all the efforts** and intentions of people dedicated to God.

Authorship

This book is attributed to "the Chronicler," a group of scribes or an individual, who drew on the memoirs of Nehemiah and continued the story of Ezra about the return of the people from exile and the rebuilding of the walls and the temple of Jerusalem.

Literary Form

Memoir: This book appears to be a story told in the first person, although it was almost surely heavily edited later by "the Chronicler."

Key Passage

8:9-10: Nehemiah, the governor, and Ezra, a priest and scribe, join the Levites in teaching the people about the importance of the temple and its liturgy. They celebrate with a joyful feast.

Food for Thought

1 and 2 Chronicles, Ezra, and Nehemiah insist on the constancy of God's providence throughout history, including even the painful period of the exile. The glory and fortification of Jerusalem and the temple are symbols of the holiness of the people themselves. What symbols of holiness help you in your life with God?

Introduction to Tobit, Judith, Esther, and 1 and 2 Maccabees

People sometimes have an otherworldly notion of holiness. In that world, the saints are seen with halos around their heads and hands always folded in prayer. In that world, many of us ordinary folks would feel lost. Fortunately for us, the biblical tradition is firmly grounded on earth, where people find God in the stuff of their daily lives. This brings us to a group of books about people facing extraordinary challenges with courage because they know that God is the source of their strength and hope. In this group, we have a little of everything to pique our interest: romance, love and marriage, illness, grief, war, and astonishing heroes. There are even angels sent to comfort, console, and heal.

Of the remaining works categorized as historical books in Catholic Bibles, only the Book of Esther is part of the canon of the Jewish (and Protestant) Scriptures, but not even all of Esther is included in that canon. These works are among the latest of the Old Testament, and the Hebrew original text, if it existed, has long been lost. Most of these works only exist in Greek and were included in the LXX; this was the basis of St. Jerome's translation into Latin, the Vulgate, which later became the official translation of the Catholic Church.

Tobit, Judith, and Esther have a common genre, that of religious fiction, a kind of religious novel. They are meant to instruct and illustrate the ways of religious piety, faith, and the importance of maintaining Jewish identity, especially in the face of obstacles and hardship. These books form a kind of bridge between the historical books and wisdom literature. They are stories of fictional persons, contextualized in historical settings, who demonstrate virtues extolled in the wisdom literature, especially the Books of Psalms and Proverbs. They pay tribute to people threatened with religious persecution who maintain their faith in God and express this faith in frequent prayers of intercession and praise. These are stories of heroes that strongly appeal to popular imagination.

The Books of 1 and 2 Maccabees conclude the "historical books" category of the Old Testament in the Catholic Bible. Set against the background of the Jewish resistance to Hellenism, which was forced upon the Jewish people by the successors to Alexander the Great, they tell of the persecution of the Jews and the atrocities visited upon them as the Seleucid rulers, with their capital in Damascus, Syria, tried to establish their dominance over the nations that had been previously conquered by Alexander. 1 and 2 Maccabees tell the stories of Jewish heroism and courage as they resist the foreign invaders and Hellenistic influence to reestablish their independence once more in 164 BC.

The popular Feast of Purim, or Hanukkah, mentioned in Esther and in 2 Maccabees, comes from this period and commemorates the rededication of the temple. Sadly, the Jews were not to enjoy religious and national freedom for long, however. The Romans would arrive a century later, in 63 BC, and their oppression of the Jews is legendary. These late Jewish works tell of the fabric of life for the Jews who had been oppressed for so long and also prepare the reader to understand the tumultuous times into which Jesus was born.

Useful Terms to Know

Angels and Demons: From the Greek term meaning "messenger," angels function as mediators between God and people. Often, as in the Book of Tobit, they bring aid and comfort to a person in distress or clarity about the right direction for his or her life. Angels are spiritual beings possessing suprahuman powers for good. For example, Raphael is an angel in disguise who serves as Tobias's guide to Media where he would find a fitting wife in Sarah (Tobit 5:4). Demons are also spiritual beings and are capable of amazing powers of disruption and evil, as in the case of Asmodeus, who killed each of Sarah's seven husbands on the night of their wedding, making her the object of much abuse (3:8).

Deuterocanonical: A term used in reference to the seven disputed books of the Old Testament that are not included in the Hebrew canon. Jews and Protestants consider these works "apocryphal," that is, interesting and significant, but not part of the inspired canon. They are included in the Catholic canon.

Feast of Purim: According to the story of Esther, the minister Haman had convinced the king to destroy all the Jews on a day chosen by lots (*purim* is the Hebrew word meaning "lots"). The feast, also called Hanukkah, which means "dedication," is based on the Book of Esther's account of the efforts of Mordecai and his niece, Esther, to circumvent Haman's plot. The feast is celebrated with a reading of the Book of Esther in the synagogue, the distribution of charity, and a festive meal to commemorate the victory of God's people despite all odds.

Hasideans, meaning "faithful ones," are first mentioned in 1 Maccabees 2:42-48. Together with the Hasmoneans, they actively oppose Hellenization. They are the spiritual ancestors of the Pharisees, who were so prominent at the time of Jesus.

Hasmoneans are the descendants of Hashmon, a Jewish family that provided military, political, and religious leadership in Judaism for most of the second century and half of the first century before Christ. This family included the Maccabees.

"Maccabee" is a name that means "hammer." The Maccabean Revolt was the Jewish rebellion against the Seleucid king, Antiochus IV Epiphanes (175–164 BC), who attempted to impose Hellenism on the Jews and then tried to suppress Judaism by outlawing central Jewish practices such as circumcision, keeping a kosher diet, and observing the Sabbath. The final straw was the king's desecration of the temple by erecting a statue of Zeus there and sacrificing a pig to it. His efforts were continued after his death by those who struggled to ascend to the Seleucid throne. These aggressive attempts to hellenize the Jews led to the Maccabean Revolt and finally to Jewish independence from Syria in 164 BC. That independence would last only a hundred years, until the appearance of Pompei and the Romans in 63 BC.

Martyr is a Greek word meaning "witness." The mother in Maccabees and her seven sons are martyrs in living and practicing their Jewish beliefs even in the face of great suffering and death; they are witnesses to their faith even unto death. Their story is told in 2 Maccabees 7.

Nebuchadnezzar is identified in the Book of Judith as the ruler "over the Assyrians," with his capital in the "great city of Nineveh" (1:1). But readers would have known that Nebuchadnezzar was actually the infamous king of the Babylonians at the time of the exile in the sixth century before Christ. Such historical inaccuracies suggest this is one of the ways that the author signaled that this work was a fictional creation; it became popular during the Hellenistic period (i.e., after the fourth century BC).

Religious Novel: The genre of Tobit, Judith, and Esther, who may all have been fictional characters. These works tell a traditional story with vivid details, meant to inspire and encourage the people to trust God unconditionally. But they may also contain geographical and historical inaccuracies. They are "fiction" in the sense that they are not meant to be taken literally or judged historically. They are nevertheless "true" and part of the canon of the Bible because their heroes exemplify the significant virtues and attitudes of a devout Israelite.

Tobit

A few years ago, my brother was diagnosed with a very rare and serious disease and had to travel to confer with a specialist. It so happened that he was seated on the plane next to a physician who was world renowned for her expertise in that exact illness. She reviewed the records he had on hand and was able to reassure him that the recommended course of treatment would help him. Sometimes it seems as if God is in the details. Despite our worries and problems, we can often find help, reassurance, and even comfort in God's providential care for us.

In the fourth century before Christ, the Jewish people found themselves surrounded by the pagan influences of Greek society, including diminishing emphasis on the importance of family and increasing belief in the notion that humans are pawns to fate and gods who act in whimsical ways. The Jews wanted to stress their religious identity as well as their dependence on a personal God who cared for them. Living in a time of religious persecution helped encourage them that God would indeed come to their aid and reward them for living according to the law, even if their prayers were not answered for some time. Marriage within Judaism, practices of filial piety, almsgiving, and trust helped maintain their identity and, they believed, would be rewarded by God's providential care.

All of these themes are evident in the story told in the Book of Tobit. Two of the main characters, Tobit and Sarah, are faithful Jews who have suffered greatly through no fault of their own—one might say, at the hand of fate. Tobit was blinded while performing a charitable deed, and Sarah suffered the death of seven husbands, each of whom died on their wedding night before the marriage could be consummated. God works in their dire circumstances, however, and because of their fidelity to their faith, each of them is ultimately vindicated: Tobit's sight is restored, and Sarah happily weds Tobias, Tobit's son.

At a Glance

Who: Tobit was a pious, wealthy Israelite living in Nineveh, exiled from the Northern Kingdom of Israel; he became blind even while he was performing the pious act of burying a stranger. In the end Tobit would sing a song praising God, in whom his faith never faltered.

What: A religious novel about fictitious people, contextualized in a time when Israel had suffered defeat under the Assyrians. In the story, vindication is finally found in the happy resolution of Tobit's own ordeals and those of his family.

When: After Israel had been conquered by the Assyrians, sometime around the end of the seventh or beginning of the sixth century before Christ.

Where: Nineveh, the pagan capital of the hated Assyrian Empire.

Why: To encourage Jews struggling under the Hellenistic regimes that were dominant after the time of Alexander (336–323 BC) to remain faithful and to maintain their own Jewish identity.

Structure and Content

1–3: The plights and prayers of Tobit and Sarah. Despite their religious piety, Tobit and Sarah are both afflicted with many problems so severe that they want to die. Providence and divine intervention come to them in the form of the angel Raphael and Tobias, son of Tobit.

4–11: Tobias acts as God's instrument to help Tobit and Sarah. While on a mission from his father, Tobias ends up falling in love with the beautiful but apparently dangerous Sarah, whose seven fiancés have died before her marriage to any of them could be consummated. After their marriage, Tobias and Sarah return to Tobit, who is cured after he follows instructions given by Raphael.

12–13: Raphael reveals his identity as an angel in God's service, and Tobit sings a song of praise.

14: Epilogue. After a farewell discourse, Tobit dies. Then Tobias and Sarah return to Media and take care of Sarah's parents until their deaths. Finally, Tobias dies with a hymn of praise to God on his lips.

Major Themes

- **Faith is manifest in the lives of ordinary people.** God's providence becomes more clear when we are open to surprises and the immediacy of grace.

- **Maintaining religious identity,** especially through faithfulness to the Law, is of paramount importance.

Authorship

Tobit is set in the seventh century BC but was written sometime in the late third century before Christ by an unknown author.

Literary Form

Religious Novel: Although not about historical persons, these stories are meant to reflect the appropriate way of a life of faith amid persecution and all kinds of trials. They are meant to encourage faith and piety as well as to entertain. These stories became very popular with Jewish and Christian audiences. Other examples include Judith, Esther, and Jonah.

Key Passages

4:3-21: Tobit's farewell discourse and charge to his son.

5:4-8: The angel, Raphael, appears and agrees to accompany Tobias on his journey.

13:1-18: Tobit's song of praise.

Food for Thought

We probably all experience some moments in our lives when things just seem too much to bear. We may feel overwhelmed and almost hopeless. God's providential care may be expressed in numerous ways, some extraordinary and some very ordinary, many times through surprises that catch us unaware. We may recognize that we have been visited by angels—messengers of God's love for us.

The Book of Tobit helps us to see God's faithfulness despite our many hardships. It encourages us to remain faithful and rely on the ultimate blessings of God. We can practice our faith in our everyday lives—for example, in our devotion to our parents and in the purity of marriage, in our reverence for the dead, and in almsgiving, prayer, and fasting. As believers, we can reflect in our daily lives the justice and mercy of God through our trust in him and in our prayer.

Judith

The unlikely hero who rescues God's people in this story is a woman. Indeed, she is even identified with God's people. Judith, whose name means "a Jewish woman," represents the very best of Judaism. She receives her mission and her strength from God, putting herself entirely at God's disposal in trust, giving God all the credit in thanksgiving once her victory over Israel's enemies is accomplished. Judith is beautiful and wise, devout and courageous; she is a widow and the model of an Israelite who relies entirely on God.

Although it is not possible to identify precisely the actual circumstances that gave rise to the composition of this narrative, the author combines lessons from several events in Israel's history that demonstrated the reliability of God's continued presence with them. As had happened several times before, the people face insurmountable odds: the overwhelming power of their enemy, this time, Assyria. One person, Achior, acts as an unwitting prophet when he warns Holofernes, an Assyrian general, not to attack Israel because God protects them (Judith 5:5-21). There is irony in the fact that oftentimes people speak the truth even while they do not acknowledge or know the source of their inspiration.

A common word found in the first part of the narrative is "fear": Nebuchadnezzar, Holofernes, the Medes, and the Assyrians all strike fear in the hearts of the Israelites. In contrast, Judith fears only God and challenges the people to "wait for his deliverance" (8:17). Before taking on the challenge to confront and conquer Holofernes, Judith first confronts her people and reminds them of how God has rescued and protected them in the past. Then she promises to deliver Israel, although she remains silent about her plans on how to accomplish this. She prays and then uses her attractiveness to seduce Holofernes, a slave to his own delusions. After she slays him, she returns to her own people with his head, the sight of which causes the condemned Achior to convert and be circumcised (14:6-10).

At a Glance

Who: A Jewish woman, Judith, who delivered the people from the Assyrians' vengeance.

What: A religious novel illustrating the concerns of Jews under Hellenistic rule to preserve their own identity even in the face of fierce persecution.
When: Set in 593 BC, the "twelfth year of the reign of Nebuchadnezzar" (605–562), ruler of Assyria, the archenemy of preexilic Israel(1:1).
Where: Israel, the Northern Kingdom, which had refused to join Nebuchadnezzar in battle against the Medes.
Why: To encourage religious piety and faithfulness.

Structure and Content

1–7: The people are terrified in the face of the pride and boasts of arrogant Assyria.

8–16: The challenge and victory of Judith. This second part emphasizes Judith's beauty, which not only attracts the archenemy, Holofernes, but is also the vehicle of her strength and wisdom acquired through prayer. Judith acts resolutely and courageously to save Israel. She then leads the people in celebration and thanksgiving to God for delivering the people just like God had done in the exodus.

Major Themes

- **Despite all sorts of fears and threats, people are called upon to put their trust in God,** who is more powerful than all of the forces that confront them.

- **Judith signifies the power of complete trust in God,** who is able to achieve mighty works through her.

Authorship

Judith's composition by an unknown author was probably sometime in the second century before Christ but could be as late as 100 BC. This popular novel manifests a Pharisaic bias in its focus on prayer and penance, strict adherence to the Law, and veneration of the temple and rituals.

Literary Form

Symbolic Narrative: A depiction of a fictional person and events set in a time of grave crisis, celebrating the protection of God for the people of Israel even in the face of overwhelming threats from foreign nations with superior military strength. This book combines images from the exodus, the exile and its aftermath, and the unexpected victory signified by the Maccabean Revolt.

Key Passages

4:8-15: All the people of Israel do penance and pray fervently to be delivered from the evils stacked against them.

8:1-8: The widowed Judith, beautiful and rich, leads an exemplary life characterized by devotion to God and prayer.

16:1-17: Judith leads the people in celebration of their victory over their enemies with a hymn of praise and thanksgiving to God.

Food for Thought

Judith represents the whole nation in personally living out a kind of exodus experience, revealing God's power and mercy even in the most threatening of circumstances. Judith personifies all of Israel's experience of bondage, liberation, and renewed commitment to God. It will probably not be necessary for us to do what Judith did. But we would do well to emulate her openness to God's will and her celebration of God's goodness once her mission was accomplished.

God protects his people despite seemingly overwhelming forces arrayed against them. God can use any human instrument to show divine power, and often God's instrument is someone judged insignificant or unimportant by human standards. God's choice often catches us by surprise. Time and again, the Bible urges people to rely on God regardless of the powers that threaten them. Judith is one such example of trust even in the face of great odds. The Gospel of Luke (2:36-38; 21:1-4), which portrays widows as a symbol of those most receptive to Jesus' teachings and miracles, could well be following in the tradition of the Book of Judith in this regard.

Esther

The Book of Esther reads almost like a classic fairy tale of a young woman who gains attention and favor with a king, apparently because of her exceedingly good looks. It is a story that starkly portrays good versus evil, with little consideration of any gray areas.

Despite the popularity of the story, from the beginning many questioned why this book should be included in the Scriptures. In fact, the history of the inclusion of the Book of Esther is complicated because the original Hebrew version was considered insufficiently religious. For example, the Hebrew version contained no mention of God or the land of Israel. Further, in that version, Mordecai and Esther, rather than God, are credited with saving their fellow Jews. However, because the book and the Feast of Purim, or Hanukkah, that is connected with the book were very popular, strong sentiment among the rabbis led to its inclusion in the canon of Scripture when that issue was debated around the mid-eighties AD.

There is more than one Greek version of Esther, and this added to the complexity of its textual history. In six additions placed throughout the book and later identified as "A" through "F," the Septuagint in particular added prayers and an emphasis that God's help made possible the survival of the Jews in a land governed by foreign powers that were constantly threatening them. Catholic Bibles include this Septuagint version as part of the canon.

Although the story is supposed to have taken place during the Babylonian Exile, it was inspired by the events of the successful struggle of the Jews against the demands of Hellenism represented in the Maccabean Revolt. The emphasis on Jewish independence and on maintaining religious identity was encouraged. Mordecai and Esther emerge as inspirational models that ought to be imitated, since their success was rooted in their faith in God.

At a Glance

Who: Esther and her uncle, Mordecai, belonged to the court of the king of the Persian Empire, who was advised by aides to eliminate all the Jews of the empire in a single day.

What: As beloved queen, Esther was in a unique position to uncover the evil plot of Haman and his wife to kill all the Jews, and to approach the king to intercede for her own people, the Jews. This is the basis for the Feast of Purim.

When: Set in the fifth century BC.

Where: Probably in the diaspora, perhaps Egypt.

Why: To show that, regardless of the overwhelming obstacles the people faced, God would provide leadership and victory for them over evil as long as they remained faithful.

Structure and Content

1–5 and Sections A–D: The ways of the powerful in Persia. Mordecai is an important and trusted minister at the court of King Ahasuerus (known in history as Xerxes I). Another minister named Haman hates Mordecai and plots to kill all the Jews in Persia. Mordecai's niece, Esther, a Jew renowned for her beauty, becomes queen after the king deposes his wife, Queen Vashti, for displeasing him. Once Mordecai discovers Haman's plot to annihilate the Jews, he approaches Queen Esther and instructs her to intercede for all Jews to her husband. At first, Esther is fearful, but eventually she does as Mordecai commands her.

6–10 and Sections E–F: Divine protection for the weak and vulnerable. When the king learns of Haman's plot, he hangs him. Rather than being persecuted and annihilated, the Jews are victorious over their enemies, and they celebrate the power that God has demonstrated on their behalf with the Feast of Purim. It would become a very popular annual spring feast in remembrance of God's faithful protection of the people in times of threat and helplessness.

Major Themes

- **God protects his people** even in the face of great danger and persecution.

- **Human responsibility to cooperate with God** is exemplified by the figures of Queen Esther and Mordecai.

- **The power of prayer** is illustrated as the people ask for God's mercy and protection from their enemies.

Authorship

Although set in the fifth century before Christ, Esther was probably composed around the time of the Maccabees in order to encourage the people to stand firm in their Jewish identity. The Greek additions might have been included in the second century BC or, as some have suggested, even as late as the eighties BC.

Literary Form

Historical Fiction: Esther is a story or short "novel" used as inspiration and encouragement to the Jews in trying times.

Key Passages

4:12-14: Mordecai's challenge to Esther that she might have arisen to a position of power precisely to exercise it to help save the Jews.

C:14-30: Esther's prayer asking God for help and courage.

9:1-23: The victory of the Jews and the establishment of Purim to celebrate God's liberation of the people.

Food for Thought

One of the reasons there was reluctance to accept the Book of Esther into the canon of Scripture was its secular nature; in fact, prayers were added at key points in the story to enhance its religious nature. Mordecai's and Esther's confidence in God and their witness to God's faithfulness despite persecution and threats make them powerful examples to people struggling to preserve their religious beliefs under difficult circumstances.

Esther presents us with the challenge of considering every day, every obstacle, or every opportunity as a moment to offer praise and thanks to God for all that has been given to us. To meet this challenge, we must pray that our talents be used for God's glory. It is not so much the actual prayers that were added to the Book of Esther that makes the story so edifying. Rather, Esther's tenacious claim to belong to the canon of our Scriptures is rooted in this holy woman's example to us, God's people, to use all the resources at our disposal to help others, to be true to our convictions, to overcome our fears, and to give glory to God with the beauty of our lives.

1 Maccabees

Nothing inspires a family or a group like the stories of heroic relatives of the past whose great acts of courage sprang from their solid convictions. This is especially true for a people as family and tradition-minded as the Jews. They celebrated their very birth as a people by recalling liturgically and historically the exodus, when they overcame the greatest odds to return to the Promised Land. Throughout their history, they had confronted Goliaths of all kinds—the nations that occupied the land and refused to let them enter, the Assyrians and the Syrians, and the Babylonians and the Greeks. Although they had suffered much from these conflicts, the Jews held on to their belief that God would vindicate them. They needed to maintain their national and religious identity and refused to be assimilated into the culture around them that kept trying to force them to abandon their religious practices.

Alexander the Great (336–323 BC) forced all the nations that had come under his power to use a single language, Greek, realizing that a universal language would help to unite his extensive empire and make these diverse peoples easier to control. Hellenistic encroachment into their lives did not sit well with the Jews, who chafed under foreign dominance throughout their history. The Seleucid Empire that succeeded Alexander's short reign was ruthless in trying to force the Jewish people to submit to Hellenism in all its forms. Finally, the outrages of a Seleucid king provoked a brave, dedicated rebellion of the Jews, who ultimately won independence around 164 BC. But their victory was short-lived: little more than a century later, in 63 BC, the Romans easily defeated Jewish resistance. The Books of the Maccabees, with their stories of heroism and resolve among the Jews during this rebellion against foreign oppression, set the stage for the birth of Jesus into a tumultuous world.

At a Glance

Who: Mattathias was an old priest who resisted the efforts of the king to force Jews to eat pork; his actions set off the Maccabean Revolt against Hellenistic interference, which was led by his sons, especially Judas Maccabeus.

What: The story of the overthrow of the Hellenistic kings and the rise of the Hasmoneans, a previously obscure priestly family, to political and religious power, with titles of both "high priest" and "king."

When: The events recounted are from the reign of Antiochus IV Epiphanes (175–164 BC) until the reign of John Hyrcanus (134–104 BC), the grandson of Mattathias.

Where: Set primarily in Modein, a town about seventeen miles from Jerusalem.

Why: To inspire Jews living under pagan regimes to hold steadfast, remain faithful, and witness to their faith even in the midst of great hardships.

Structure and Content

1–2: The Maccabean Revolt. This book begins with a short reference to Alexander the Great, who spread his kingdom from Greece throughout the known world. On his way home to Syria after waging war on the Egyptians, a Seleucid king plunders the temple in Jerusalem and imposes outrageous sanctions on the Jews. Finally, Mattathias, an old priest from Modein, a town not far from Jerusalem, and father of five sons, kills a Jewish man about to eat pork and also kills the messenger of the king. His example rallies the rest of the Jews.

3–16: Leadership of Judas Maccabeus and his brothers, Jonathan and Simon. The victories of the brothers and the purification and rededication of the temple are recounted in these chapters. The book ends with the accession of John Hyrcanus, grandson of Mattathias, who becomes ruler and high priest of the Jews from 134 BC until his death in 104 BC.

Major Themes

- **Absolute monotheism.** There is no other God but Yahweh, the one, true, living God.

- **The leadership of the Maccabees** is yet one more example of God's faithfulness.

Authorship

The book is attributed to an anonymous Jewish nationalist, an admirer of the Hasmoneans, who wrote around the beginning of the first century BC.

Literary Form

Historical Narrative: An account of the rise of the Hasmonean dynasty.

Key Passages

3:42–4:25: Judas Maccabeus leads the army in prayer and supplication, begging God to bless their efforts, and then leads them into battle against King Lysias' army; they strike a mighty blow against their enemy.

4:36-59: The temple is cleansed from its desecration; the altar is rebuilt and rededicated, and sacrifices are offered to celebrate the victory of the Jews.

Food for Thought

Depicting events that set the political scene for Jesus' birth, 1 Maccabees explains the rise in power of the political dynasty known as the Hasmonean dynasty, ancestors to the high priests who ruled in Jesus' time. 1 Maccabees also provides background for understanding the relationship between Jews and foreign occupiers such as the Greeks, the Seleucids, and, finally, the Romans. This book thus helps us understand why the Jews of Jesus' day looked for a Messiah who would fulfill the functions of both priest and king.

As human beings, we tend to forget things quickly and fall back into old habits of complacency. We can be inspired by the courage of those who came before us and had to struggle for religious liberties that we take for granted. Give thanks today for your faith. Identify today the spiritual ancestors you can draw on for inspiration and strength. Celebrate today that you are free to worship the living and true God. What forms does your thanksgiving for the freedom to practice your religion take?

2 Maccabees

Sometimes history's most potent lessons are learned through the story of an exemplary individual. 2 Maccabees is more of a supplement than a sequel to 1 Maccabees, and it singles out Judas Maccabeus as the personification of the leadership and courage of Judaism's struggle against its pagan oppressors. One of the ways the author makes this example stick is that he places the heroic leadership of Judas just after the inspiring story of the courage of a mother and her seven sons who are tortured and finally killed one by one as they refuse to reject their Jewish heritage in order to save themselves. The mother encourages each son, from the oldest to the youngest, to remember their identity as Jews, to believe that God takes notice of their sacrifice and courage, and to be strong even as they accept death. The unforgettable and moving testimony of the mother and her children weakens the threat of the pagan enemy while exemplifying the strength of the unbreakable will of those who trust firmly in God. 2 Maccabees is also a very powerful statement of the emerging Jewish belief in the resurrection from the dead that was gaining currency in the two centuries before Jesus.

At a Glance

Who: 2 Maccabees focuses on the son of Mattathias, Judas Maccabeus.

What: A narrative of the success of the Maccabean revolt and the popularity it held for Jews struggling under foreign domination.

When: Covering the time period of about 180 BC to 161 BC. That time period encompasses the beginning of the reign of Antiochus IV Epiphanes (175–164 BC) and his atrocities against the temple, the city of Jerusalem, and the Jewish people. It also includes the revolt of Judas Maccabeus, which succeeded in expelling foreign occupiers from the land, and the rededication of the temple in 164 BC.

Where: In and around Jerusalem.

Why: To encourage heroism and even martyrdom for the sake of preserving Jewish heritage.

Structure and Content

1–2: Letters to the Jews in Egypt and author's preface. This book begins with two letters inviting Jews in Egypt to share their joy from their victory over the Seleucids by celebrating the Feast of Hanukkah (meaning "dedication"), a jubilant feast to rededicate the temple. The author adds a preface that gives an overview of the book.

3–7: Profaning the temple and other persecution. The author reviews the history of the decline of the high priesthood and the high priests themselves, thereby introducing and allowing Hellenism to take root even in Jerusalem. Antiochus, a Seleucid king, ravages the city of Jerusalem and raids the temple treasury because the priests have not paid him homage. He forbids the Jews to keep the Sabbath, to celebrate the traditional feasts, or even to admit that they are Jews. The story of the martyrdom of a mother and her seven sons illustrates the extent of the king's evil ways. But the king's power is no match for how God would transform their witness into strength beyond imagination.

8–15: Judas' victories and purification of the temple. The remainder of the book recounts the extraordinary successes of Judas and his followers because they trust in God. God delivers all of the people's enemies into their hands. The enemies are destroyed, and the temple and the city are rededicated.

Major Themes

- **Freedom and strength are found in trust in God**, even for the very vulnerable.
- **Martyrdom is exalted** as a willingness to live and die as observant and faithful Jews.
- **It is good to pray for those who have died** in view of the resurrection from the dead.

Authorship

The anonymous, or unidentified, author, writing in Greek, says he based his account on the five-volume work of Jason of Cyrene (2:23). Dating sometime around 124 BC, 2 Maccabees may be a little older than 1 Maccabees.

Literary Form

Historical Narrative: A historical account of Judas Maccabeus' leadership of the Jews in their rebellion, accompanied by moral reflections.

Key Passages

1:9-10: A reminder to celebrate the rededication of the temple in memory of those who have struggled against their oppressors.

7:1-41: The stirring dialogue between a mother and her sons as they courageously face martyrdom for their faith.

12:42-46: Offerings and prayers of atonement are asked for those who have died in battle. The author makes the point that if the fallen were not to rise again, it would be useless and foolish to pray for them in death.

Food for Thought

Certainly, 2 Maccabees is the Old Testament's clearest portrayal of belief in the resurrection of the dead. We also see here references to the intercession of saints for the living as well as the power of praying for those who have died. New Testament portrayals of martyrs, including Stephen (Acts 7) and even Jesus (as seen in Luke's Gospel), may have been influenced by the example of the woman and her seven sons. The extreme demands of religious faith as expressed in 2 Maccabees provided an example that was especially well received later among Christians as they came to understand Jesus' death and as they underwent persecutions of their own.

Since the time of the earliest Christian martyrs, the idea of being willing not only to die for the faith but also to live as a "witness" (the meaning of the term *martyr*) of that faith has been a motivating factor for Christians as they seek to live responsibly and courageously in a complex world full of temptations to abandon their ideals. The Catholic tradition has always maintained that devotion to the saints as models is a worthy pursuit. Readers can draw inspiration from 2 Maccabees for the significance of a person's witness to his or her convictions. In our daily lives, even when we are not threatened with persecution or death, we can still witness to our beliefs and thus help others to stand firm.

Introduction to the Wisdom Books

A foreign cleric visiting the United States wanted to go to a bookstore. He browsed the shelves, moving from the religious to the self-help section nearby. Amazed at the sheer volume and scope of the titles there, he commented, as if to himself, "I thought Americans believed in God." I demurred that a lot of us do. "Then why do you need all these books," he replied, gesturing in the direction of the self-help section, "when you have this?" he asked, holding up the Bible. His reaction gave me pause. Faith actually has everything to do with living well, with having joy in a most profound sense, with living a satisfied, productive, and fulfilled life. Israel's wisdom literature functions as a guide for wise, pragmatic living. The "wise" not only believe but also trust in God, whereas "fools" do not. This is so not because of some threat or promise about the afterlife. The wise person is just and lives well in the here and now.

Yet wisdom also suggests a connection between what we do in this life and our life hereafter. The human search for immortality became more popular and pressing in the wake of the Greek philosophical tradition that dominated the world after the death of Alexander the Great in 323 BC. It is understandable that despite their fear of assimilation into the Greek culture, Jews would have been affected by Hellenism, not necessarily to their detriment. Philo, the first-century Jewish teacher in Alexandria who wanted to show the superiority of the Jewish Law, famously said that Plato was "Moses speaking Greek." Moses taught that acting according to the Torah was life. People were often rewarded for acting justly and punished for sin. Wisdom literature struggled with this simplistic notion of retribution and the realization that oftentimes there is no direct connection between good and reward, evil and punishment. Sometimes the wicked succeed brilliantly and the good languish in suffering and failure. Still, this life is not all there is. It makes good sense to believe that an all-knowing, good God gives life even after death.

The expression "fear of the Lord" is one of the most oft-repeated and characteristic ideas of wisdom literature: "To fear the Lord is the beginning of wisdom" (Sirach 1:14, cf. Proverbs 1:7). "Fear" is to be taken in the sense of awe, reverence for the mystery of God beyond human understanding—in a word, faith. God's wisdom is inextricably linked to creation as well as the story of Israel's choice as God's people. All of this is beyond human comprehension.

The timelessness of wisdom literature makes it all the more difficult to date. Some psalms, for example, were intended for use in the temple liturgy, so we can assume a post-temple date. But others can be so universally applied to almost any historical period that dating seems impossible. The Book of Job deals with universal religious issues such as the problem that innocent suffering poses for faith in a just God. The same can be said for the Book of Proverbs, which offers generalized wisdom for people trying to live faithfully in a complex world. Such timelessness can work to our advantage since the issues and answers are never out of date; we still have some of the same questions wisdom literature addresses.

The Catholic canon lists seven works in the category of wisdom literature: Job, Psalms, Proverbs, Ecclesiastes, Sirach, the Song of Songs, and the Wisdom of Solomon. Sirach and the Book of Wisdom are not part of the Jewish or Protestant canon.

Useful Terms to Know

Diaspora: Refers to Jews living outside of Palestine from the time of the Babylonian Exile in the sixth century BC.

Hellenism: The influence of Greek culture that was prevalent especially with the Golden Age of Greece in the fifth and fourth centuries BC. This was particularly pronounced and treated as both a problem and an asset after the time of Alexander the Great (336–323 BC), who promoted all things Greek in an effort to unify the lands he had conquered.

Immortality: The notion of life after death developed late in the Old Testament period and became increasingly popular in the time after the exile. This is the situation described in wisdom literature.

Proverb: Often a short, pithy saying that conveys meaning symbolically. It is not meant to be taken literally but connotes truth through images. The root word also means "parable" or sometimes "riddle." Proverbs are instructions that must be studied and practiced in order to become wise; fools will fail to grasp their meaning, and that failure will lead to misery.

Psalms/Psalter: From a Greek word, "psalms" means hymns of praise; the "Psalter" refers to the collection of hymns or originally to a musical instrument that accompanied the singing of these hymns. The Book of Psalms in Hebrew is called *Tehillim,* meaning "praises."

Righteousness or Justice: These are synonymous attributes of God shared with humans through revelation.

"Satan": A fairly late term, Satan is portrayed in Job as a personified adversary of humankind; he acts out the role of a prosecutor in a heavenly court, challenging God to note that Job, who represents humankind, is only righteous because his life is good and full of blessings.

***Tanak*:** This refers to the tripartite division of Jewish scriptures. Its name refers to the *Torah* (the Law), the *Nevi'im* (the prophets), and the *Ketubim* (the writings). This division is first mentioned in the prologue of Sirach.

Theodicy: Defense of God's goodness and justice. In the Book of Job, there is tension between God's justice and the innocence of Job who, like God, is also "righteous." The mystery of suffering, especially innocent suffering, challenges faith in a God who is good.

Theory of Retribution: The practical notion that "what goes around comes around," that everything is explainable as a matter of cause and effect.

Wisdom: A gift God shares with humans, and they respond by living justly. In this literature, wisdom is personified as a woman-companion to God who participated in the creation of the world and delights in walking among human beings.

Job

Job represents everyone who has ever struggled with the dilemma of why bad things happen to good people. Job is a fictional rather than historical person who, despite his righteousness, suffers immensely from loss of fortune and family, personal illness, and pain. He also endures loneliness as he is surrounded by misunderstanding, including suggestions from his family and friends that he himself is somehow responsible for what is happening to him. Job refuses to curse God for injustice (as his wife challenges him to do), nor will he admit that he has done some wrong that has brought disaster on himself (as his friends imply in their responses to him).

The antagonist of the book's prologue is called "Satan," a term meaning "adversary," a role rather than a proper name. The term appears relatively late in Jewish literature. Here it is used in the discussion between God, depicted as an enthroned monarch surrounded by servants called "the sons of god" (his ministers), and this adversary or prosecutor whose task it is to report human transgressions to the monarch. Satan is not to be confused with or identified with the devil, a concept of personified evil that comes later. It is probably the King James Version translation of James 5:11 that provided the basis for the expression "the patience of Job," a characterization that is misleading and inaccurate. The word "perseverance" rather than "patience" is more accurate and truly descriptive of Job, who perseveres in his faith in God despite suffering all kinds of calamities.

At a Glance

Who: Job is best understood as a fictional character seeking an answer to the mystery of innocent suffering. Because he is righteous, his suffering could not be due to sin.

What: Job wrestled with his faith in God in the light of his personal misfortunes and suffering.

When: Composed sometime after the fifth century BC, the Book of Job depicts Everyman struggling with the problem of evil and of innocent suffering.

Where: Postexilic Israel.

Why: To encourage wisdom as faith in God despite personal circumstances and suffering.

Structure and Content

1:1–2:10: The prologue depicts a heavenly scene that envisions a conversation between God and the prosecutor, "Satan," concerning Job, a righteous person. The adversary claims that Job's apparent faithfulness proceeds from self-interest and that if all the good things are taken from Job, he will sin. God wagers that even if Job experiences nothing but misery and loss, he will remain faithful. All of Job's children then die, and he himself is covered in sores from head to foot; even his wife tells him to "Curse God, and die" (2:9).

2:11–28:28: Three friends of Job defend God's justice, with the consequence of accusing Job of some sin he ought to confess because otherwise he would not be so severely afflicted. In dialogue with them, Job protests his innocence while still maintaining faith in God. Yet in his own moments of solitude and tortured self-examination, Job demands that God give him an explanation so that he can answer his and God's critics.

29–31: Against the backdrop of a supposed trial, Job summarizes his case and, still insisting that he is innocent of wrongdoing, challenges God to explain what has happened to him.

32–37: Another character enters the scene, Elihu, whose name means "My God is he." He speaks out against Job, pointing out that God can speak in many different ways, some of which may bring them temporary pain so that in the end, God can redeem them. He defends God's justice and rebukes Job for rebelling against God and being self-righteous.

38:1–42:6: God's speech challenging Job. God walks Job through creation, asking him repeatedly where he was when the earth was made and populated and when the mountains and the seas were formed and stocked with life. God reminds Job of the wonder of it all and reduces Job to silence.

42:7-17: The epilogue, or afterword, reestablishes Job as a person rich in possessions, family, and personal prestige. But these are not to be considered as a reward or recompense for his faithfulness, or the whole project of the book would be nullified. Job is far more blessed, wise, and virtuous than he was before he experienced adversity because now he "knows" and has "seen" for himself that God is faithful.

Major Themes

- **God is just** even though we do not always understand God's ways.
- **God has faith in humans,** despite the sins of many and the challenge that many are only living good lives out of self-interest.
- **Suffering, especially innocent suffering, serves as a test of faith** and sometimes threatens to break the fragile thread of trust in a caring and just God.
- **Yet, mysteriously, people have also plumbed depths of goodness and trustworthiness** through suffering and emerged stronger, more convinced of their own unshakeable faith.

Authorship

The author of the Book of Job is unknown. Although widely debated, many interpreters suggest a postexilic date for Job, that is, sometime after the exile of the fifth century before Christ.

Literary Form

Folktale: This story has a dramatic setting—in a kind of court where God's justice is on trial, and Job is a witness. It also includes dialogue and poetic speeches.

Key Passages

1:20-22: God is the giver of every good. Job also professes God's right to take away blessings. In all things Job gives praise to God.

42:1-6: Job's profession of faith that God is the ruler of the universe. God's ways are beyond human comprehension. Job accepts God's will and thus shows that God was right to have taken Job's side against Satan.

Food for Thought

The belief in the universal sinfulness of all people is fundamental in the Bible. Still, the question persists: what if someone suffers, and there is no possible cause-and-effect explanation? Innocent suffering puts a strain on faith in a righteous God, and that is the problem that the Book of Job addresses. How can a just God allow innocent people to suffer? The image and dilemma of Job, a righteous person, may have helped the early church wrestle with the problem of evil's apparent triumph, especially in the passion and death of Jesus. Jesus is depicted in the Gospels, especially Luke, as the innocent, just one who, like Job, refuses to submit to the temptation to either curse his Father as unjust for allowing him to suffer or to accept responsibility for personal wrongdoing that accounts for his suffering.

It is sometimes very difficult to accept all that happens in our lives. How do we navigate the channel between blaming God and feeling guilty about the events in our lives that cause us pain? Job helps us appreciate the fact that rational explanations are seldom really satisfying. Like Job, we can hold on to the assurance that God is always good. We can even use the experience of suffering as an opportunity to deepen our trust in God.

Psalms

As I was making a day trip in Germany with a nun friend some years back, we got caught in a sudden, unpredicted snowstorm. We stayed in a small hotel without luggage, with little money, and not much to distract or entertain us. When Sister Rita proposed that we could pray some psalms, I pointed out that we had no books, not even a Bible. No problem—she had learned several of the psalms, she said, "by heart." It was a wonderful prayerful experience we shared, with me listening in a way I never did when I was reading the words, and with her speaking them with such conviction because she had made their sentiments so completely her own.

Jesus' disciples, seeing him at prayer, asked, "Lord, teach us to pray, as John taught his disciples" (Luke 11:1). People have always looked for guidance about how to pray. Perhaps because God is awesome and transcendent, people have recognized that their approach must be respectful and reverential. But Israel's God is also approachable, and instances of prayer have punctuated the long history of Israel's relationship with God. For example, Moses spoke to God "face to face," as an intimate friend (Exodus 33:11). God made a covenant with David that remained unbroken no matter how grievously David sinned (2 Samuel 7:8-17). Whereas most of the books of the Bible are said to be God's word to the people, the Psalms often express the people's prayers to God. The word "psalm" means "hymn." "Psalter" is a term used for the collection of hymns such as we find in this wisdom book. The psalms manifest all of Israel's faith, in times of celebration as well as in times of great confusion and need. The psalms are Israel's treasury of faith, and whether recited as a community or as individuals, the psalms are the rich expression of a lifetime of believing and knowing that God remains close to his people.

There seems to have been some editorial arrangements to the collection of psalms contained in the canon. A rather loose arrangement has laments clustered generally in the first half and hymns of praise in the second. The lament-praise sequence is also present in a number of individual psalms that begin with complaints but conclude with professions of faith and trust. It is possible that a five-part division, mirroring the five books of the Law, the Pentateuch, can be observed in the formation of the Psalter.

At a Glance

Who: Almost half of the psalms (seventy-three of them) are specifically attributed to David, and thirteen more refer to incidents in his life.

What: Poetic songs expressing the gamut of religious experience, from hope, praise, petition, and thanksgiving to laments and complaints addressed to God. They are part of the religious heritage of the chosen people. The psalms were composed over a long period of time and reflect long use in the liturgy and in the personal religious lives of the people of Israel.

When: Since the psalms are timeless prayers, it is difficult to date them. Many of them were designated for use in the temple liturgy, implying a composition date close to the construction of the temple in the tenth century BC. The process of composition, use, and the inclusion of other psalms and prayers probably continued for some time, at least until the return of the people from Babylon in the sixth century BC.

Where: In Israel, centered especially around the temple in the South.

Why: To serve as a collection of common prayer for communal and personal use.

Structure and Content

1–41: Book 1 describes the way of righteousness. This collection includes psalms known as "wisdom" psalms (e.g., Psalms 1, 19, and 37), using language and imagery characteristic of wisdom literature and useful for teaching about the way of righteousness and the justice of God.

42–72: Book 2 depicts difficulties and challenges in following the way of the Lord. Many of the psalms in this section include communal laments describing troubles experienced by the community, often in relation to a common enemy (e.g., Psalms 44, 48, and 60).

73–89: Book 3 reflects on turning to God, from whom all blessings flow. Psalms of several different types appear here. For example, Psalm 74 appears as a lament for the troubles faced by the community. Psalms 77 and 78 are of a mixed type, not fitting into any particular category.

90–106: Book 4 focuses on reliance on God as the sole source of salvation. Many of the psalms in this part of the collection express confidence in

God, who alone is powerful enough and willing to come to the aid of his people.

107–150: Book 5 includes hymns of praise and thanksgiving. Many of these psalms praise God for all of the things God has accomplished. Thanksgiving is expressed by individuals (as in Psalm 138) as well as by the community (Psalm 124). This final section is probably the most uniform of all, with mostly songs of praise and thanks.

Major Themes

- **The psalms express the spectrum of experiences and reactions to life** considered appropriate for a people who believe they share an interpersonal relationship with God. There are hymns of praise for creation and redemption, for life and all its goodness.

- **Laments express complaint and confusion** because of suffering and distress, but they also confess faith, thanksgiving, and praise despite everything.

- **Royal psalms reflect the popular notion that the dynasty begun in David** symbolizes God's faithfulness to the covenant with Israel and the promise that it shall be restored.

- **Wisdom psalms deal with such topics as the opposition between good and evil** coupled with concerns about retribution; they emphasize practical living in everyday life as a righteous and faithful person.

- **Psalms celebrating the Torah** review the history of Israel from the creation of the world to the covenant that lasts forever.

- **Penitential psalms recognize the need for God's mercy** and advocate humbly asking for God's forgiveness.

Authorship

A long tradition links the psalms with King David, and with very good reason. David was known as a musician and poet, famous for his range of emotion and sentiment, from his persevering faithfulness to Saul despite the king's homicidal jealousy to his friendship to Jonathan, his lust for Bathsheba, and his sorrow over the deaths of Saul, Jonathan, and his own sons.

Literary Form

Poetry: Many of the psalms use such devices as parallelism, symbolic imagery, inclusion, chiasm, rhythm, and meter. It is also evident that music influenced the formation of the psalms.

Key Passages

22: The psalmist begins, "My God, my God, why have you forsaken me?" He goes on to lament that his sufferings are so great that he "can count all [his] bones" (22:17). Others stare and gloat over him, even dividing up his clothes as they watch him die (22:17-18). This psalm helped to formulate the Evangelists' passion narratives.

23: This psalm visualizes God as a shepherd caring for his flock.

51: Called by Catholics *"Miserere,"* from the Latin for "Have mercy, (Lord)," it likely expresses the sentiments of David, king and sinner, when he is confronted by Nathan after his adulterous affair with Bathsheba.

119: The longest of the one hundred fifty psalms, it extols the blessings of the Torah and of God's people who walk in the way of righteousness.

Food for Thought

Catholics are accustomed to liturgical and personal prayers that are well-known, often committed to memory. We would do well to regularly read and pray the psalms as an expression of our continued faith in God's goodness and care regardless of hardship and suffering. We stand shoulder to shoulder with the holy men and women who have found their own religious sentiments expressed in the psalms for thousands of years. What changes in our prayer life might we experience if we learn to pray the psalms "by heart" like Sister Rita does?

Proverbs

We probably all have a relative known for speaking in proverbs. With my family it is Mum, my great-grandmother, an emigrant from the Old Country, who had a proverb for any occasion. I think of her fondly as a teacher of such maxims as "If you can't say anything good, don't say anything at all" and "If you don't use your head, you have to use your feet."

The Book of Proverbs takes its name from the first word in 1:1, the Hebrew term *mishle,* meaning "to rule or govern." In this sense, "proverbs" act as standards of behavior. Generally, proverbs are short, pithy sayings that convey meaning symbolically. The term can also be used to refer to a parable, which means a similitude, or comparison, taken from common experience or nature and meant to convey a nugget of wisdom. The Book of Proverbs became for Israel general rules of conduct, a practical guide for life. Truth is told in short word pictures.

Some of the proverbs are distinctly Hebrew, and others appear to have parallels in other Ancient Eastern literature. In Proverbs, there is no story line. The book is a collection of wise sayings, most ascribed to Solomon but some to other sages. At the beginning of his reign, Solomon asked God to give him "an understanding mind," and the Lord was pleased that he asked for wisdom rather than a long life or riches or revenge against his enemies (1 Kings 3:7-9; Wisdom 7:1-22). From then on, Solomon was renowned for his wisdom in judgments and in governing his people.

Wisdom was meant to confront the chaos of life and introduce order. For the Israelites, the highest form of wisdom was found in the Law, which needed to be revealed. We cannot find wisdom by ourselves; we need God's help, the divine word ordering our thoughts just as God governs all else.

Readers will immediately notice the male perspective from which the proverbs were written, a perspective expressing the patriarchal view that dominated the culture. What is more remarkable is that often the motivation for wise and just living is the teachings of mothers as well as fathers. Not only that, but Proverbs depicts wisdom personified as a woman who noisily makes her entrance in the marketplace, calling out for all to hear (1:20-33). Those who answer her call are invited to dine with her and nurture themselves with truth.

At a Glance

Who: Attributed to Solomon who was known for wisdom, but actually an anthology from many sources.

What: A collection of sayings and teachings, many very short, drawn from experience and observation; there are also some longer instructions and poems.

When: Collected over a long period of time from multiple sources and passed down from the tenth to seventh centuries before Christ through families, clans, and tribes.

Where: Some proverbs were drawn from other cultures, and some were innate to Israel.

Why: To provide wise guidance in everyday life, in a way accessible to all.

Structure and Content

1–9: This is a prologue to the teachings of wisdom, extolling the value and blessings of wisdom and understanding. It includes a description of wisdom as a woman, the companion of God at the creation of the world, who offers delights to all who seek her. Wisdom is as food and drink to those who desire to be filled.

10–29: This section contains a series of short sayings attributed to Solomon and other sages. These extol the dignity of work and the importance of discipline for children while condemning the evils of greed and laziness and the folly of self-deception and cheating. Some wisdom found here is common sense, while other portions seem to be the product of Israel's faith.

30–31: The epilogue is composed of wise sayings and a poem celebrating wisdom as a "good wife," with all the attributes of wisdom. The wise are like Solomon, who chose to ask for wisdom above all else and, when given it, received all else of value besides.

Major Themes

- **A good life is its own reward.** Proverbs does not deal with an afterlife but suggests that those who live wisely live well. Conversely, sinners' misdeeds will be visited upon them as retribution.

- **Human contentment is found in a life of virtue,** especially in honesty, integrity, discipline, chastity, devotion to God (called "fear of the Lord"), care of the defenseless and afflicted, and honor to the family. These are virtues that parents are meant to teach their children.

Authorship

Proverbs is traditionally attributed to Solomon, who was known for wisdom (see 1 Kings 1–3). The book contains wisdom sayings going back to the thirteenth century, and some are as late as the seventh century BC.

Literary Form

Proverbs: Concise sayings of wise advice often presented as teachings of parents to children (that is, father to son, consistent with the patriarchal environment of the time) that convey the proper training for life.

Key Passages

1:1-7: In the opening words of this book, the proverbs are ascribed to Solomon.

8:1–9:6: Wisdom is portrayed as a desirable woman; this description is particularly remarkable in these chapters where Lady Wisdom appears calling out to all and promising, "I love those who love me, / and those who seek me diligently find me" (8:17).

31:8-9: Kings must protect and assure the rights of the afflicted, needy, and poor.

31:10-31: A wise man extols the virtues of his good wife, whose value is far beyond pearls and other riches.

Food for Thought

For the Greeks, wisdom could be achieved through study of the universe. But for Jews and Christians, wisdom is revealed by God. The Jews consider the Torah the highest expression of wisdom. Christians understand Christ as God's greatest revelation, the closest expression of the image of God, wisdom personified. The Gospel of John apparently drew on Proverbs' portrayal of Lady Wisdom in its depiction of the Word: Wisdom was with the creator in the beginning, begotten before the world was made. God delights in her from the beginning, and she delights in living among human beings.

The Book of Proverbs contains memorable short sayings that express wisdom as faith in a loving and personal God who guides our actions with providential care. We can learn from Proverbs to make faith practical and evident in our daily lives.

Ecclesiastes

Many people familiar with the phrases "Vanity of vanities" or "For everything there is a season" or "Send out your bread upon the waters" may not know that they come from the Book of Ecclesiastes (1:2; 3:1; 11:1). Such ideas seem to be timeless reflections on the futility of human endeavors to change things for the better. The initial observation of the author, Qoheleth, is that all is vanity, meaning emptiness. "Vanity of vanities" means the superlative of emptiness. Where is the wisdom here? We have to read further to discover that Qoheleth insists that only God can fulfill all our human aspirations. St. Augustine's famous saying, "Our hearts are restless until they rest in you, O God," could easily have been penned by Qoheleth. The author investigates the purpose and value of human life, only to demonstrate the vanity or emptiness of all things created.

Despite what may appear to be a fruitless effort to find meaning, Ecclesiastes represents an advance beyond the conventional wisdom of the theory of retribution, which, simply stated, taught that virtue would produce happiness whereas suffering was an indication of some wrongdoing. Ecclesiastes insists that amidst all the vanity of life, there is only one possible avenue of meaning, that is, offering thanks and praise to the creator of all. This insight opens the door to the possibility of a future life beyond this one, where God rules with true wisdom.

The name of this book as found in the Catholic Bible, "Ecclesiastes," means "a convener, one who convokes assemblies." Ecclesiastes is a rough Greek translation of the Hebrew name "Qoheleth," which appears in the first verse and later in 12:9 as "Teacher," as the one whose teachings are recorded here. Qoheleth is further portrayed as "the son of David, king in Jerusalem" (1:1) and as a wise and learned teacher, descriptions that fit Solomon and carry on the tradition that he is the source of wisdom literature.

At a Glance

Who: Attributed to King Solomon but probably the work of a sage many years later. A royal persona is asserted only in chapter 1 and then dropped.

What: A reflection on life's meaning in view of the universal experience of death. An anonymous teacher who has lived a long time shares his acquired wisdom with his younger students.

When: After the exile, probably in the third century BC due to the style and language.

Where: Israel.

Why: To reflect on life and remind readers that the highest wisdom is to live respecting the order that God has ordained for the world.

Structure and Content

1:1-11: The prologue is a soulful lament that "all is vanity" (1:2), and human beings cannot find peace or satisfaction. This is particularly troublesome in view of the universality of death. After a time, there is not even a memory of people who have gone before.

1:12–12:8: A treatise showing that everything "under the sun" (1:14) is empty, vacuous, and unsatisfying. Desire is frustrated, and life, with all its riddles, is disillusioning. Yet wisdom is superior to folly, and virtue is far better than sin.

12:9-14: Qoheleth, "the Teacher," declares that God is the judge of all and points to a higher wisdom that rests with God.

Major Themes

- **The philosophy "Eat, drink and be merry, for tomorrow we die" is a senseless way to live.** Since we are all faced with death, it is incumbent upon us to search for a meaningful way to conduct our lives.
- **Faith in our creator is our hope** and the only path that leads to happiness.
- **Justice and peace cannot be achieved in this life.** But God judges the human heart.

Authorship

It is implied that Solomon is the author, but this book was probably composed much later, around the third century before Christ. Most of the work is from a single author, but an editor and follower of Qoheleth is probably responsible for the epilogue in 12:9-14.

Literary Form

Philosophical Treatise: Ecclesiastes is written to support the thesis that nothing created can satisfy the human spirit's longing for meaning.

Key Passages

1:1-14: "The Teacher," Qoheleth, says that everything "under the sun" is vanity; he has seen it all, and human endeavor is like trying to capture the wind.

5:13-20: Why seek riches or material things when they don't survive past death? Live well in the present, for life is short.

9:17: Heed wisdom above all, even when it is shouted down by foolishness.

12:13-14: The only goal of a good life is keeping the commandments of God, who will judge every human deed.

Food for Thought

Perhaps written partially in response to the searching questions and answers of schools of Greek philosophy, Ecclesiastes teaches that God's wisdom far surpasses human reasoning and that trust in God is our hope. By recognizing the endless vanity of human endeavors, we can turn our hearts and minds to faith in God, our creator and redeemer.

Ecclesiastes seems to echo, at least in the beginning, the often unspoken but real fears of many people that life seems without purpose or direction and might even be meaningless. Such fears may be even more powerful in today's world with so many threats to our peace of mind. But the real lesson of the Teacher is that God does not make junk, that trust in God is our hope and meaning, and that there is no other way to peace of mind than faith. All of our busyness, our plans, and our attempts at self-importance are for naught if we do not have faith in God and commend our lives to God's care.

Song of Songs

When it comes to art and music, most of us defend the superiority of our personal preferences and taste. But the Bible puts before us a very special song whose title is a superlative; the implicit meaning is that this is the greatest of songs or poems. Some may wonder why this obviously erotic love poem is included in Scripture. God is not even mentioned, and the starkly physical nature of some of the poem's language has caused later interpreters, especially Christian writers, to blush at the literal meaning and strongly emphasize a more symbolic, religious interpretation.

But this is not how it was first interpreted within the wisdom tradition itself. It echoes the Jewish understanding of creation, of sexual love, from the beginning. In the Book of Genesis, the mutual attraction or love of man and woman is the best way that humans experience the image and likeness of God and reflect that to others. Despite all of the imperfections of marriage as it has been practiced in society, the ideal of the mutual respect, honesty, attraction, and love has endured as the perfect image of God's creative intention and God's image in creation.

The religious nature of this poem is best understood as depicting the covenant relationship between God and his people as a marriage, just as Isaiah and other prophets presented it. At the same time, this poem can also be seen as presenting the ideal marriage, characterized by unconditional love, forgiveness, and fidelity.

At a Glance

Who: The first verse serves as the title and attributes the song to Solomon, in keeping with the wisdom tradition.

What: A poem extolling human love, dramatic in its dialogue and emotional in its expressions of mutual yearning.

When: Based on its language and style, it probably comes from the sixth or fifth century before Jesus, after the Babylonian Exile.

Where: Israel.

Why: To present the ideal image of human love mirrored in the Genesis story of creation.

Structure and Content

Because it is presented in the style of a dialogue between lovers, it is difficult to overlay a logical structure to this poem. Nevertheless, we may see the poem in two parts:

1–3: Seeking and finding love. In praise of mutual love, the song shows that the yearning is experienced by both the woman and the man.

4–8: Lovers' dialogue. Love is praised as stronger than floods or other disasters, including death. It will conquer and outlast all else.

Major Themes

- **Sexual and physical attraction is good,** and the love between a woman and a man is the greatest blessing of all.

- **The ardent, faithful love of God for his people** is seen through this relationship between a man and his beloved bride.

Authorship

This song is ascribed to Solomon, and its title suggests that this is his greatest composition. But its style and the fact that it uses some vocabulary from Persia suggest that this song was probably composed sometime after Persia conquered the Babylonians and ended the captivity of the Jews in Babylon.

Literary Form

Love Poem: It uses sensual images meant to convey complete and unconditional devotion and the powerful force of love.

Key Passages

2:10-17: Nature tells the story of life. After the trials of winter, spring is all the more refreshing. Human beings find great solace in love.

6:3; 7:10: The lover and beloved are one.

8:6-7: Love, being stronger than death, conquers all.

Food for Thought

Many prophets presented marriage as a symbol of the powerful love God has for Israel (see Isaiah 54:4-8; Jeremiah 2:2; 3:1-2; Ezekiel 16:6-63; Hosea 1–3). New Testament writers likewise used marriage as symbolic of the extent and depth of Christ's love for the church (see Matthew 9:15; 25:1-3; John 3:29; 2 Corinthians 11:2; Ephesians 5:23-32; Revelation 19:7-8). St. Jerome expressed concern over the sexual language of the song and feared readers might get the wrong idea. But other writers, such as Origen and St. Bernard, extolled the song as an exquisite and fitting expression of Jesus' love for the church.

The love story reflected in the dialogue of the Song of Songs can be used as the basis for meditating on the Sacrament of Marriage. What a challenge and a grace to realize that marital love allows us to see and to reflect God's own image in our world! Today marriage seems to get a bad rap. The example of happily married people who respect, support, and truly love one another is needed more than ever. Consider the great gift that is bestowed on us in our sexuality, our mutual attraction, and our ability to love one another faithfully regardless of all the distractions, temptations, and trials of life in today's world.

WISDOM

Ascribed to Solomon, this book is probably a much later composition invoking the king's fame and reputation for wisdom and envisioning him as a teacher of all those who want to live well. In fact, the Wisdom of Solomon is probably one of the latest compositions of the Old Testament, written in the first century before Christ. It is familiar to Christians because we read selections from the Book of Wisdom in the liturgy throughout the year, and some passages celebrating the lives of the just are well suited for use in funeral liturgies.

Wisdom teaches that the good life cannot be achieved through our own works but depends on a relationship with God, who gives wisdom as a gift to those who seek it. No one can ultimately be satisfied with the successes of this world. We will always be disappointed by the passing glitter of fame and fortune, luck and temptation, greed, lust, and pride. The wise place all their confidence in God who "love[s] the living" (11:26) and whose immortal spirit is accessible to us.

At a Glance

Who: Attributed to Solomon in keeping with his reputation as a sage teaching the ways of wisdom.

What: A description of the good life as the virtuous life with justice as its main characteristic, in contrast to the folly of the wicked who want to enjoy the good things of life with no thought for how they are oppressing the just ones (2:6-10).

When: One of the last books of the Old Testament, perhaps composed not more than a generation or two (some fifty years) before Jesus.

Where: For Greek-speaking Jews of the diaspora.

Why: To encourage people to live well so as to enjoy the afterlife.

Structure and Content

1–5: Justice is lived wisdom and leads to immortality. The first verse addresses the "rulers of the earth," telling them to "love righteousness" [or justice], which means wisdom in practice. The instructions of the wise person are addressed to all, implying that the greatest gift and most effective way to rule the world is to learn wisdom, to practice it in everyday life, and thus to achieve immortality.

6–10: Solomon teaches wisdom. This king and exemplar of wisdom speaks in the first person, praising wisdom as the gift that should be sought above all others. This section includes a reminder that instead of asking for wealth or power or prestige, Solomon sought wisdom through prayer (7:7), and God was so delighted with this request that everything else was given to him besides (see also 1 Kings 3:5-15).

11–19: The exodus illustrates the lessons of wisdom. Although there are no explicit references to either Egypt or Israel, the exodus is used as an example from history that generalizes the obvious differences between the responses to events of the wise and the foolish, or the just and the wicked.

Major Themes

- **Immortality** is the reward of the just.
- **The thinking of the wicked is contrasted with that of the righteous.** The opposition can also be seen in the exodus story.
- **God loves human beings and wants to grant us wisdom.** The wise are saved and given a lasting life, far more valuable than this one, whose pleasures do not endure.

Authorship

In the middle section, the author takes on the identity of King Solomon, but Wisdom is probably a much later composition. The anonymous author, speaking as Solomon, is familiar with ideas prevalent in the world post-Alexander. The work was probably composed in Alexandria, a major Egyptian city on the Mediterranean where many Jews had migrated after the exile.

Literary Form

Proverbs: A collection of short, pithy sayings on wisdom in the form of a long instruction by King Solomon to others who would "rule over multitudes" (6:2).

Key Passages

1:16; 2:10-11: Wicked, foolish people consider the vulnerable fair game for oppression. They think that might makes right, and weakness is useless.

7:7, 11-12: Wisdom is God's greatest gift to us. To acquire wisdom, prayer is necessary.

Food for Thought

Wisdom literature recognizes that this world is passing. Life on earth must be a prelude to a better life after death. In this world, the vulnerable often suffer while the powerful thrive. The theory of retribution only explains a small part of reality. There must be more. Biblical wisdom includes faith that God, creator of the whole world and giver of life, will judge human beings with justice and reward those who are just with lasting life. By the end of the Old Testament era, many Jews believed in an afterlife and resurrection from the dead. Christians adopted these beliefs, which were realized in Jesus. Jesus' resurrection brought blessings for humankind far beyond the sin and death that all have experienced since Adam.

For Jews, wisdom is not gained through personal study, as the Greeks thought. Rather, wisdom is granted to those who seek God. This is a huge difference. How do I persevere and nurture my quest for wisdom and right living? How do I demonstrate that I cherish wisdom above all other blessings?

Sirach

Like many others can attest, I have been blessed with exceptional teachers who still influence me in my life choices today, even though my school years are long gone. My own teaching career has been completely satisfying, and my prayer is that I have done more good than harm. Sometimes it seems that in teaching, the subject matter taught is incidental. Of more importance are the relationships formed and the mutual example, inspiration, and admiration shared.

The Book of Sirach reflects the thinking of a teacher in Jerusalem about two hundred years before Christ, at a time when Greek thinking and culture had become very attractive to many young Hebrews in Palestine. It is sometimes called "The Wisdom of Sirach." It is also called "Liber Ecclesiasticus" or simply "Ecclesiaticus," a name that means "church book." This name, from the Vulgate's translation of the Greek, suggests the importance it had in the early church and continues to have in the liturgy of the church even today.

Many lessons are addressed to "my son," suggesting that the students of these teachings are disciples and heirs of the wisdom of Israel. The lessons are directed at young boys. Using lessons he himself learned as an extensive traveler, student of the world, and teacher of young men, Sirach shows that the Jewish ideal found in the Law is superior to Hellenistic views of wisdom. Sirach uses his impressive knowledge of Hellenism to teach the young minds before him to resist the temptations of the worldliness of Greek culture. He also addresses contemporary topics such as friendship, wealth, and the virtues and makes observations from the world of nature, demonstrating that all good things point toward God. For Sirach, wisdom is a practical way of life rather than an academic study or intellectual pursuit. While the book contains lessons primarily for Jewish students, there is a universalist and a salvation-historical perspective of the book, two ideas rarely found in the Old Testament. Sirach meant for this wisdom to be taught and learned by all who seek right living.

At a Glance

Who: A sage from Jerusalem, Sirach, who accumulated wisdom from the Scriptures and from his extensive travels. His teachings were translated by his grandson into Greek.

What: The teachings of a scribe who had dedicated his life to studying the Scriptures and who founded an academy to teach them to young men as superior to Greek philosophy.

When: Around 200 or 180 BC.

Where: Sirach was a native of Jerusalem, but his grandson wanted to make his teachings about the superiority of Judaism over Hellenism known to all Jews, even those living in the diaspora.

Why: To make the sage's teachings available "for all who seek instruction" (33:18).

Structure and Content

Prologue: This introduction, lacking numbered verses, contains information about the origins of the teachings, about Ben Sirach, and about the translator, the author's grandson. The concern of Sirach's grandson was to give those living abroad, outside of Palestine, an opportunity to acquire wisdom and to live their lives according to the standards of the Law.

1–43: The importance of wisdom. A collection of proverbs resembling more class notes than chapters of a book, Sirach covers a number of themes, such as praise of wisdom as right living according to the Law; justice; lessons on sin and divine judgment; the importance of friendship; duties of parents and children; women's subservience to men; property and slaves; and women's culpability for sin and death. Sirach teaches that judgment comes at death and that human beings are responsible for their own actions.

44:1–50:24: Praise of ancestors who exemplify wisdom. The list includes many famous and several lesser-known male leaders of Israel, including the patriarchs Moses, Nathan, David, Solomon, Elijah, Elisha, Hezekiah, Isaiah, and Josiah. Finally, Sirach praises Simon, a Jew whose term as high priest was characterized by a great number of liturgical and other reforms.

50:25–51:30: The epilogue combines two endings, the first in 50:25-29 and an appendix in chapter 51. Both endings include encouragement to follow Sirach's teachings by putting them into practice, along with the promise that such efforts will be rewarded by God. Chapter 51 brings all of these musings to a conclusion that celebrates and praises God with thanksgiving.

Major Themes

- **The superiority of Judaism over Hellenism** drives the author's writing; Sirach teaches that the Jewish ideal found in the Law is superior to Hellenistic views of wisdom.

- **Duties of both children and parents** are enumerated at length and upheld as a path to wisdom.

- **Warnings about individuals' responsibility for actions** and judgment at death are illustrated by holding up for imitation the examples of many ancestors.

Authorship

Mention of the high priest Simon, son of Onias, in 50:1 suggests that Sirach was teaching sometime around the beginning of the second century before Christ. Sirach's grandson circulated the teachings in writing in the Greek-speaking capital of Alexandria. His grandson may have been referring to the Septuagint when he says, in some manuscripts of the Prologue, that he found a reproduction of the valuable teaching of his ancestors and then felt duty bound to translate his grandfather's teaching to add to this.

Literary Form

Proverbs: Many of these short, pithy, and wise sayings on a variety of topics are presented in Sirach as an instruction of an elder to youth or as a teacher to his disciples. There are also poetic material, prayers of praise and petition, autobiographical material, lists, and other teachings of the sage.

Key Passages

1:14: Fear of God, in the sense of awe and respect of the Lord, is the beginning of wisdom.

51:23-30: Students should stay close to the teacher, taking upon themselves the "yoke" (51:26) of instruction. God is revealed in the teachings of wisdom, and God judges the hearts of the wise with mercy.

Food for Thought

Written at a time when Jews were very anxious to assert their own identity and faith in a world dominated by Hellenism, Sirach represents the attraction of faith in God and the wisdom in following the Law. Sirach's instruction is meant to build up the community of faith grounded in its relationship to the personal and caring God revealed in the history of Israel. Sirach advocates faithfulness to the covenant and a wary attitude toward this passing world with its temptations to sin.

Sirach's invitation to "draw near to me" and take on the "yoke" of the Law (51:23, 26) might have inspired Matthew's record of Jesus' words, "Come to me, all you that are weary and are carrying heavy burdens. . . . Take my yoke upon you. . . . For my yoke is easy, and my burden is light" (11:28-30). Our relationship to Christ is like a "yoke" joining us to him and to one another. We study the Scriptures to learn how to live the gospel. How do we preach the gospel by the example we set for others? What Scripture teachings do we invoke to help us live in today's world?

Introduction to the Major Prophets

People commonly think of "prophecy" as a prediction, a foretelling of things to come. In the Bible, a prophet is one who speaks and acts on behalf of God. In changing times, prophets interpret the will of God for the present. Only later, when the words of the prophet were interpreted in the light of Jesus Christ, did prophecy seem to mean a prediction of things to come.

The concept of prophecy is not unique to Israel, although its idea of a "true prophet" as one who speaks for God and whose words are confirmed by events is unique. One of the main functions of the prophets was to interpret the Law under changing circumstances. The prophets of Israel were not part of the organized government, so they could speak with some independence. They served as the conscience of the nation and of the king in particular.

We can trace a trajectory of the increasing prominence and finally the decline of prophecy from the first kings and early prophets such as Samuel and Nathan, through the eminent careers of Isaiah and Jeremiah, to the limited successes of Daniel or Malachi in their own time. There also seems to be something of a progression: from early plain-speaking prophecy about specific events, such as the rain or drought Elijah spoke about, to the cryptic language of Ezekiel who, in the midst of the misery of captivity, prophesied about apocalyptic visions revealing the ultimate victory of God, to Daniel, the only full-fledged apocalyptic book of the Old Testament. As a sign, perhaps, of the freedom of the Spirit, at times women were referred to as prophets. For example, the first time the title appears in the Bible, it is in reference to Miriam, sister of Moses (Exodus 15:20). Deborah (Judges 4:4) and Huldah (2 Kings 22:14) are also called prophets.

Prophets speak with the authority of God. The prophetic calling, as described by Israel's prophets, is usually unexpected and unsought. It often involves a mission, not necessarily to the prophet's liking. Jeremiah, for example, protested that he was too young for his prophetic mission (1:6). Jonah complained that he didn't like the people he was sent to (4:1). Isaiah is an exception in that he enthusiastically volunteered, telling God, "Send me!" (6:8). Although each of the prophets had his own emphasis, standard themes characterized the message of the prophets. Some of the main themes found in many of the prophets include a demand for strict monotheism and a rejection of idols; social commitment to the defenseless, represented by widows and orphans; a call for true leadership and for righteousness according to the Law; and the Torah and the temple as unifying sacred realities.

In Catholic Bibles, the prophets appear after the writings and just before the New Testament. This is consistent with the idea that the prophets prepare the way for the coming of Jesus Christ and contain many of the descriptions and expectations for the Messiah. The prophetic books are usually divided into major and minor prophets, probably stemming from the fact that the major prophets (e.g., Isaiah, Jeremiah, and Ezekiel) were each written on a separate scroll while the twelve so-called minor prophets shared a common scroll. Lamentations, Baruch, and Daniel are included with the prophets in Catholic Bibles, while the Hebrew Bible, which does not include Baruch, categorized Daniel and Lamentations as writings.

Useful Terms to Know

Apocalypticism: Classical prophecy, with its emphasis on the word of God directed to the people through the prophet, gave way to prophetic visions expressed in cryptic language devised so that only believers, not their foreign oppressors, understood their true meaning. The flavor of such visions shows the progressive popularity of apocalyptic literature in Judaism after the exile; for example, Ezekiel's visions are designed to encourage those who are suffering oppression while promising that the grip of their captors will be broken. In the centuries of persecution and oppression by the Romans, Christians employed and adapted apocalyptic imagery to express their understanding of Christology and eschatology.

Call Narrative: A description of the prophet's call from God, following a pattern seen consistently since the call of Abraham. This narrative usually consists of many of the following elements: an appearance of God or an angel/messenger, usually to someone who is not expecting God's call; a stated reason for the apparition; a commission of the person and their objection(s); and reassurance followed by a sign.

Cherubim: In Ezekiel, these are not the fuzzy, huggable little angelic beings linked to romantic life and featured in card shops around Valentine's Day. Rather, they are weird creatures with human, animal, and mechanical characteristics, with faces, wings, and wheels that move in the midst of a fiery scene meant to express an otherworldly reality presided over by God. The prophet's call and subsequent visions are witnessed by these creatures, who do everything God commands them to do. In Ezekiel 1:4-14 the cherubim are of "human form," with four faces—human, lion, ox, and eagle—and four wings with human hands. This imagery is perhaps connected to the winged sphinx of the ancient Near East.

Confessions of Jeremiah: Complaints about the hardships and loneliness of being a prophet. Examples are found in 12:1-4; 15:10-21; 17:14-18; 18:19-23; and 20:7-18.

"The Day of the Lord": This phrase is a prophetic reference to a day of judgment, a time to be feared, and a warning of the coming punishment of God. Within the context of apocalyptic thinking, it also means the promised vindication and reward for the innocent and the faithful. Suffering is not in vain but is counted as evidence of faith, often at great cost.

Lament: A complaint addressed to God about the people or the situation of the prophet. Jeremiah is called to preach warnings to the people, who are relatively prosperous and fairly smug at the time. Jeremiah "laments" his lot—that he has to preach doom and gloom to the people who do not want to hear it and who persecute the prophet for speaking it. But more than a complaint, a lament acknowledges the sad state of affairs resulting from the people's failure to heed divine warnings, coupled with a plea for mercy and a confession of faith in God's eternal goodness.

Oracle: A divine revelation communicated to the people through the prophet.

Scribe: One who could read and write. Scribes were employed by prophets to record oracles and often to communicate them to the people in a public reading.

Seraphim: The word *seraph* means "fiery" or "burning" and refers to spiritual beings depicted as servants of God, carrying out the divine will. For a prophetic description of the seraph who brings a burning coal to sear Isaiah's lips, see Isaiah 6:2, 6.

Servant Songs: Interpreters have identified this "servant" God promises to send in a number of ways: as historical, collective Israel; an ideal Israel; the prophet Isaiah; or some other Old Testament person or anonymous prophet. The Evangelists and Christians since that time have identified Jesus as the Servant of God and a fulfillment of these prophecies. (See Isaiah 42:1-4; 49:1-7; 50:4-11; 52:13–53:12).

"The Son of Man": The phrase means "a human being" and is the ordinary way God addresses some of the prophets (e.g. Ezekiel 36:17). The NRSV rather awkwardly translates this expression as "Mortal." "Son of Man" emphasizes the difference between the omnipotence of God and the obedience of the servant-prophet who can only speak the word God tells him to speak. In the Gospels, this is the term or title most often applied to Jesus and the designation Jesus seems to prefer for himself, most probably because of its prophetic connotations.

Isaiah

Isaiah may be called the prophet of simplicity. When all around him were calling for war and big guns, Isaiah spoke of peace rooted in reliance on God. Amidst some brutal, violent language about a people enslaved with a "bar across their shoulders, . . . the boots of the tramping warriors and all the garments rolled in blood," Isaiah inspired hope by prophesying, "A child has been born for us" (9:4-6). When others demanded signs, Isaiah presented his wife and children, who were given symbolic names and roles meant to communicate the truth that God was with them.

As the book opens, the Lord has decided to set things aright (see 1:10) and has chosen Isaiah as the prophet who will speak to the people. Isaiah enthusiastically accepts his role as God's spokesman, crying out, "Here am I; send me!" (6:8). Yet Isaiah, like Moses long before him, sometimes appears to run out of patience with the people he has been called to serve.

Isaiah lived in the kingdom of Judah, threatened from all sides by foreign powers, a nation already decimated because of problems with Israel to the north. Isaiah was awestruck by Jerusalem, the capital of Judah. He gloried in the temple that represented so many of Judah's aspirations to serve God in holiness and integrity. The prophet's family members, especially his children, are featured in the first part of the book, and they symbolize God's judgment, mercy, and the remnant of Israel that remains true to the covenant. Isaiah preached complete and total confidence in God to the point that he believed Judah should enter into no alliances with its neighbors but should rely on God to protect and shield it from its enemies. Isaiah advocated that Judah should, as the psalmist said, "Be still, and know that I am God!" (46:10).

Unfortunately, all three of the kings whom Isaiah advised (Jotham, Ahaz, and Hezekiah) preferred the more apparent safety of human alliances. For example, King Ahaz leaned toward an alliance with Assyria; he sought protection from the Syrian consortium with Israel to the north. Isaiah protested such an alliance, insisting that Judah ought to place her confidence wholly in God. The weak and vacillating king refused to listen to the prophet and entered into his unholy alliance with Assyria. Finally, Hezekiah ascended the throne and, at first, instituted many religious reforms. But when Assyria became more of a threat than a friend, Judah turned to Egypt in desperation, a move Isaiah denounced as a "covenant with death" (28:15). These kings opted for temporary and false security that either folded like so many cards or, worse, backfired and brought about destruction. Isaiah foretold the exile in Babylon, a prophecy that came to pass a little more than a century later. Because Judah refused to listen to Isaiah's message, Judah would suffer the greatest crisis of the people's history: the fifty years of captivity in Babylon (587–539 BC).

At a Glance

Who: Isaiah was highly educated, a prophet called by God around 742 BC to advocate Judah's resistance to the promises made by powerful Assyrian kings.

What: The oracles of Isaiah, who prophesied with God's authority.

When: Scholars suggest that the Book of Isaiah comes from two or possibly three periods. First Isaiah, composed between 742–701 BC, comprises chapters 1–39. Chapters 40–55 come from the time of the exile, and 56–66 appear to be postexilic.

Where: Judah, focusing on Jerusalem and the temple.

Why: To advocate trust in and dependence upon God and to denounce the temptation of the king to seek refuge in alliances with Syria and the Northern Kingdom of Israel against the Assyrians.

Structure and Content

First Isaiah:

1–5: Indictment of both Israel and Judah. The book begins with Yahweh's complaint about his rebellious children. Israel and Judah are invited to "hear the word of the LORD" (1:10), but it is a word of accusation and warning. The land is full of idols, and "that day" (2:11), a time of judgment, is coming. Yahweh has treated the people like a well-tended vineyard, but it has not borne fruit (5:1-7).

6–12: Immanuel prophecies. This section begins with Isaiah recounting his divine call; he says that the seraph burned his lips so that his sin was blotted out, and he speaks only the message God wants the people to hear. Isaiah tells King Ahaz to ask for a sign, but Ahaz refuses to "put the LORD to the test" (7:12). Isaiah then tells him that a son born to a young woman will be called *Immanuel,* meaning "God with us" (7:13-15).

Isaiah prophesies that the rule of Immanuel will bring universal peace, and "on that day" (7:18), the people will celebrate the salvation of God.

13–23: Oracles against the pagan nations. Israel and Judah are not alone in their sin, and so all the pagans will see God's justice and will be punished for their sins, from the great nation of Babylon to the neighboring cities of Tyre and Sidon.

24–35: The apocalypse (or revelation) to Isaiah includes a prophecy of the destruction of the world, though a remnant faithful to Yahweh will be saved. Yahweh's triumph is celebrated in liturgy and song. There is a second song of the vineyard, and the day of the Lord is described as one of reward for good and punishment for sin.

36–39: Promises of future salvation. Hezekiah the king becomes seriously ill, but he repents of his sin and is restored to health as Isaiah has prophesied. Hezekiah sings a song of thanksgiving.

Second Isaiah:

40–48: Israel's liberation. This "book" begins, "Comfort, O comfort my people, says your God. / Speak tenderly to Jerusalem" (40:1-2). The difference in tone and the apparent situation of the people provide a basis for the view that these oracles occur while the people are exiles in Babylon. Jerusalem has been destroyed, but Isaiah promises a brighter future.

49–55: Promises of restoration. Jerusalem is comforted and moves from sorrow to hope and redemption. Zion, the mountain upon which Jerusalem is built, is portrayed as mother of the people and spouse of Yahweh, her creator and redeemer.

Third Isaiah:

56–66: Restoration. The people have returned from exile and understand that they have been given another chance to live worthy of the covenant with God that was first expressed in the Law and was advocated by the prophet.

Major Themes

- **God is wholly other,** referred to as "the Holy One of Israel" (30:15).
- **Complete confidence in God alone** is required of the people of Judah.
- **Jerusalem and the dynasty of David** have a special place in God's plan of restoring the people.
- **An obedient servant of God** will bring about a renewed relationship between God and the people in justice and peace.

Authorship

This book is attributed to an educated and trusted adviser of three kings of Judah. Isaiah's prophecies begin under King Jotham (742–735 BC) and continue to cover the reigns of Ahaz (735–715 BC) and Hezekiah (715–687 BC). The circumstances of the second half of the book change so much that it seems clear that the people have not only suffered fifty years of captivity but have returned to their homeland by the time the book is completed. Thus, Isaiah is probably the work of at least two and possibly three prophets who all spoke with one voice.

Literary Form

Oracles: These are direct messages from God, given here in the form of poems; there are also biographical references that feature highlights from Isaiah's own life as symbolic elements of Judah's present and future.

Key Passages

5:1-7; 27:2-6: God's relationship with the people is likened to that of a man with his vineyard. This became a very popular image, familiar to us as one Jesus used to urge people to repent (Luke 20:9-18).

6:3-8: The call of Isaiah. The prophet protests his sinfulness in the light of God's great holiness. Isaiah's lips are purified when a seraph touches them with a burning coal. Then Isaiah calls out eagerly for God to send him to speak to the people.

7:14-16: Although Isaiah referred to the child of King Ahaz's young wife, this prophecy about a woman who would bear a son named *Immanuel* ("God with us") would appear in Matthew's infancy narrative in reference to Jesus (see 1:21-23).

10:20-21: Promise of the survival of a remnant of Jacob. Isaiah and the small group around him, including his wife and two sons, represent the faithful remnant, symbolic of God's faithfulness and of the people's eventual salvation.

11:1-9: Promise of peace. A "branch" will grow out of the "stump of Jesse"(11:1) father of David. The spirit of the Lord shall be upon him, and he will lead with righteousness and faithfulness. The peace of his reign is portrayed as a return to the beginning of creation.

25:6-9: The messianic banquet. God sets out a banquet for all people and destroys sadness and death. This is a celebration of the salvation of humankind.

61:1-3: Proclamation of the jubilee. The prophet is anointed by the Spirit of God to bring mercy and grace, a fulfillment of the jubilee year set out in Leviticus 25. Jesus used this passage to inaugurate his mission as the Messiah (see Luke 4:16-21).

Food for Thought

Isaiah is one of the most used and quoted books of the Scriptures. As Christians, many passages are familiar to us. Isaiah is full of promises of universal salvation, restoration, and fulfillment. Many passages in Isaiah are seen as messianic. Isaiah's influence on the New Testament writers to express Christology, especially the "Servant Songs" of Second Isaiah (42:1-4; 49:1-7; 50:4-9; 52-13–53:12), cannot be overestimated.

Complacency, self-justification, and resting on our laurels all subject us to a rude awakening when we encounter the prophet's demand for us to search honestly within ourselves. Yet God is faithful and answers those who call out in trust. The long Book of Isaiah traces the experience of the people from haughtiness and pride, through suffering, and finally to a restoration far more glorious than their initial state. Believers can see their own story of forgiveness, mercy, and healing in this book.

Jeremiah

When we casually ask others, "How are you?" we might be surprised when people actually answer the question! And when they do, we often learn that things are not good. The prophet Jeremiah told his tales of woe to anyone who would listen. In fact, Webster's dictionary informs us that a tale of woe might be called a "jeremiad," an allusion to the type of lamentation we find in the Book of Jeremiah.

It is sometimes said that a prophet's task is to comfort the afflicted and afflict the comfortable. Jeremiah's prophecies appear to be quite pessimistic at a time when the people were settled and things seemed to be going along rather well. Thirty years before Babylon first attacked Jerusalem, Jeremiah was predicting gloom and doom at the hands of Babylon if the people of Judah did not repent with sincerity. Jeremiah did strange things like parade around Jerusalem with a wooden yoke on his shoulders to symbolize how the Babylonians would treat the people of Judah. Jeremiah remained unmarried and interpreted this lifestyle as a warning to the people that "both great and small shall die in this land; they shall not be buried, and no one shall lament for them" (16:6). When Jeremiah prophesied about the suffering to come, authorities mocked, threatened, and punished him. The people did not want to hear bad news or dire warnings.

Jeremiah accused the false prophets of seeking only the approval of people, of saying, "'Peace, peace,' when there is no peace" (8:11). Jeremiah complained loudly and often to God, even bemoaning the day he was born, complaining that he was the object of laughter and mockery among the people, denounced and hated because he was always the bearer of bad news that people refused to hear. Jeremiah is a good example of how difficult it is to be a prophet of the true and living God. One fellow professor visualizes a very frustrated Jeremiah pleading with God to give him just one "prince-of-peace saying" as beautiful as those that Isaiah was privileged to speak almost routinely.

But the Book of Jeremiah represents an excellent example of the big difference between optimism and hope. Optimists can often merely refuse to see the warnings, the signs of the times that can lead to disaster. Jeremiah upbraided the false prophets who were unrealistically optimistic and more interested in courting human favor than channeling the word of God. Hope rests in certainty; the Book of Jeremiah is full of hope because the prophet's confidence was in God, not in any human force or power.

At a Glance

Who: Jeremiah lived in tumultuous times; his prophetic ministry lasted about forty years.

What: Oracles warning the king and the people about disasters to come.

When: From his call as a young man around 627 BC to his death in Egypt soon after the destruction of Judah and the beginning of the exile in Babylon (ca. 587 BC).

Where: Judah.

Why: To remind the people of King Josiah's reforms from 621 BC and of the consequences of not following them, namely, destruction at the hands of the Babylonians.

Structure and Content

1–20: Prophecy mixed with history and autobiography. King Josiah of Judah implements a reform that Jeremiah endorses. But when the king dies on the battlefield of Meggido in 609, official reform efforts fizzle; the people prefer the optimistic predictions of the false prophets who court their favor rather than the pessimistic-sounding prophecies of Jeremiah, who continues to call them to integrity and repentance.

21–33: Final years in Jerusalem. Jeremiah 31 speaks of the new covenant God will make with the people. Jeremiah comes to understand that only God can change human hearts.

34–45: The fall of Jerusalem. Jeremiah predicts death in captivity for King Zedekiah and mercy for some who have remained faithful. Zedekiah shows himself to be duplicitous, seeking the counsel of Jeremiah and then betraying him and leaving him to his enemies. Jeremiah continues to denounce his enemies even in exile in Egypt, where it is assumed that he eventually dies, either of natural causes or at the hands of others.

46–52: Oracles against the nations and conclusion. Beginning with Egypt and moving from west to east, Jeremiah boldly continues his oracles of judgment against all the nations, including Babylon, interspersing denunciations with some words of hope for Israel.

Major Themes

- **The people are disobedient and rebellious, but God is steadfast and faithful,** like a potter with clay, fashioning it and refashioning it until it becomes a beautiful work.
- **The suffering of the prophet** is evidence that he is called by God and speaks on God's behalf to promote and encourage true repentance on the part of the people.
- **Hope in God's awesome faithfulness** overwhelms the prophet's pessimism about the obstinacy of the people.

Authorship

Jeremiah dictated his oracles to the scribe Baruch during the seventh and sixth centuries before Christ.

Literary Forms

Confessions: Jeremiah includes many complaints about the hardships and loneliness of being a prophet; examples are found in 12:1-16; 15:10-21; 17:14-18; 18:18-23; and 20:7-18.

Parable: A parable is a simile or metaphor, taken from nature, common experiences, or the daily lives of people, with a strange twist designed to capture the imagination and lead the hearer to a new awareness, a change of mind or behavior. Jeremiah often relayed his oracles from God as parables; these include the linen loincloth in 13:1-11, the potter and the clay in 18:1-12, and the potter's flask in 19:1-15.

Key Passages

1:5-9: God calls Jeremiah to be a prophet from his mother's womb, that is, even before he is born.

7:1–8:3: The temple sermon, in which Jeremiah exposes the people's hypocrisy; they will face condemnation and destruction for their wickedness, just as Israel did.

16:1-7: The Lord instructs Jeremiah to remain celibate as a sign that this life is passing.

31:31-34: The new covenant, which will be written on the hearts of the people.

Food for Thought

The prophet Jeremiah stressed that God's will may be manifest in new, unexpected ways at various points in history, altering how we view positive and negative occurrences in our lives. For example, Jeremiah understood Babylon as an instrument of God to discipline and reshape the people as a potter works with clay. False prophets wanted the people to think that Babylon's power over them would be short-lived and that Judah would rise up and conquer, perhaps with the help of other foreign powers. Jeremiah's message that Judah would succumb to Babylon was not well received, and the prophet was persecuted for teaching that the people of Judah ought to be examining their own role in their destruction at the hands of the Babylonians.

Jeremiah's image of the new covenant was used extensively by early Christians to interpret what God had done in sending Jesus into the world. This image is also used in relation to the Eucharist, as well as to the whole of the New Testament.

Jeremiah saw his whole life as service to God, symbolized by his call to celibacy—the only such example in the Old Testament. We would do well to meditate on whether we are full- or part-time believers and how our faith in God affects all of our lives, including the way we act, talk, and pray.

Lamentations

Based on its name, it might seem that this is a depressing book, designed to make us beat our breasts in guilt and sorrow. But that is neither the meaning nor the purpose of the book. Anyone who has ever experienced pain and loss, homesickness and regret, suffering of any kind, or confusion about the sad state of a chaotic world can identify with the sentiments of Lamentations. Here the author expresses anguish over the state of Jerusalem after it has been conquered, humiliated, and abandoned by its people, many of whom have been taken into captivity in a foreign land.

Beginning in the first chapter, Jerusalem is depicted as a mother and a grief-stricken widow. The people are like broken pieces of pottery that now litter the abandoned streets of the city. The author recalls how the people did not heed the warnings of the prophets that such terrible occurrences would result from their neglect of the truly important things in life. At this point, the people have lost all confidence in their own future and in God. They are coming to realize that God is their only hope, a God who is ever faithful, steadfast, and full of mercy. Thus, Lamentations is not truly depressing but offers a reflection on the pain of the exiles; it can also serve as a mirror for readers today as an expression of their solidarity with others who have suffered loss and survived through faith. Lamentations helps readers to know that they are alone neither in their suffering nor in their hope.

Although Lamentations has always been considered part of the canon, its place varies among the traditions. In the Hebrew Bible, it appears among the writings, finding its home as part of the *Megilloth,* or five "scrolls," that are read on various Jewish feast days. In Catholic Bibles (based on the Greek and Latin traditions), Lamentations is placed among the prophets, following Jeremiah, its supposed author, and preceding Baruch, a book also linked to Jeremiah, since Baruch was his secretary.

At a Glance

Who: Ascribed to Jeremiah according to a very long tradition, perhaps based on 2 Chronicles 35:25 that says Jeremiah composed laments after the death of King Josiah and that these were collected and preserved in "the Laments."

What: A collection of five poems expressing the pain of the survivors in the aftermath of the destruction of Jerusalem.
When: The end of Jeremiah's lifetime, around 587 BC.
Where: Judah, soon after the return of the exiles.
Why: To help the exiles as they struggled to understand their recent history in the light of perceiving themselves as God's people.

Structure and Content

1: Lament over a deserted Jerusalem. Jerusalem is portrayed as an abandoned mother, clothed in rags, a stark contrast to the beautiful clothing she once wore.

2: Acknowledgment that God had warned the people. The day of the Lord is a day of wrath; the people of Zion respond in an outpouring of grief. In vivid imagery, the dead lie in the streets while the enemies of mother Jerusalem mock her for the loss of her children.

3: God is steadfast and faithful, and this provides hope for the people. The extreme sufferings of the prophet and the people strengthen their resolution to return to the Lord.

4: The punishment of Zion. Reflections on a city besieged and distressed reveal the vanity of human efforts to protect or shield Zion.

5: Plea for God's mercy. The prayer of the prophet and the people for restoration.

Major Themes

- **Praise of God's justice and faithfulness** runs throughout Lamentations.
- **Acknowledgment of sin and due punishment and pleas for mercy** are interspersed with the author's praise of God.

Authorship

Lamentations is traditionally attributed to Jeremiah, which accounts for its placement in the Catholic Bible. The strong images and language suggest composition soon after the city of Jerusalem was conquered and after the people were taken into exile but before the return from captivity in 537 BC.

Literary Form

Lament: A formal expression of sorrow as well as a plea for divine mercy. Although linked to the prophetic books, Lamentations is closer to the Psalms in form. For example, although impossible to reflect in translation, the first four of these five laments are constructed and arranged so that each verse begins with a successive letter of the alphabet.

Key Passages

1:1: Jerusalem is deserted and sits like a lonely widow, though she was once glorious.

3:1-20: The prophet complains about his affliction, which eats away at him like a cancerous disease.

3:21-33: The prophet expresses hope in the steadfast love of God, whose mercy is without end.

Food for Thought

Psalm 137 begins, "By the rivers of Babylon— / there we sat down and there we wept / when we remembered Zion . . . / For there our captors asked us for songs, / and our tormentors asked for mirth, saying, / 'Sing us one of the songs of Zion!'" (137:1, 3). Perhaps among the songs the people sang was Lamentations, a lament for the fate of Jerusalem because the people did not heed the warnings of God, and yet also an expression of the hope that is based on God's goodness and mercy rather than any human quality or power or merit.

The sentiments of the speaker in Lamentations could have inspired the passion narratives of the synoptic Gospels. On the cross, Jesus expresses his anguish at the apparent abandonment of God (Matthew 27:46; Mark 15:34). Yet Jesus is a model of faith and hope despite the temptation to despair elicited by extreme suffering. During Holy Week, the songs in Lamentations are sung as part of the Tenebrae service recalling the passion and death of Jesus. In the course of the ritual, candles are snuffed out so that participants experience darkness, which is symbolic of pain and loss. But there is always hope rooted in the God who loves us.

The biblical tradition assures us through many examples that it is okay to wrestle with God, to complain about things that cause pain in our lives, and to repeatedly ask God to take care of us, protect us, and deliver us. In just such prayers, we learn to place our hope and trust in God's loving care.

Baruch

Presented as the words of Jeremiah's trusted servant, Baruch assumes a time frame near the end of the exile, promising that the exile is nearly over (1:1). The people need to take responsibility for their captivity as punishment for sin and resolve that such suffering will never happen to them again. This resolution will be lived out in true confidence in God. Baruch looks back on the history and experience of Israel and praises God for the Law, which guides the people toward wisdom. We cannot achieve it by ourselves. This is a fundamental idea in all the Scriptures and one that sets the wisdom of Israel apart from that of others, particularly the Greeks, who taught that wisdom could be found through human efforts. The biblical authors maintain that wisdom is God's revelation and that we are dependent on God's mercy and grace in obtaining it.

Baruch is a six-chapter collection of parts that were originally distinct but were probably grouped together because they were too short to be preserved individually. Although there are indications that some parts of Baruch were originally composed in Hebrew, the earliest extant manuscript of this book is in Greek. Catholics, while considering Baruch part of the canon and therefore inspired, have not attributed major significance to this work. Protestants consider Baruch one of the apocryphal books.

At a Glance

Who: Baruch is the scribe of Jeremiah, but this attribution is probably pseudonymous.

What: A composite book of prayers, sections of prose, and poetry ascribed to Baruch and linked to Jeremiah. The last chapter is written in Jeremiah's name; this was supposedly a copy of a letter from the prophet warning the people about falling back into idolatry.

When: At least a generation after the end of the exile, reflecting the sentiments of those who had experienced the exile upon their return, although the prayers of Baruch are supposed to be the prayers of exiles just after the destruction of Jerusalem in 587 BC.

Where: In Judah, reflecting on the devastation of the exile.

Why: To warn against the dangers of idolatry.

Structure and Content

1:1–3:8: Confession and prayer of the exiles. Baruch explains the reasons for the captivity and invites the people to repent.

3:9–4:4: Praise of wisdom identified with the Law. Here is a poetic description of wisdom, illustrating its importance and asserting that no one can find wisdom unless God reveals it.

4:5–5:9: Encouragement and hope for Jerusalem. The prophet addresses believers in the diaspora, as well as Jerusalem and Jerusalem's neighbors, in a message that bewails the captivity and consoles the captives by saying that it will soon end.

6:1-73: Letter of Jeremiah denouncing idolatry and urging confidence in God.

Major Themes

- **Confession of sins and prayers for deliverance** are encouraged by the prophet.
- **True wisdom,** which means renouncing idols and placing all trust in God, is extolled.
- **Hope for a brighter future** must be based on God's promises.

Authorship

This book is attributed to Baruch, the scribe of the great prophet Jeremiah. The book supposes the situation to be at the time just before the return of the people from exile, around 537 BC. It is actually more likely that Baruch came later, during the Maccabean Revolution, when the people of Israel were trying to express their uniqueness as the people of God and to resist the temptations of assimilation into the society defined by Hellenism.

Literary Form

Letter of Encouragement: The final chapter is presented as a letter from Jeremiah, demonstrating the significance of letters purported to have come from noted authorities for the sake of giving direction to the community. This letter follows a report of the weeping of the people and their resolution to do better if they are allowed to return to Jerusalem.

Key Passages

1:3-9: The writer envisions assembling the people to celebrate the Feast of Booths with penitence and prayer.

3:9-15, 32–4:4: Israel is urged to learn wisdom, walking in the way of God.

6: A copy of the letter that Jeremiah sent to the exiles in Babylon to give them the message that God had commanded him to give.

Food for Thought

Even though a passage from the third chapter of Baruch is one of the seven Old Testament readings used for the Easter Vigil each year, the Book of Baruch is not given great prominence overall in the liturgy. However, Baruch is an extraordinary work that deserves our reflection. Perhaps written far later than the events described, Baruch keeps alive the trials of the exile and the resolution that the people had to never again commit the same errors that led to their captivity. Baruch also repeats the truth that wisdom is found in God's ways and in God's Law, not in human endeavors or empty ambitions.

Baruch's use of letters to offer direction and guidance to communities may have served as an example to Paul. The Book of Baruch invokes the authority of Jeremiah, even though it may well have been written some three centuries after Jeremiah and his scribe, Baruch, lived. The practice of attributing a work to an admired person had both the effect of honoring that person and also of lending authority to the message of the actual authors. Imagine the significance of finding a letter addressed to contemporary Americans from the secretary of George Washington or a lost letter addressed to Catholics from St. Francis or St. Dominic.

Ezekiel

God sent the prophet Ezekiel with a message so surprising that no one, not even a prophet, could ever have made it up. In contrast to how Jeremiah spoke a message of warning to a smug people who thought the good times would roll on and on, Ezekiel buoyed up the people in exile just when they thought things would never improve because God had abandoned them. The messages of Isaiah, Jeremiah, and Ezekiel were actually pretty similar and basically very simple: "Rely on God. Repent of your sin, and keep faith with the God of our ancestors, who is steadfast and merciful."

Although prophets are usually understood as interpreters and communicators of God's word, Ezekiel is best known for his *visions,* which were often very strange and certainly complicated. It is as if Ezekiel was trying hard to put into words experiences that were divinely inspired and beyond extraordinary, experiences that took him right out of this world and opened for him the heavenly realm in which God resides. Ezekiel sounds like a wild man, a primitive prophet like Elijah and Elisha, describing incredible creatures such as cherubim with wings appearing amid fire and lightning, moving on wheels within a wheel (1:5-21). Yet although the realities Ezekiel described are very radical, his language and metaphors are earthy and common and therefore easy to understand. God is like a shepherd who tends to Israel as a compassionate caretaker, as one who finds and adopts an abused child. The creator and giver of all life shows Ezekiel that even lifeless, dry bones strewn in the desert can live (37:1-14). Thus, Ezekiel delivers a message of hope.

At a Glance

Who: The priest and prophet Ezekiel was among the first of the exiles to be deported to Babylon after Jerusalem first fell to Nebuchadnezzar around 597 BC, that is, about ten years before the attack that leveled the city, the temple, and the hopes of a reprieve for Jerusalem's inhabitants.

What: While previous prophets referred to God's word communicated to them, Ezekiel experienced divine revelations in visions, some of them quite bizarre-sounding and difficult to picture in our understanding of this world. Ezekiel employed a new form of literature called "apocalyptic."

When: The period of the exile, in the sixth century before Jesus.
Where: Set in Babylon at the beginning of the exile.
Why: To convince the people that God was using Babylon as an instrument of punishment and then to offer solace and hope that they would never be abandoned by their God.

Structure and Content

1–3: The call of the prophet. Ezekiel is called to be a "sentinel for the house of Israel"(3:17), a watchman or witness of God's faithfulness to the people who may be wondering if, at last, God has abandoned them. The prophet eats the scroll of God's word as God commands him to do. Then he is lifted up by the spirit of God and taken off to Babylon. For seven days—a symbolic period of time signifying some period of hesitation, doubt, and confusion—the prophet remains on the banks of a river before he is told to speak as a witness, warning the people in exile of its meaning. Ezekiel listens to God, who tells him that he is to help the people understand that God is still with them. First, though, Ezekiel is made speechless; his inability to speak and his restoration are clear signs of God's power working in him.

4–32: Judgments against Israel and the other nations. Ezekiel explains why Israel has been exiled but also affirms that God has still not abandoned her. Ezekiel announces that the temple, which everyone thought was inviolable because it was holy and represented God's presence with the people, would be destroyed. God's glory would leave the temple and come with the cherubim, Ezekiel, and all the rest of the people to the shores of the river Chebar. The crimes of Israel and of Jerusalem will be punished by the sword of Babylon, which will act, for a time, as the instrument of God. The prophet also speaks God's judgment against all the peoples who have repeatedly done all kinds of evil.

33–48: The new Israel. The watchman-prophet speaks of the restoration of the people. There will be retribution for those who have not turned to God, who is like a shepherd to the people. After all this time of suffering, however, the covenant between God and his people will be restored; even bones lying in the desert will be given new life at God's word. There will be a new temple and a new Jerusalem.

Major Themes

- **Salvation and unconditional forgiveness** are extended to the captives from the God who will never abandon them.
- **The hope of the people** rests in God.
- **A new temple and a new Jerusalem** will be given to the people, who will experience a resurrection of sorts, just as the dry bones in the desert were raised to new life.

Authorship

Ezekiel was a priest living in Jerusalem and was also one of the first to be taken captive into Babylon around 597 BC, about ten years before the beginning of the exile of the whole population.

Literary Form

Oracles: Direct messages from God, often in the form of visions. We see in Ezekiel the beginning of Jewish apocalyptic literature.

Key Passages

34:1-31: The leaders are the "shepherds" of Israel. Because they have misled the people, God will become the shepherd of the people.

37:1-14: The dry bones prophecy.

47:1-12: Ezekiel envisions living water flowing from the temple.

Food for Thought

More than any other prophet, Ezekiel and his visions function as a kind of bridge between other prophets and images very familiar to later readers of the New Testament. Just as Elijah went up to heaven in a fiery chariot, Ezekiel landed in Babylon in a fiery chariot, an image of some out-of-body experience hard to express in human terms. When it comes to encouragement and hope, Ezekiel sounds like many of the prophets that came before him, like Isaiah and his contemporary, Jeremiah, who also lived in the land of exile. Ezekiel built on the words, careers, and images of these prophets, just as future prophets and the New Testament writers would build on his words and visions. The prophecy of the dry bones was later used by Jewish teachers as a prophecy of resurrection. It is featured implicitly in the Gospels as the background for belief in the resurrection of Jesus. Jesus himself used Ezekiel's image of living water (see John 7:38). In the Book of Revelation, we are treated to visions of the new Jerusalem (21:1-27). Thus, we are indebted to Ezekiel for giving us these images in the first place.

In the Book of Ezekiel, God is the hope of the people, and restoration is promised them because God is always faithful. It seems easy enough to believe in God when things are going our way. But if our hope is rooted in God rather than in passing fortunes, we will trust God and be an example for others of God's power, love, and way of life, even in trying times.

Daniel

Who is Daniel, and what is he doing in that lion's den? Here we have a great example in the form of a young man and his friends who are willing to sacrifice everything for the sake of their Jewish traditions and way of life. They are featured as the servants of the infamous Nebuchadnezzar, king of Babylon, a figure of great power and authority who, at a stroke, could have them executed. However, Daniel and his friends actually lived some four hundred years later when it was the Hellenists, rather than the Babylonians, who were oppressing the Jews.

True to the apocalyptic tone that would become synonymous with his name, Daniel uses cryptic images to convey his message. In a time of persecution, the first thing to go is freedom of speech. So the authority Daniel resisted was referred to as the dreaded Babylon of bygone years, a kind of code language that was safer than a direct attack on the reigning monarch, who was making it impossible for Jews to freely practice their religious customs, particularly circumcision, dietary restrictions, and Sabbath observance.

The placement of Daniel in the Bible is somewhat controversial, as seen by its history. Unlike the other prophets with whom he is often grouped, this book is not really named for the author so much as for the protagonist. In fact, "Daniel" is a name that appears earlier in the Scriptures. It may be used here for its familiarity, as an amalgamation of all of the sages who have relied on God. Yet in the style familiar to the prophets, the apocalyptic visions of Daniel are narrated in the first person (see chapters 7–12). In the Hebrew and Protestant Bibles, an abridged version of the Catholic Book of Daniel (i.e., without chapters 13 and 14, which appear only in Greek) is included with the writings. In the Septuagint and in most English translations, Daniel is listed with the prophets and sometimes referred to as the fourth major prophet after Isaiah, Jeremiah, and Ezekiel. Yet Daniel is significantly different from the other prophets and almost forms a category by himself as a representative of apocalyptic literature, one of the last genres to be developed in the Old Testament.

At a Glance

Who: Daniel, a prophet and seer, and his friends, who were persecuted for holding fast to their Jewish traditions.

What: Exemplary and edifying stories of Daniel and others who were willing to undergo persecution while maintaining faith in God. Daniel also contains the promise of rewards for perseverance based on belief of vindication by God and suggestions of life after death.
When: Set in the time of the exile.
Where: Israel.
Why: To encourage resistance to assimilation into Hellenistic culture.

Structure and Content

1–6: Daniel and his companions in Babylon. This is a collection of six short stories recounting the trials of Daniel and his companions at the hands of Nebuchadnezzar, king of Babylon.

7–12: This section details Daniel's four visions: the vision of the four beasts; the vision of the ram and the he-goat; Gabriel and the seventy weeks; and the vision of the Hellenistic wars.

13–14: The appendix. More stories from the time of Daniel—Susanna, Daniel, Bel, and the dragon—which ridicule the ways of idolatry.

Major Themes

- **Courage under persecution and confidence in God** enable Daniel and his friends to withstand great persecution.
- **Hope for a life beyond suffering** comforts those who are persecuted.
- **Those who faithfully witness** through their lives or their deaths will earn great rewards.

Authorship

Since Daniel 7–12 is written in the first person, it was long believed that Daniel was written by someone who had lived through the experience of persecution that the book describes. However, telling edifying stories of heroism and persistent faith through hardships is a well-known rabbinic teaching technique. Thus, Daniel is probably a composite work of the second century, popularly used to encourage Jews suffering in a hostile world.

Literary Form

Apocalypse: A vision described as an out-of-body and out-of-this-world experience.

Key Passages

7:9-14: The vision of the son of man, who is given power and authority by the "Ancient One" over all creation.

12:1-4: After a period of great distress, "Michael, the great prince"(12:1) shall appear, and those who have died will awaken to life. The wise and the righteous will enjoy everlasting life.

Food for Thought

The Book of Daniel is a good example of how to compare and contrast the content of a book with the historical context of when it was composed. The setting for the Book of Daniel is the time of the exile, a time of great suffering for the Jews, who were being persecuted by the king of Babylon. However, Daniel was not written until after the time of the Maccabees, near the end of the second century before Christ. It was written to encourage the Jews who had known great suffering during so many periods of their history to persevere as they suffered under the successors of Alexander who aimed to impose Hellenism on everyone and eliminate Jewish beliefs and practices.

Daniel is essentially a testimony about martyrdom; a *martyr* (from the Greek) is one who "witnesses." Amidst many threats against practicing Judaism, Daniel and his companions represent those who stood up to the power of the king who ordered them to eat pork and deny their Jewish ways and roots. Daniel was used in Christian circles to encourage perseverance in the face of great persecution and suffering. Martyrdom became a powerful and popular image for the commitment required to be a Jew or, later, a Christian living in a hostile and often intolerant world. Although today most of us are not required to give up our lives for our religion, we are asked to *live* our lives according to our faith. Martyrdom, in the sense of giving testimony daily to what we believe, never goes out of style.

Introduction to the Minor Prophets

There are twelve prophets known as "minor," not because their influence or importance is minimal, but because these books are shorter than those of the major prophets; traditionally, they all shared one scroll. Geographically, Hosea and Amos preached to the Northern Kingdom of Israel while the other minor prophets addressed Judah or the people after the exile. Chronologically, the minor prophets span the centuries, from the eighth century to the postexilic period, as late as the second half of the fourth century BC. The oldest trio, who preached in the eighth century BC (also the time of First Isaiah), include Amos, Hosea, and Micah. Zephaniah, Nahum, and Habakkuk preached toward the end of the seventh century BC, when Babylon was on the rise. Haggai and Zechariah were prophets in the time of the rebuilding of the temple near the end of the sixth century BC. Joel, Jonah, Obadiah, and Malachi also came after the exile, somewhat later, although their exact dates are difficult to establish.

The minor prophets share a number of characteristics with one another and with the longer so-called major prophets. They contain oracles of warning, salvation, judgment, and complaint. Some common themes of these prophets include the call to conversion of heart, the priority of social justice, and the essential link between true worship and true justice. Some prophets used their own life experiences, such as political leadership, marriage, and parenthood to communicate God's message to the people.

Some, like Hosea and Micah, are well-known to us for their beautiful imagery and hopeful message. Others, like Amos and Joel, may make us squirm in discomfort as they warn of judgment and retribution even for the chosen people. They were meant to. Isaiah stressed that God's thoughts are not our thoughts and that God's ways are not our ways (55:8). The twelve who make up the kaleidoscopic mosaic called the minor prophets illustrate and repeat this lesson. The word of God came to the prophets in different times to guide the faithful in the ways of justice, not merely to console and comfort. We need to listen to God's word as prodding us to change, to become more responsive as people who hear God's word and keep it.

Paramount among the common themes of the prophets is the vision of "the day of the Lord." This concept often suggests a threat and a warning to Israel before the exile (see Amos 5:18-20; Isaiah 2:10-12; Zephaniah 1:14-15). Amos related this term to God's judgment, which would spell punishment, doom, and destruction for Israel and Judah as well as other nations. In the postexilic period, "the day of the Lord" conveyed hope and a promise of vindication (see Isaiah 63:4; Joel 3:4-21). Those who call upon the Lord and repent shall experience it as a day of rescue and restoration in the sight of all those who have oppressed and mocked them. It is a time when God will be victorious, and God's judgments will reverse all the values and fortunes that people have established in this world. This is a fundamental concept dominating Jewish apocalypticism. Eventually, classical prophecy in Israel gave way to apocalyptic thought as the ideas of judgment and salvation were extended to include belief in an afterlife and resurrection from the dead.

Useful Terms to Know

Chaldeans: The Babylonians, whose power was on the rise when Habakkuk spoke.

Darius I: This Persian emperor enjoyed a long reign (521–486 BC) and assumed a conciliatory stance toward the Judeans that was a marked divergence from the way his predecessor had treated them. Haggai began preaching in the second year of Darius' reign, urging the people to trust that the initial signs of the freedom they were beginning to enjoy would last because they would be blessed by God in their efforts to rebuild the temple.

Edom: A people related to Judah through their common ancestry; both descended from Abraham. From the time of the exodus, when Edom refused passage to the Israelites returning from Egypt, hatred between the two peoples was fueled by mutual aggression and acts of war.

Ephraim: The heartland of the Northern Kingdom, known alternately as "Israel," following the split between the North and the South.

***Hesed*:** The Hebrew word meaning "covenant" that conveys God's enduring love and mercy. The prophet Micah emphasizes this *hesed,* the consistent and steadfast love of God.

Judgment by Fire: Many understand this to refer to a scorching drought of the land. It may have become symbolic of hell for divine punishment of evil through eschatological use.

Nineveh: Famous from the book of Jonah, Nineveh was the capital of Assyria, the great enemy of Israel, known for its cruelty and torture of its many foes. Nineveh was located in modern-day Iraq, not far from the present-day city of Mosul. The Ninevites represented all that was hated about the pagans, although Jonah attested that the people of Nineveh would repent far sooner than the Israelites. Isaiah 10:5-16 depicts Nineveh as the instrument of God's punishment of Israel. Nahum takes some comfort in prophesying the utter destruction of Nineveh, a prophecy that would come to fruition in 612 BC. But not too many years afterward, Jerusalem would also learn the impact of disaster from events similar to those that Nineveh had experienced.

Plumb Line: A symbol of God's justice as defined by the Torah, this is a line that hangs down from the heavens, measuring a straight trajectory. The Jews understood that justice was a property of God and could not be attained except through obedience to God.

Remnant: At times the term signified Israel, as excluded from God's wrath because of the covenant, a wrath other nations would feel because of their sins as Israel's enemies. Amos used the term "remnant" as a warning that a complacent and sinful Israel would be reduced to a small number of those who remained faithful to the covenant. Thus, for Amos, it was no longer a term of comfort but of warning.

Zerubbabel: A king who descended from David and bore the messianic hopes of the people. Haggai prophesied to him and to Joshua, son of Jehozadak the high priest (1:1).

Hosea

There is a saying that God writes straight with crooked lines. Certainly that seems to be the case with Hosea. The man had a nontraditional marriage with a harlot not known for her faithfulness. And yet Hosea's words to or about her represent some of the most romantic, tender, poetic, and beautiful love language in the Bible.

Hosea was a prophet to the Northern Kingdom of Israel, also sometimes called Ephraim, during its final days. He used his marriage to the harlot, Gomer, to symbolize the relationship between Yahweh and the faithless Israel, who acted the prostitute. Israel's infidelity was idolatry and the ruthless oppression of the poor. Hosea prophesied that God would strip Israel of the ornaments with which false gods had bedazzled her, like the lovers of an unfaithful spouse.

After the demise of the Northern Kingdom, Hosea's prophecies were known and used in the South as a warning to the people there. Hosea's strong indictments against the priests could suggest that Hosea was himself a priest. However, little is known about the man except for his marriage to Gomer. Hosea's preaching career was roughly contemporary with that of First Isaiah (chapters 1–39).

At a Glance

Who: Hosea, son of Beeri, was a prophet in the last days of the Northern Kingdom of Israel.

What: Warnings of disaster for the sins of the kingdom to the north that Hosea calls Israel or sometimes Ephraim.

When: Second half of eighth century BC, between 750–732 BC.

Where: The Northern Kingdom, but the Book of Hosea was also remembered and circulated in Judah when the prophet's warnings came to pass.

Why: To warn the people, especially the priests, of the possible consequences of their sins, but also to reveal to the people that God acts as a faithful husband who will punish Israel but never abandon her.

Structure and Content

1–3: Hosea's marriage and children are part of his "call." Prophetic lessons about God's fidelity are taken from Hosea's tragic marriage to Gomer, a harlot. The names of Hosea's children are also symbolic of the fractured relationship between Israel and Yahweh.

4–14: Israel's sin and God's judgment against her. In Hosea we see a pattern that is pronounced throughout the prophets; that is, denunciations of the sins of the people are interspersed with promises of restoration.

Major Theme

- **God is faithful even though Israel is not.** God's love for Israel knows no bounds, and even though Israel has rejected God time and time again, God will never abandon his people.

Authorship

Little is known about Hosea, who is identified in 1:1 as the "son of Beeri," prophesying throughout the reigns of four kings in Judah, just before the dissolution of the Northern Kingdom. Together with Isaiah, Micah, and Amos, Hosea is one of the great prophets of the eighth century BC.

Literary Form

Oracles: A good example of classic prophecy in Israel, Hosea conveys direct messages from God of judgment and salvation.

Key Passage

11:1, 3-4: Israel is referred to as God's son whom God loves and called out of Egypt. God is depicted as a doting father, teaching Israel to walk, lifting him up to kiss his cheeks, and bending down to feed him.

Food for Thought

Hosea continues a tradition of comparing God's love for Israel to marriage. Hosea helps us understand that our human experiences of marriage and parenting provide insight into the power of God's love for us, which knows no limit or condition. It would have been shocking in Hosea's time to use the image of an unfaithful wife to illustrate the extent of God's love for the chosen people. But Hosea's tender language involves the way God has responded with great compassion and forgiveness to Israel's infidelity.

Hosea may be the first biblical author to describe God's love for Israel as the love of a parent for his young child learning to stand and walk. We can probably all relate to this experience, which helps us comprehend just how boundless such love is. Too often we focus on the ways in which lovers and spouses exemplify the limits of love, or we cite many examples of ways children disappoint parents with thoughtless and ungrateful behavior. Instead, we can magnify the great love people show every day in our families and neighborhoods and see these actions as so many examples of the far greater love God has for each one of us.

JOEL

There is a difference between optimism and hope. Optimism can be uninformed, stubborn resistance to reality. But hope, as described in the Bible, is rooted in God. Hope emphasizes God's fidelity, experienced time and again even though we have sinned and neglected faith. Joel is a perfect example of biblical hope. Joel interprets the natural disaster of a locust infestation as an opportunity and an invitation to "wake up," (1:5), to be appalled at the catastrophe, and to turn to the Lord, who will take "pity on his people" (2:18). The day of the Lord, Joel says, is near. It is not a day of joyous expectation, but a "day of darkness and gloom," full of fiery flames from which there is no escape (2:2-3).

Yet the prophet's message is one of hope and promise. Despite the fearsome imagery, Joel repeats that we need not fear when we turn wholeheartedly to the Lord. What we know for sure is that our God is "gracious and merciful, . . . abounding in steadfast love, and relents from punishing" (2:13). Joel issues a call to join God in waging war on all that threatens us: farmers fight pestilence and famine; priests vanquish idolatry and sin; even newlyweds join battle against every form of sin. Joel is a prophet of hope rooted in God's tender love, not in false hopes or naïve fantasies.

Not much is known about Joel, although he represents a model of Israel's prophets. His prophecy is democratic and egalitarian, calling on everyone and everything—farmers and priests, elders, infants and brides, even the wild animals and the soil itself—to join in the lament, prayer, and repentance for Israel's sins in seeking God's mercy. The Book of Joel is truly a universal and timeless celebration of God's steadfast love.

At a Glance

Who: Joel, son of Pethuel; his name, *Yo'el*, means "Yahweh is God."

What: Prophecy interpreting a natural disaster as a symbol for the coming day of the Lord.

When: Sometime in the latter part of the fifth century or the first part of the fourth century BC, a late date suggested by the prevalence of apocalyptic imagery. Joel's dating is much debated, but most agree that Joel is postexilic, as shown by the absence of reference to a king.

Where: References to priests and the temple cult indicate that the prophet preached in Jerusalem.

Why: To call the people to repentance, lest something even worse than their current natural disasters should happen to them.

Structure and Content

1:1–2:17: A drought and a plague of locusts prompt the prophet's call to prayer and repentance. Joel describes the "day of the LORD" (1:15) as a day of judgment for Israel and all her neighbors. He calls on the priests to lead a solemn assembly in the temple to acknowledge and repent for the sins of the people. The people must "rend [their] hearts and not [their] clothing" (2:13) and pray that God will spare them. The description of a swarm of locusts afflicting the countryside becomes a metaphor for a military attack on the city (2:1-17).

2:18–3:21: The end of the plague is symbolic of the victory of God over all of Israel's enemies. God answers the sincere prayer of his people, and the people celebrate joyfully in the countryside as they are filled with "grain, wine, and oil" (2:19). The spirit of God is poured out upon all, men and women, old and young, who have seen the signs of the day of the Lord and have repented. Yahweh vindicates Israel in the assembled view of their archenemies, including the Phoenicians and the Philistines.

Major Themes

- **The day of the Lord is a day of reckoning** for everyone but is especially ominous for Israel's enemies.

- **True repentance of the heart, with prayer and fasting,** is an absolute necessity.

- **God's blessings go beyond the people's requests,** and God sends the spirit on all people.

Authorship

Dating this prophecy is determined through hints in the text itself. For example, parallels with other postexilic works suggest it was written after that event, and Joel's emphasis on the temple implies that the temple had been rebuilt (i.e., after 515 BC). The mention of Sidon implies that Joel wrote before that important city was destroyed around 343 BC.

Literary Form

Oracles: Messages from God, occasioned by a crisis of nature that was interpreted as a sign of the day of the Lord and its consequences. A naturally occurring event thus takes on cosmic significance in the perspective of the prophet.

Key Passages

2:28-29: Prophecy of universalism, promising that all, men and women, old and young, slave and free, will be included in the outpouring of the Spirit of God.

3:9-10: Reversing the images used in Isaiah 2:4 and Micah 4:3, Joel calls on all to beat "plowshares into swords, and your pruning hooks into spears"(3:10) as they join God in battle against God's enemies.

3:14b-15: The day of the Lord will mean devastation for sinners, but a new age of joy and abundance for God's people, as Joel warns that the "sun and the moon are darkened, and the stars withdraw their shining."

Food for Thought

According to Acts 2:16-21, Peter used the idea from Joel of God's spirit being poured out on all the people in his speech on Pentecost. He affirmed that the day of the Lord is not only a day of judgment and fear, but also one of promise for all those who repent: "Then everyone who calls on the name of the Lord shall be saved" (Acts 2:21; cf. Joel 2:32). Just as the Evangelist Luke presents the birth of the church as the time of fulfillment of all the prophetic promises, so we today should meditate on our time as a time of fulfillment. The prophets always insisted that God does not act alone but requires human cooperation through grace. For this to truly be a time of universal fulfillment, we need to convert our hearts and minds through true repentance and openness to the spirit. Joel is particularly appealing in our world, which desperately needs holy people to join the battle against injustice of all kinds: poverty, discrimination, and a disregard for the sanctity of human life. Is our hope strong enough?

Amos

We've probably all had at least one experience in our lives that caused us to wonder, "What am I doing here, and why am I doing this?" Sometimes it seems as if we just have to go out on a limb, even when our better judgment tells us that someone is trying to cut down the whole tree! That's something like what happened to Amos.

Amos is the first literary prophet in the traditional sense, meaning that this is the oldest written prophetic book; it is ascribed to a shepherd who was called by God to speak to the people in God's name. As such, Amos represents the long line of prophets who would come after him, claiming that he was minding his own business when God intervened, interrupted his life, and mandated a mission to preach in God's name in order to persuade the people to convert their lives.

Amos was from Judah, but he was called to prophesy to the people of Israel in the north. Amaziah, a priest of the North, sent word to Jeroboam, king of Israel, that Amos was a conspirator from the South, and he tried to have Amos exiled. In 7:14-15, Amos responded to Amaziah, saying, "I am no prophet, nor a prophet's son; but I am a herdsman, and a dresser of sycamore trees, and the LORD took me from following the flock, and the LORD said to me, 'Go, prophesy to my people Israel.'" The true prophets base their authority on their call from God, not on any credentials or talents they themselves possess. And the true prophets can speak only God's word, not words of appeasement or ones designed to gain human approval.

The greater part of the Book of Amos is unmitigated warning of impending judgment and doom. Well-meaning editors later apparently added an ending to soften the message and promise that God would indeed visit mercy on his people. But perhaps the prophet's words should be read without this about-face conclusion so that Amos' message can penetrate people's hearts and minds and shock them into conversion. Israel, in fact, suffered all that the prophet foretold and more. The people just didn't listen. But if Israel (and we) would have taken Amos' message seriously and literally, without the reservation that "God might not really mean it," it could have become for us a strong message, motivating us to change our ways, convert our hearts, and be saved. It could become a prophecy of mercy and healing.

At a Glance

Who: Amos, a shepherd from Tekoa in Judah, was called to convey and interpret visions by preaching conversion to the people of Israel.

What: A fire-and-brimstone warning against the nations like Philistia and Tyre, including his homeland, Judah, and against Israel, with even more calamitous effects. Amos railed against social injustice, especially while people hypocritically offered sacrifices as part of their cult, or ways of worship.

When: In the eighth century BC, probably 760–750, after a severe earthquake during the otherwise prosperous reign of Jeroboam II (786–746 BC).

Where: The prophet from the South preached to the people of the North and was denounced by the priests there as a traitor.

Why: To call the people of Israel to repentance by prophesying about the downfall of Israel and the judgment to come on "the day of the LORD."

Structure and Content

1:1–2:5: Judgment against the nations. Amos first pronounces judgment against Israel's neighbors, including Aram, Philistia, Tyre, Edom, Ammon, Moab, and even Judah. Readers can almost hear Israel applauding as her neighbors are all called to task by the prophet, himself a Judahite.

2:6–6:14: Judgment against Israel. When Israel herself is condemned, especially for her abuses against the poor, her priests protest to the king and charge Amos as a traitor.

7:1–9:8a: Visions interpreted with threats and promises. Amos describes five visions that will mean judgment for Israel. These visions function as parables, warning the people of impending doom.

9:8b-15: The epilogue depicts the Messianic restoration. This prophetic book concludes with God's promise to "raise up the booth of David that is fallen" (9:11) and to "restore the fortunes of my people Israel" (9:14).

Major Themes

- **God's sure and coming judgment** will also include the chosen people.
- **Social injustice and hypocrisy** evoke the prophet's outrage.
- **God's word is efficacious,** and Amos' prophecies will come to fruition.

Authorship

Amos was older than Hosea but prophesied around the same time Hosea did; these were the only two prophets sent to the Northern Kingdom of Israel. All but the final seven-and-a-half verses come from Amos in the eighth century BC. The concluding epilogue may have been written by a disciple centuries later, after the return of the exiles.

Literary Form

Oracles: During a time of prosperity, the prophet expresses God's message and visions of judgment foretelling Israel's impending doom.

Key Passages

2:6-12: Indictment of Israel for sins against the covenant with God, including neglect and abuse of the poor (tantamount to "selling" them for a trifle), as well as rejecting and trying to silence the prophets sent from God.

5:12-17: Amos laments the many sins of Israel, especially social injustice against the needy and the powerless. Amos reminds the people to hate evil, love good, and establish justice so that perhaps God will be "gracious to the remnant of Joseph" (5:15).

5:18-24: Amos warns that the day of the Lord will be darkness, rather than light, for those who do evil. He prays for justice to "roll down like waters" and righteousness to be "like an ever-flowing stream" (5:24).

Food for Thought

The prophets assert that God will answer the prayers of the poor and needy who are righteous and will punish those who oppress them. Older prophets like Amos proclaim that God's victory over evil will be evident in this world. In contrast, later apocalyptic writers would use imagery fashioned by such prophets as Amos to describe a retribution that comes in the next world and judgment that is delayed perhaps until after death. When reading Amos, there is something to be said for lingering on the truth of the literal. All that Amos foretold came about for the people. And the genius of the prophet was to identify the sins that brought about this judgment as injustice against the poor and the downtrodden. These sins, combined with a careless and hypocritical attitude toward religious feasts, sacrifices, and offerings, are rejected by God as worthless and "hated" (cf. Amos 5:21).

In the Gospels, Jesus paraphrases Amos, echoing God's rejection of empty religious acts and sacrifices and warning against injustice (see Matthew 23:1-36). Amos stresses the priority of social justice and calls for sincere worship. These must play a major role in the formation of a Christian conscience, since they provide the essential basis of the church's social teaching and actions. We need to ask ourselves how the connection between our works for justice for the powerless and our participation in the liturgy is manifest and serves as an example to others.

Obadiah

We may think of sibling rivalry as a very natural, harmless thing. However, there are several cautionary tales throughout the Bible about the dangers of sibling rivalries. For example, the rivalry between Cain and Abel reached such depths that Cain committed fratricide (see Genesis 4:1-8); Cain was then condemned to a life of wandering (4:10-16). The rivalry between the people of Israel and Edom was likewise legendary. Edom, a small state south of Judah whose people had descended from Abraham's grandson Esau, was especially hated by the Jews for taking advantage of Judah's suffering under the Babylonians. But their mutual animosity went back further. From the time of the exodus, when Edom tried to prevent the Israelites from passing through their territory, to the more recent attempt to deny passage to the Israelites returning from exile in Babylon, Edom had hindered Israel at every turn. Because of such treacherous actions, Edom was condemned by the Book of Obadiah, which warned, "For the slaughter and violence done to your brother Jacob, shame shall cover you" (10).

Obadiah is the shortest (only twenty-one verses) and appears to be among the most strident of all the prophecies in the Old Testament. Obadiah applies the principle of retribution, warning that Edom will suffer greatly for gloating over Israel's suffering. Although Edom has conspired even against the holy city, Jerusalem will escape destruction and remain a sign of God's protection. Obadiah ends with the exclamation, "The kingdom shall be the Lord's," a profession of faith that the inevitable victory over Judah's enemies belongs solely to God (21).

At a Glance

Who: Nothing personal is known about the prophet Obadiah.
What: An oracle against Edom, a perennial enemy of Judah.
When: Probably written sometime in the fifth century BC.
Where: Composed in Judah, perhaps Jerusalem.
Why: To warn Edom that she will be punished and destroyed for her many sins against God's people.

Structure and Content

1-16: Short oracles against Edom (verses 1-14) and all the nations (verses 15-16) who have harmed Israel. Edom is doomed, as her own actions have come back to haunt her.

17-21: Judah's final triumph. The day of the Lord is a day of judgment against all those who have persecuted God's people. Finally, God rules as king and rescues the faithful.

Major Themes

- **Edom represents a negative example of the Golden Rule:** what she has done to others will be done to her. Edom shall "drink" of God's wrath (15-16) and, ultimately, on the day of the Lord, will be obliterated.

- **The day of the Lord is one of judgment against Israel's enemies.** Ultimately, God will be victorious, and the "kingdom," that is, all the people, shall belong to God.

Authorship

Obadiah is mentioned only in the superscription. Nothing is known about the prophet himself, except that he probably lived and prophesied during the fifth century before Christ.

Literary Form

Oracles: Obadiah speaks God's message, expressing hope that the suffering of God's people will be vindicated and that Edom, one of the most obstinate of Israel's enemies, will be punished.

Key Passage

13: There are several parallels between this passage and Jeremiah's oracles against Edom; they both condemn Edom for gloating over the destruction of the Israelites (see Jeremiah 49:7, 14-16).

Food for Thought

Obadiah seems to exult in the concept of revenge that he sees is justly due Edom. The theory of retribution implies that people reap what they sow. The Book of Obadiah not only speaks to Edom but contains a message for all time. If, for a while, we evade the consequences of our actions, inevitably, evil deeds are redressed. Often people suffer the very consequences of actions they have perpetrated on others.

Many religions have something akin to the idea of *karma,* a Sanskrit term borrowed from Hinduism that literally means "weight" and signifies that any action we do in life functions like a boomerang. We are meant to reap the benefits of good actions and the bad consequences of evil ones. The Book of Obadiah is thus not so much about revenge on Israel's enemies but a reminder that human beings are responsible for their actions, especially those that affect others. Do I realize that all my actions have consequences?

JONAH

The Book of Jonah is a classic story of the lengths to which people go to resist God's call. In fact, Jonah's reluctance was extreme, as he illustrated the futility of trying to evade the "Hound of Heaven." The rhetorical question of the psalmist to the creator of the universe explores the same impossibility of trying to hide: "Where can I flee from your presence?" (139:7). Jonah tried running away on a boat, but when it almost capsized, he was thrown overboard and swallowed by a "large fish" (Jonah 1:17), which coughed him up on the shore of the land where God wanted him in the first place.

There are several other stories in the Bible that depict the reluctance of people to recognize a call from God. Moses protested that the people wouldn't believe him and that he was "slow of speech" (Exodus 4:10). Isaiah and later Peter protested that they were unworthy sinners (Isaiah 6:5-8; Luke 5:8). Even Mary of Nazareth found it necessary to remind God that she was a virgin as she wondered how it could be that she would conceive the long-awaited Messiah (Luke 1:26-34).

The Book of Jonah is probably best characterized as a story, but one that has much to teach us about the nature and use of the prophetic tradition in Israel. The obvious exaggerations in the story—the comic depiction of the prophet's reluctance to preach to the hated Ninevites, the parabolic way the story focuses on the theme of God's will being enforced despite Jonah's attempts to escape it—all show that the story serves a primarily theological purpose. Our contemporary understanding of history, often too narrow, should not prevent us from seeing the real contribution that the Book of Jonah makes to a better comprehension of the role and purpose of the prophets. Jonah presents a theodicy, a defense of the justice of God in view of his mercy, which are not conflicting but coexisting qualities of God; this is a mystery best illustrated in stories rather than in abstract formulas.

Above all, this book focuses on God rather than on a human being. The power of prophecy is not inherent in the prophet, his personality, his abilities, or even his willingness to serve God. God's message will be preached with or without the participation of human agents. Even the apparently unworthy will repent and respond to God's message.

At a Glance

Who: Jonah ben Amittai was a prophet called by God to preach to the people of Nineveh; he was probably a fictional legendary character, perhaps based on a name found in 2 Kings 14:25.

What: A parable showing the centrality of God's will and his choice of human instruments as prophets and, even more important, God's justice and the need for repentance for all.

When: Difficult to date since the work does not refer to any historical event, but Jonah seems to be at home in the postexilic milieu of the end of the sixth century or the beginning of the fifth century BC.

Where: Postexilic Judea.

Why: To show the need for repentance as well as the enduring forgiveness and mercy of God.

Structure and Content

1–2: The first mission. The word of the Lord comes to Jonah, who at first tries to evade his mission but, after being swallowed by a fish, sings a song of thanksgiving to the Lord and vows his obedience. Jonah is then spewed out on the shore of Nineveh.

3–4: The second mission describes the conversion of Nineveh. Jonah is full of obstinate anger at the people's conversion, and the Lord reproves him.

Major Themes

- **God's justice and mercy are universal,** meant for non-Israelites as well as Israel.

- **The prophet is an instrument of God,** speaking God's word.

Authorship

The author is unknown. It was probably written sometime in the fifth century BC, near the end of the age of the prophets, when there was a waning of prophecy and skepticism about God's continuing faithfulness to the people.

Literary Form

Extended Parable: Although it is placed among the prophets, Jonah illustrates some of the qualities of wisdom literature as well as some of the legendary heroes of old such as Samson, Judith, and Esther, as it teaches universal truths through a story.

Key Passages

1:6: The ship's captain demands that Jonah ask his God to save them all.

4:2: Jonah acknowledges in prayer that God is a "gracious God and merciful, slow to anger, and abounding in steadfast love."

Food for Thought

As a parable, the story of Jonah teaches great truths about the universal mercy of God, the unworthiness but usability of the prophet, and the necessity of relying on God's protection, providence, mercy, and kindness in our lives. The Book of Jonah illustrates that a story can be true without being historically factual. The fantastic story of Jonah in the belly of the fish for three days is used by Jesus as a foreshadowing of his resurrection (Matthew 12:38-42).

Some say that there are no instances in the Bible where God or Jesus laugh. But Jonah, like the incident with Zacchaeus in Luke, shows that God and Jesus must have a marvelous sense of humor. Who can think of poor Jonah trying to avoid doing what God asks of him without smiling in sympathy, identifying the times we have tried to avoid doing what we know we should (and will, in the end) do? Or consider Zacchaeus, who runs ahead to get a good vantage point from which to spy Jesus unobtrusively, only to become the center of attention when he is sighted and called down out of a tree by Jesus (Luke 19:1-10). Zacchaeus winds up promising all sorts of good resolutions, and we, as readers, are left to smile knowingly to ourselves when we recall parallels in our own experience. We, too, have been "caught" by the gratuitous choice of divine providence granting us the opportunity to do greater things than we could imagine. The creator of the world has the most fantastic sense of humor of all. They say if you want to make God laugh, tell God your plans. Inspired by Jonah, we might paraphrase, "If you want to show how far you can go, tell God your limits."

Micah

It seems hard and lonely to be a prophet. We tend to like people who agree with us and shun those who don't. The prophets to Israel and Judah spoke many gloomy messages of impending doom and destruction and castigated both kings and commoners alike for their sins. None of these messages won them any popularity contests, and they must have tired of being disliked. Micah, a contemporary of Isaiah, excoriated many leaders of his time—the rich who exploited the poor, the merchants who robbed the people, the corrupt priests and judges, and the "yes-men" prophets on the take. Nonetheless, Micah is most remembered for his summary of God's will for the people: "to do justice, and to love kindness, and to walk humbly with your God" (6:8).

There are some parallels between Micah and some other important prophets, namely, Isaiah and Jeremiah. Micah seems to borrow some ideas and even some passages verbatim from Isaiah, who probably just preceded him. Later, when the prophet Jeremiah was threatened with death by the king, some influential elders stepped forward to plead for his life, citing the example of "Micah of Moresheth, who prophesied during the days of King Hezekiah" (Jeremiah 26:18). Their reasoning was that since Hezekiah did not put Micah to death, even though the prophet had indicted the king for many sins, neither should Jeremiah be put to death. Rather, the king should repent like Hezekiah did. Although this book does not say so expressly, this plea apparently worked, for Jeremiah survived the threat and lived to prophesy for quite some time after that. This interaction among the literary prophets adds to their interest for us.

At a Glance

Who: Not much is known about the man named Micah, except that he lived around the same time as Isaiah and came from Moresheth, a small village of Judah (1:1).

What: His oracles were especially concerned with social justice and were especially aimed at the evils practiced against the poor and lowly, women, children, and all who were vulnerable. He singled out the capitals of Samaria and Jerusalem.

When: Toward the end of the eighth century BC, around the same time as or just after the great prophets of Amos, Hosea, and First Isaiah.

Where: Rural Judah.

Why: To indict the leaders in Judah for their lack of social justice and for the hypocrisy and emptiness of their religious practices. Micah warned of God's impending judgment against them but did not preclude the possibility of receiving mercy if the people would repent.

Structure and Content

1–3: A theophany depicting the coming of God as a judge. The prophet indicts the leaders of the people, who will be punished just as Samaria was punished. Jerusalem will not be spared, although Micah laments what will happen there. The evil that befalls the people will be punishment for their sin, especially sins of social injustice and indifference to the poor and the needy.

4–5: A remnant shall be spared and their opponents destroyed. The people will be restored after the exile. The oracles of these chapters express messianic hope. Here Micah seems to borrow from Isaiah's description of Immanuel (see Isaiah 7:14-16 and Micah 5:2-5).

6–7: The compelling case against Israel and a prayer for mercy. In Micah 6, God brings a suit against the people of Judah, calling on creation to witness against them. They have heard of and know what God asks of them, about doing justice and walking with God, but have refused to do these things. A later editor after the exile might have added the more positive conclusion of 7:8-20 with its promise of restoration if the people repent and show their trust in God.

Major Themes

- **God will punish Jerusalem** as Samaria was punished.

- **God is both just and merciful,** and these characteristics are not incompatible.

Authorship

Micah's style and language suggest a more rural life setting, as compared to Isaiah. All except for the last oracle of restoration (7:8-20) seem to come from Micah, who wrote near the end of the reign of Hezekiah.

Literary Form

Oracles: Messages from God spoken to the leaders and people in the Southern Kingdom. These were preserved even though they challenged the ways of the people. This implies that despite their unpopular and impolitic message, the people continued to respect the role and the message of the prophets.

Key Passages

4:3b: An oracle of peace and security, reversing the preceding oracle of doom. Images borrowed from agriculture are used in the promise that the people will no longer need instruments of war. These images also appear in Isaiah 2:4 and Joel 3:10.

5:2-5: Micah evokes the covenant between God and David, promising that one from Bethlehem, the city of David, will come to bring peace. A woman will give birth to this ruler who will feed his flock and whose majesty will extend to the ends of the earth.

6:8-12: Using vivid imagery to show the injustice of lies and deceit, such as using dishonest weights on scales to rob the poor, Micah insists that God's will remains unchangeable: God requires that we do justice and act with compassion and integrity toward one another.

Food for Thought

Micah mixes the message of sure judgment with hope in God's unending love. Justice and mercy are compatible in Israel's God. It is easy to see why Micah's insistence on social justice as a reflection of the covenant relationship with Yahweh finds echoes in the prophetic message of Jesus. Like Micah, Jesus deplored empty religion and demanded a sincere conversion of heart, requiring his disciples to "be perfect, therefore, as your heavenly Father is perfect" (Matthew 5:48). Like Micah, Jesus excoriated the leaders of his time for hypocrisy while they neglected the needy and the poor.

We could spend a lifetime reflecting and acting on the implications of living according to Micah 6:8. The rabbis taught that this verse is a summary of the Torah. How do our actions as individuals, as a church, and as a nation illustrate that we take to heart Micah's instruction on living according to God's will?

Nahum

Nahum is the only prophetic book that celebrates the imminent defeat of the enemy rather than focusing solely on the corruption and sin of Israel. At face value, Nahum seems to delight in the impending devastation about to befall the dreaded enemy, Assyria, and especially its capital city, Nineveh. This seems to be a prophecy of revenge and of pleasure felt at other people's misery. "Where's the revelation or inspiration in that?" we might legitimately ask. But the fact that this prophecy was preserved by believers and made part of the canon suggests that they actually took a much longer and deeper view of its contents.

There is a tension throughout the Old Testament between belief in the choice of Israel as God's people and the universality of the power and authority of the one true God. The election of Israel as God's people involves a responsibility to live according to the covenant. When the people sin, they are punished, just as Israel suffered at the hands of the Assyrians. Yet Israel's God will relent and restore the people; he will not endure the sins of Israel's enemies forever. And even while the people might have taken some satisfaction in the demise of Assyria, the fact that they kept this book, especially in light of subsequent events (when Babylon would prove to be an even more oppressive regime), implies that the people understood that their lives were always in God's hands. They were called to live the covenant. The prophets challenge people to examine their own conscience in good times and in bad, to look to themselves for improvement when things are tough, and to thank God and recognize God's goodness whatever the times are like.

At a Glance

Who: Little is known about the prophet, who identified himself as from Elkosh.

What: This is the only prophecy, called a "book of the vision of Nahum," about the downfall of Nineveh. Nahum's optimism surrounding the anticipated destruction of Israel's archenemy was short-lived. Soon Babylon would pose a much greater threat and wreck havoc on Jerusalem.

When: Sometime in the late seventh century, probably in the years immediately preceding 612 BC when Nineveh was destroyed.

Where: Jerusalem.

Why: To predict and even celebrate the impending destruction of Nineveh, capital of the hated Assyrian Empire.

Structure and Content

1:1–2:1, 3: The Lord, the avenger, is coming. This first part of Nahum falls easily into two subdivisions. The first part, 1:2-14, urges Judah to recognize that God has indeed avenged the atrocities against the people committed by Assyria. In a second part consisting of two short verses (2:1, 3), Nahum invites all of Judah to celebrate the impending disaster that will fall upon Nineveh. Nahum rejoices at the arrival of one bearing the good news of peace.

2:2–3:19: Nineveh will be punished and destroyed. Nahum is asserting two articles of faith. First, Yahweh will not endure forever the injustices practiced by the Assyrians. God has used Assyria as an instrument of punishment for the people, but Assyria's reign of terror will also be addressed and avenged. Second, Judah will celebrate the defeat of her enemy, but in the midst of their celebration, Judah should take the fate of Assyria as a warning and examine its own conscience according to the covenant.

Major Themes

- **God's just vengeance** will come upon Nineveh.
- **God still provides shelter and hope** for those who repent and turn back to God, despite the destruction of Israel's foe.

Authorship

This book is attributed to an otherwise unknown author sometime just before the destruction of Nineveh in 612 BC. The author declares that he is from Elkosh, whose much-debated location ranges from near modern-day Mosul in Iraq (which suggests Nahum was an expatriate living near Nineveh) to the outskirts of Jerusalem (a location that seems more probable).

Literary Form

Oracles: This is a classic example of prophecy, foretelling things to come, thus demonstrating the prophet's credibility.

Key Passages

1:15: A celebration of the arrival of the messenger of peace; Judah's woes are at an end.

3:1-5: Images of degradation and death are used in an oracle of woe depicting God's judgment against Nineveh for her epic cruelty to conquered nations.

Food for Thought

Nahum's prophecy makes clear that Israel's God is also the Lord of the universe. Israel has suffered because of Assyria's oppression, and God is not indifferent to injustice, whether it is practiced by other nations or by Israel. Assyria will be punished, and God's people will exult. Yet the prophet knows that Assyria is not the only evil regime. Another, Babylon, will cause even more suffering. The people of God see in every historical event the hand of God calling them to greater faithfulness to the covenant.

The historical context for Nahum and the preservation of this short prophecy in the canon of the Bible temper the prophet's satisfaction that the enemy is finally facing consequences. At a deeper level, there is always the lesson for honest believers to focus on the covenant and its responsibilities and areas for self-improvement. We have no time for smugness or complacency, no enthusiasm for judging others. The Book of Nahum reminds us of this saying attributed to St. Ignatius of Loyola: "Work as if everything depends upon you, and pray as if everything depends upon God."

Habakkuk

A small child was disciplined, unjustly he felt, by his father. The boy then complained to his grandmother that he had, in fact, behaved, whereas other children at the party did not. Then he asked, "Did God see that?" When his grandmother assented that God indeed sees everything, the little boy, still feeling wrongly accused, demanded, "Then what did God say?"

When faced with suffering or loss or the confusion that comes from witnessing evil triumph over good, we all have entertained questions such as "Why?" or "How can a good God allow this?" We have Habakkuk to thank for the precedent of challenging God when things don't seem to be going right. Among the prophets, Habakkuk seems to complain to God the loudest that there is no justice and that good people are suffering while evil is becoming more rampant and more ominous; the Book of Job, written after Habakkuk, later elaborated on these themes. The Babylonians (Habakkuk calls them "Chaldeans") are eating up nations and threatening the tiny nation of Judah. Habakkuk does not understand how God can see all this and not act in favor of Judah. Yet even though the issue he raises is not settled, Habakkuk concludes his reflection with a prayer, expressing trust and even joy. Although he remains in the midst of continued suffering and the threat of more to come, Habakkuk gives praise to God.

At a Glance

Who: We know only that Habakkuk was a prophet.

What: A lament and complaint of the prophet, who spoke with God about the alleged injustice of the times.

When: It dates from sometime in the late seventh or early sixth century, after the death of Josiah, king of Judah, in 609 BC, and just before the fall of Jerusalem to the Babylonians and the beginning of the exile in 587 BC.

Where: Judah.

Why: To lament the injustices he had observed the Babylonians committing and to seek justice. Habakkuk complained about the sins of his own people but pointed out that the Babylonians were even worse. He complained about God's silence and inertia.

Structure and Content

1–2: Dialogue between Habakkuk and God. Habakkuk begins by asking how long he must suffer without a response from God. Habakkuk vows to "stand at [his] watchpost" to await God's answer (2:1). Meanwhile, he complains that the wicked are getting meaner and the people are turning to idols. God's response to Habakkuk's complaint is that he is "rousing the Chaldeans" (1:6) to use as an instrument of punishment for Judah's sins.

3: Habakkuk's prayer. Despite not yet hearing from God a logical and adequate answer, Habakkuk nevertheless expresses his faith in a prayer of trust and joy. The state of the world is still dreadful, but Habakkuk knows that God is the answer and that he is in charge. Even though "the fig tree does not blossom . . . ; though the flock is cut off from the fold," Habakkuk's source of joy and hope is God (3:18).

Major Themes

- **God's apparent silence and inaction are cause for complaint** as the people face severe oppression from the Babylonians.
- **Faith is the only and greatest answer** to all of life's questions.

Authorship

Little is known about the prophet except that he witnessed the increasing threat of Babylon as it swallowed other nations and approached Judah. These events date this work sometime around 600 BC.

Literary Form

Dialogue: Habakkuk challenges God's justice in the face of oppression and then listens as God responds to his laments. The Book of Job will elaborate on this theme. Habakkuk's prayer of thanksgiving and hope echoes sentiments in many of the Psalms.

Key Passages

1:2: Habakkuk's complaint that his cries for help to God go unanswered.

2:1-4: Habakkuk testifies that he will continue to watch and wait for God's answer, insisting that "the righteous live by their faith" (2:4).

Food for Thought

Habakkuk echoes the complaints and the language of previous prophets such as Isaiah and Jeremiah. What Habakkuk adds to the prophetic tradition is to directly question God about justice and about God's treatment of those who are threatening Judah. Later writings, especially the wisdom literature such as the Book of Job, followed Habakkuk's lead and provided a biblical basis for the theological lament that questions divine retribution and attempts a theodicy that reconciles a caring, provident God with the apparent injustices that the faithful experience in the world. Habakkuk's questioning is abandoned because of his insistence that trust and celebration of God's providence are required.

The idea of balancing this challenge with an expression of faith even though things have not improved or the dilemma expressed has not been resolved is part of Israel's tradition. We can see the same balance in Psalm 22, for example, that opens, "My God, my God, why have you forsaken me?" The author goes on to complain that his enemies gloat while he suffers. He uses all kinds of imagery to illustrate the extent of his misery: animals encircle him, his energy is "poured out like water," and his heart melts "like wax" (22:14). But before the psalmist concludes or any change in his situation is made, he also says to God, "In you our ancestors trusted; / . . . and [they] were not put to shame" (22:4-5). The psalmist confesses that he stands on the shoulders of generations of believers before him, and like them, he knows his faith will be vindicated.

The best argument for faith is that we are spiritually linked to generations of saints before us for whom faith was the answer. While Jesus, on the cross, echoes the psalmist's cry, he also provides an example of persistent faith. We have the option of complaining that justice does not seem to prevail, but the Bible encourages us to never give up on faith: God, indeed, will neither abandon nor fail us.

Zephaniah

We have probably all seen cartoons that depict people carrying signs announcing the end of the world. They may seem foolish because the sun continues to rise and set and there really is no change and no end. The prophet Zephaniah preached at a time of religious degradation, when idols flourished. With Isaiah's help, King Hezekiah had actually attempted some religious reform, but it was too little, too late, and Hezekiah's reforms were later reversed by his son and grandson (2 Kings 21:1-24). Josiah, who would eventually try reform one more time, was only eight years old when he became king; this also marked the beginning of Zephaniah's preaching. Zephaniah's message of gloom and doom involved not only Judah but the pagan nations as well. His message of hope for the future also included Judah and all other people, who would all have access to the one true and living God. Zephaniah is no cartoon, speaking only of doom and destruction; he is a prophet of hope and restoration.

At a Glance

Who: A prophet during the reign of Josiah, king of Judah.
What: Oracles of imminent judgment and future salvation.
When: Sometime between 640 and 625 BC. Zephaniah immediately preceded Jeremiah, who seems to have been influenced by him in language and ideas.
Where: Jerusalem.
Why: To warn of the trials coming under the Babylonians, who would be used as God's instrument of punishment for Judah and Jerusalem.

Structure and Content

1–2: Oracles announcing the "day of the LORD" (1:7) as a day of judgment and doom for Jerusalem as well as for her pagan neighbors. Zephaniah protests against the false gods and the authorities who allow the old idolatry to reappear. God's power will be manifested in terrifying forms, as darkness and black clouds, as fearsome noises and alarms, and as a consuming fire that will threaten the whole world and all who live in it.

3: Accusations and the promise of redemption for Jerusalem and Judah. Jerusalem is described as "soiled, defiled, oppressing" (3:1). God has tried to teach her with the destruction of other nations, but she has not changed her evil ways. Ultimately, however, God will gather the people again and bring them home. Yet again, a prophet expresses faith and hope even before the promise of restoration is fulfilled.

Major Themes

- **The day of the Lord** is a day of judgment and suffering.
- **God is always faithful,** and after suffering for a time, Judah will be restored.

Authorship

The superscription provides the ancestry of Zephaniah four generations back and makes him a descendant of King Hezekiah (the king when Isaiah, Hosea, and Amos prophesied). It also explains that Zephaniah was a contemporary of King Josiah.

Literary Form

Oracles: God's messages to the people through the prophet speak of judgment as well as of hope.

Key Passages

1:14-18: The coming day of the Lord will be a day of wrath, a day of distress and anguish, a day of ruin and devastation, a day of darkness and gloom.

3:14-20: God promises to save the poor and the outcast, to turn their sorrow and pain into joy.

Food for Thought

Zephaniah prophesies about a time of universal judgment and suffering for Judah as well as other pagan nations. But after this time of suffering is over, there is restoration and salvation for all, for other pagan nations as well as for Judah. Zephaniah might be the first truly "universalist" prophet. He tells of salvation first being enjoyed by a faithful remnant, the few who make up the poor and the lowly who remain faithful to God. But after a time, salvation will be accessible to all. For Christians, these promises were fulfilled in Christ.

The Christian hymn known as *"Dies Irae"* (Latin for "day of wrath") is inspired by Zephaniah 1:15-18. But Zephaniah is most of all a prophet of hope, telling of a day when the people and all the nations of the earth will "call on the name of the LORD / and serve him with one accord" (3:9). It does not require faith to observe the evil in the world, but it does require faith to be an example of hope even amidst almost overwhelmingly negative circumstances. Hope is not naïve wishful thinking. It is rooted in our covenant with God.

HAGGAI

Living in a small rural town while I was growing up, my family belonged to a "mission" church that longed to become a full parish with its own priest and a "real" church building. To the original ten Catholic families of the area, the celebration of Sunday Mass by a visiting priest in the local grange hall just wasn't appropriate. Our parents and the other adult Catholics echoed the longing, even shame, that David expressed to Nathan the prophet: "See now, I am living in a house of cedar, but the ark of God stays in a tent" (2 Samuel 7:2). From David's time, the temple came to represent the importance of worshipping God worthily.

Haggai echoes David's sentiment when the people are reluctant to undertake the task of rebuilding the temple after their return from exile: "Is it a time for you yourselves to live in your paneled houses, while [the temple] lies in ruins?" (1:4). When David wanted to build a temple, God blessed him and promised him that his dynasty would last forever. Similarly, God promises the people that the rebuilt temple will surpass the previous one destroyed by the Babylonians (2:9). Haggai addresses the "people of the land" (2:4), the common people, and offers them hope and encouragement. Through Haggai, God says, "From this day on I will bless you" (2:19).

At a Glance

Who: Haggai, the postexilic prophet, spoke to king and priest alike and challenged them, as leaders of the people, to put their responsibilities to God above all else; then everything else would be added to them.

What: A combination of oracles of rebuke and promise, inspired to provoke shame, action, and hope.

When: Haggai began his career around 520 BC, in the second year of the reign of Darius I over the Persian Empire (521–486 BC); his prophecies seemed to have come within a few months of each other (2:2, 10, 20) and then ended abruptly.

Where: In and around Jerusalem.

Why: To remind the Judeans of the importance of rebuilding their religious identity and independence, as symbolized in the reconstruction of the temple, and to move them to action.

Structure and Content

1: The call to rebuild the temple in Jerusalem. The people are hesitant to begin this task, wary of the ways of the foreigners who still rule over them. They are at first full of enthusiasm, but then fear and doubt set in amidst threatening economic times.

2:1-9: The new temple will surpass the old in glory. The prophet reminds the people that none of them have seen the old temple of Solomon that was destroyed but that holds such a cherished place in their memory. The new one they will build will be filled with the glory of God and will far surpass the old one.

2:10-14: A priestly instruction on the unworthiness of some people to offer sacrifice in the new temple. Haggai might have been referring to the Samaritans here who, although related to the Judeans, were considered suspect ever since the division of the kingdoms into North and South.

2:15-19: A promise of agricultural prosperity. Haggai promises that better economic times will be one of the blessings of rebuilding the temple.

2:20-23: A promise to King Zerubbabel, a descendant and representative of David. God is faithful, and David's successor will enjoy the fulfillment of promises made to David. "I am about to shake the heavens and the earth," God says, for "I have chosen you" (2:21, 23). God's promises are reliable.

Major Theme

- **Making God and the temple their first priority** will enable the people to experience real prosperity and blessing.

Authorship

An otherwise unknown prophet encourages the people to undertake the rebuilding of the temple after their return from exile during the reign of Darius I of Persia.

Literary Form

Oracles: God's message to the people through Haggai is very concise.

Key Passages

1:4-5: Haggai asks rhetorically if it is fitting for the people to live in nice houses while the temple lies in ruins. Selfish pursuit of their own fulfillment leaves the people unsatisfied.

2:15-19: Before rebuilding the temple, the people can barely eke out a living from the land. But if they make the temple their priority, God will reward them with abundant blessings.

Food for Thought

In the Bible, sometimes it seems as if there is some ambivalence about the temple as an appropriate religious symbol. For example, David vowed to build a temple but through the prophet Nathan, God dissuaded him (see 2 Samuel 7). Solomon did build a temple in Jerusalem, but many of Solomon's achievements were considered too materialistic and ambitious. Many of the prophets excoriated the people for hypocritical practices connected with the temple while they neglected the poor and the needy among them. Later, Herod would try to ingratiate himself with the people by building a spectacular temple. But when Jesus' disciples admired its form and beauty, Jesus told them, "Not one stone will be left here upon another" (Mark 13:2). And so it happened that the temple was not even finished when it was destroyed, along with the rest of Jerusalem, by the Romans in AD 70.

Haggai advocated the temple's reconstruction, and so the story of the temple reminds us of the need for religious integrity. It is good to have a building appropriate for religious worship, as long as the people maintain the balance between dedication of the building and attention to all the other demands of true worship, especially care for the poor and the needy. Does the way we worship reinforce our dedication to the social requirements of the gospel? Our temples and our churches might be only brick and mortar, or they can be symbols of our religious dedication. How do we determine and measure their real value? The Book of Haggai can help us get perspective on such issues.

ZECHARIAH

A woman whose small house was leveled by a tornado returns home to find her husband and eight children safe. She blesses herself and them in gratitude. Her first words are full of comfort as she notes, "It's an ill wind that doesn't do any good." Now she sees an opportunity to build a house better suited to her family's growing needs. She could have taken a page out of the Book of Zechariah.

The prophet Zechariah was a contemporary of Haggai in the sixth century BC, soon after the people had returned from the exile. The Books of Haggai and Zechariah share common concerns about encouraging a weary and dejected people to rebuild the temple and reestablish their commitment to the covenant on a firm foundation of faith. Zechariah describes his hope in chapters 1–8, a section of the book sometimes called "First Zechariah." Chapters 9–14 were actually the work of an anonymous author some one hundred fifty to two hundred years later. These chapters do not mention Zechariah and emphasize different themes, although the two sections do share some themes in common, such as the promises of a new age and the central role of Jerusalem in the restoration of the people. The Gospels, especially Matthew, found inspiration in this so-called "Second Zechariah," especially his depiction of a messianic figure as a just savior who would come to lead the people in justice and peace.

At a Glance

Who: Actually two postexilic prophets; the first was preaching soon after the return of the people from exile, and the second was added about two hundred years later.

What: First Zechariah repeatedly called for the people to turn from their evil deeds and return to the Lord (1–8). The apocalyptic language and imagery of Second Zechariah envisioned God as the warrior leading the people to victory and peace (9–14).

When: The prophet in First Zechariah began preaching in the same year as Haggai, i.e., 520 BC, "in the second year of Darius" (1:1; cd. Haggai 1:1). Although Haggai's preaching career lasted only a few months, Zechariah's lasted almost two years, concluding in 518 BC. Second Zechariah was composed sometime in the fourth century BC.

Where: Judah.

Why: To encourage the people returning from exile to reestablish their religious identity and to stay committed to Yahweh.

Structure and Content

1–8: Three oracles of First Zechariah. The first oracle interprets the destruction of Jerusalem as punishment for sins of the people who now must return to God (1:1-6). The second oracle consists of eight dreams and visions, addressing the disappointment of the people and encouraging them with hope and promise (1:7–6:8). The third oracle shows the need to prepare for the coming Messiah with conversion and fasting (7:1–8:23).

9–14: Second Zechariah, presented in two parts, consists of God's judgments and the restoration of the people. The first part, 9:1–11:17, intersperses divine judgments with promises of future restoration. These oracles contrast good and bad shepherds and describe the promises of restoration in terms of the exodus relived. The second part, 12:1–14:21, is composed of a collection of oracles about future restoration "on that day." God's spirit will be poured out like water that cleanses.

Major Themes

- **A future hope that seems distant at times but sure** is foretold by the prophet.
- **Messianic promises** are communicated in symbolic terms and images.

Authorship

This book had two distinct authors who were separated by about two hundred years of Judah's history. One wrote just after the return of the exiles to Judah, and the other, a couple of centuries later.

Literary Form

Oracles: A collection of prophetic words and visions from the Lord, with many images familiar to Christians because of the Gospels' (especially Matthew's) use of the Book of Zechariah.

Key Passages

7:9-10: God's will is that the people render justice and mercy especially toward the widow, the orphan, the alien, and the poor.

9:9: "Daughter Zion," or Jerusalem, is called upon to rejoice greatly at seeing the king coming, riding on a donkey.

12:10–13:1: God promises to "pour out" like water "a spirit of compassion and supplication" on the people (12:10). They will be cleansed from all sin and impurity.

Food for Thought

Zechariah illustrates how some images, especially of a priestly and royal Messiah, were developing in the centuries approaching the messianic era of Jesus Christ. Through all of their trials, God's people held on to the belief that God would not abandon them. The imminent time of the Messiah would usher in a new age. Texts in Zechariah originally referring to historical events and people (e.g., the high priest, Joshua, and the governor of Jerusalem, Zerubbabel, whom they hoped would be made king) were interpreted to point to a messianic figure and a new age. At the same time, Zechariah shows the increasing popularity of apocalypticism in Judaism and lays the foundation for its influence on Christian writers.

Zechariah repeats the people's belief in the ultimate victory of God against evil. We must hold onto faith even when it does not seem to change anything. Our commitment to social justice in view of the new age of Jesus Christ must not waver despite its hardships. We live according to our values as Christian believers, not because they are solutions to problems in the world, but because we believe that we participate, through grace, in helping to bring nearer the kingdom of God.

MALACHI

Most people have heard of the oft-quoted slogan that there are three important things in real estate: "location, location, location." The location of the Book of Malachi, placed as it is at the end of the prophets and just before the Gospel of Matthew that opens the New Testament, seems, well, inspired. With his series of oracles questioning God and then listening to the Almighty's response, Malachi, whose name means "my messenger," sums up the history of the chosen people's remarkable and tumultuous relationship with God. The people challenge God, and God reminds them again and again of the ways in which they have experienced his love. Yet Malachi is quite appropriate as a bridge to the New Testament with the myriad ways it foreshadows Jesus, who fulfilled all the expectations of the Messiah. This short three-chapter work is thus given new depths of meaning because of its location in the Bible.

Malachi promises God's continuing help and guidance through the messenger that the New Testament authors, especially Matthew (see 11:10), linked to John the Baptist. The preceding Book of Zechariah described priestly and royal messianic figures; now Malachi speaks of the prophet Elijah who will return before the "great and terrible" day of God's judgment (4:5). In these two final books of the Old Testament, we see the roots of the Christian expectations of a messiah who will be priest, king, and prophet.

At a Glance

Who: The composer or editor appears to have wanted to remain anonymous and thus made a proper name out of the Hebrew word for "my messenger" (see 1:1; 3:1).

What: A series of six oracles in the form of questions from the people answered by God.

When: In the fifth century BC, after the return of the people from exile, when their religious enthusiasm was beginning to wane.

Where: In Judah.

Why: To stir up and rekindle the religious spirit of the people and encourage them to have faith and hope in God.

Structure and Content

1:1–4:3: Six oracles in question-and-answer form. The exiles have returned to Jerusalem, and their early fervor is beginning to waver. The people are disappointed and fatigued, and they begin to wonder if there is any use in trying. They pose a series of questions to God, who responds with firmness and compassion.

4:4-6: Short appendices. The author calls for a return to the Law of Moses, a fitting conclusion not only to Malachi but to all of the prophetic books. Verse 4:5 identifies the divine messenger as Elijah, who will return "before the great and terrible day of the LORD comes."

Major Themes

- **God is faithful** despite the people's sin.
- **God is consistently patient and compassionate,** even in the face of the people's accusations.
- **The prophet attempts to rouse a discouraged people** to return to God.

Authorship

This book is attributed to an anonymous author writing in the fifth century BC; it is included among the prophets with a name construed from the Hebrew word for "my messenger."

Literary Form

Oracles: Here God alternately listens and then speaks in a series of questions and answers.

Key Passages

2:10: We have but one father, one God who created us. We are "profaning the covenant of our ancestors" when we are faithless to one another.

3:6-7: God does not change, and we have not perished. Our salvation rests in God's faithfulness. We are asked only to return to the God who loves us.

Food for Thought

Malachi is an example of how prophetic oracles that originally addressed specific historical situations could be and were, in fact, used to apply to other circumstances just as appropriately. Although this book is out of place chronologically, it is appropriately placed as the last book of the Old Testament, just before the beginning of the New Testament. It makes a fine conclusion to the Old Testament and provides a bridge to the New Testament.

We are encouraged as Catholics to practice an examination of conscience as a way to better serve God in our lives. Malachi is one of the prophets who can guide us in this spiritual exercise. The people's series of questions leads readers into an examination of their own faith journey. When the people ask, "How have you loved us?" (1:2), we can remember all the ways in which God has graced our lives. When we ask, "How have we despised your name?" (1:6), we may find ways to improve our thoughts and actions. The people follow up the prophet's accusation of sin by asking why God does not regard their sacrifices as worthy of the covenant. Their question can make us ponder whether we worship with a sincere heart fixed on social justice. When they wonder, "Where is the God of justice?" (2:17), they are assured that God will soon be manifested. If we ponder their question "How shall we return?" (3:7), we will learn of ways to hear and obey. Our reward and our challenge is in the message of the "LORD of hosts," who promises, "They shall be mine" (3:17).

Introduction to the New Testament

There are twenty-seven books in the New Testament. Compared to the Old Testament, these books were written within a relatively short period of time. Paul was the first Christian writer, composing letters usually to Christian communities in major cities of the Greco-Roman world that he had already visited and that had already accepted the gospel. Paul wrote most of his letters in the fifties AD. He was executed sometime early in the sixties (AD 62–64) under Nero in Rome. Between AD 65 and 70, Mark wrote the first Gospel, a theological narrative recounting some of Jesus' words and deeds, his passion, death, and the empty tomb. Matthew and Luke used Mark and other sources to compose their accounts sometime in the eighth decade of the first century AD. Finally, the Gospel of John was written in the nineties. The Book of Revelation and possibly the Letters of John were also written around that time. The remaining letters of the New Testament were composed sometime between the mid-sixties and the early second century.

There are four basic types of literature in the New Testament: Gospels, history, letters, and apocalyptic literature. The Gospels offer four perspectives on the significance of the life, ministry, death, and resurrection of Jesus the Messiah. Acts of the Apostles provides a kind of history of the early church as it spread out from Jerusalem to all known parts of the world during the first century AD. The bulk of the New Testament is categorized as "epistles," or letters, written to guide the early Christian communities. The Pauline correspondence, consisting of thirteen letters either written by Paul or in his name, gave ongoing guidance for the fledgling, predominantly Gentile Christian communities Paul had founded that were concerned with living the gospel in the hostile environment of the Roman Empire. A subgroup of letters, 1 and 2 Timothy and Titus, are ascribed to Paul and are known as the "pastoral letters"; these works illustrate the special bond between the apostle and the next generation of his associates, who were charged with the leadership of early Christian communities.

Hebrews follows Philemon in the order of the canon and is unique in that its author is unknown and its form resembles more a sermon than a letter. Seven other epistles comprise a collection called the "catholic letters" because they were addressed to all believers, unlike the letters of Paul, which were addressed to communities in particular locations. The catholic letters are known by the names of their supposed authors—leaders of the early church such as Peter, James, John, and Jude. Finally, the Book of Revelation is particularly appropriate as the last book of the New Testament since it uses images from all the previous Scriptures to bolster hope in the final gathering of the faithful and promises the ultimate victory of God over evil.

The books of the New Testament are presented in the following order:

—Books of the New Testament—

THE GOSPELS:

Matthew
Mark
Luke
John

HISTORY:

Acts of the Apostles

THE LETTERS:

Romans
1 Corinthians
2 Corinthians
Galatians
Ephesians
Philippians
Colossians
1 Thessalonians
2 Thessalonians
1 Timothy
2 Timothy
Titus
Philemon
Hebrews
James
1 Peter
2 Peter
1 John
2 John
3 John
Jude

APOCALYPTIC:

Revelation

Introduction to the Gospels

The New Testament, beginning with the Gospels, is familiar reading to us. A Gospel, or "good news," is an interpretation of events that tells the story of Jesus of Nazareth, who held throngs of people spellbound with his teaching about the kingdom of God. His enemies conspired to put him to death and succeeded in doing so after Jesus' very short preaching career. This would not be "good" news except for the fact that believers linked Jesus' message to the fulfillment of God's promises made to the patriarchs, Moses, and the prophets, and for the fact that they believed that Jesus rose from the dead and continued to live in the church, that is, the community of believers. No human power was sufficient to silence them or stem the growth of the body of people who came to believe that Jesus was the Messiah that God had promised to send them.

Readers of the Gospels may immediately note that three are very similar, while the fourth is quite distinctive. Matthew, Mark, and Luke are known as the "synoptic" Gospels because they can be compared ("seen together" is the meaning of the term "synoptic"), and they have striking similarities. The framework of all three shows Jesus' journey from Galilee, where he performed a number of miracles and preached the arrival of God's kingdom, to Jerusalem, where he was put to death. The synoptics give very little indication of any time period for Jesus' ministry, although all three agree that Jesus arrived with his followers in Jerusalem just before the Passover celebration. Throughout these accounts, reference is made to Scripture passages fulfilled in Jesus' life, works, and death. Despite his opponents' attempts to put an end to the claim that Jesus was the Messiah, the synoptic writers agreed that no tomb could contain him, since he was raised from the dead.

The fourth Gospel, John, has a distinctive story line. In John, there are accounts of three Passover celebrations, and Jesus' most significant works and preaching are set in Jerusalem. John showed that from the beginning, Jesus confronted his enemies, who resolved to put him to death. John's Gospel uses symbols, irony, and misunderstanding in a special and unique way to separate believers who "knew the truth" from those who refused to believe and preferred lies, darkness, and death to the gospel of truth, light, and life that Jesus had brought.

Useful Terms to Know

Apocalypticism: The New Testament authors adapted Jewish apocalypticism, with its characteristics of dualism, imminence, universalism, and vindication. Christians understand that all the expectations related to God's promises as expressed in the Scriptures were fulfilled in Jesus Christ. In some sense, all the New Testament writers had an apocalyptic perspective.

Apostle: Luke described the role of the apostles when he recorded Peter's speech about the election of a successor to Judas, indicating that an apostle was one "who [has] accompanied us during all the time that the Lord Jesus went in and out among us, beginning from the Baptism of John until the day when he was taken up from us" (Acts 1:21-22). "Apostle" comes from the Greek word *apostolos,* meaning "sent out."

Christology: The understanding of Jesus as the Messiah and the ways in which he fulfilled and even surpassed Old Testament expectations.

Church: The word *ekklesia* (a term literally meaning "call out," that came to signify an assembly or gathering) appears many times in Paul, who used it in reference to the community of those who believed that Jesus is the Messiah. The only Gospel to use this term is Matthew where it appears three times (once in Matthew 16:18 and twice in 18:17). **Ecclesiology** is the understanding of the identity, mission and structure of the church as it developed from its roots in the New Testament.

Eschatology: From the Greek word *eschaton,* meaning "last things." Nineteenth-century Christian theologians developed the meaning of this term to refer to the various descriptions of the end time and afterlife in the Scriptures. Some New Testament authors seem to describe the end-time as having already begun in Christ; this is called "realized eschatology."

Gospel: A compound Greek term from two words, *eu,* meaning "good," and *angelion,* meaning "message" or "news." The compound appears first in Isaiah (i.e., 52:7; 61:1), but Mark gives it a new meaning in applying it to the story of the words and deeds of Jesus. For Paul, writing before Mark, the term "gospel" meant "the power of God for salvation" (Romans 1:16).

"I am" Discourses: A series of long speeches in John in which Jesus claimed divine identity and authority and also claimed to be greater than many Old Testament figures and symbols. For example, Jesus says, "Before Abraham was, I am" (8:58) and "I am the way, and the truth, and the life" (14:6).

Incarnation: A Latin word whose meaning, "in the flesh," was inspired by the prologue of John's Gospel (1:14).

"Mighty works": Like the prophets, Jesus performed miracles to show that he possessed the power of God. The Gospel accounts of these works follow a three-part pattern: first, there is an insurmountable problem of health or nature (e.g., a person born blind or a huge storm); Jesus then intervenes with a word or sometimes by touching the afflicted person or through some other gesture; finally, there is solid evidence that a positive change had taken place (e.g., the blind man can see, or the sea is calm).

Parable: According to a classic definition, a parable has four elements: first, it is a metaphor or simile, i.e., a comparison; second, it is familiar to the audience in that it is drawn from nature or common experience; third, it has a "twist," a strange, unexpected outcome aimed at causing the hearers to rethink presuppositions; and finally, it is meant to elicit a commitment from the hearers to a change of mind and behavior.

Parousia means "coming" or "arrival," but in Christian parlance, it refers to the return of Jesus at the end of time. Paul used this term in this new Christian sense. Matthew is the only Gospel to do so (see 24:3, 27, 37, 39).

The Pharisees were a Jewish sect at the time when Jesus lived. Their name meant "the pure ones" or "the separated ones," and they believed that the writings of the rabbis adequately interpreted the Law and that the traditions that the rabbis passed on had authority comparable to that of the Law itself. They taught strict adherence to the Law, the prophets, and the rabbinical teachings. The Pharisees were teachers, and their influence was especially great in synagogues. Together with the scribes, the Pharisees came under particular criticism from Jesus, who opposed their narrow interpretation of the Law as hypocritical and self-serving.

The Sadducees were another sect within Judaism during Jesus' time; they were a group of priests and their dependents and supporters who were mainly connected with the temple. They were also prominent in the Sanhedrin, the Jewish court involved in temple matters, at the time of Jesus' trial. The Sadducees were politically liberal, sensing that their power was dependent on their cooperation with Rome. The Sadducees tended to be more religiously conservative than the Pharisees; however, they did not believe in angels or in the resurrection from the dead, for example, as the Pharisees did, because the Sadducees did not find convincing evidence of these in the Scriptures. Although they did not agree with the Pharisees on many issues, the Sadducees did join forces with them to put Jesus to death.

Scribes were Jewish religious leaders who could read and write and were considered experts of the Law. Scribes were aligned with various groups of Jews, including the Pharisees and the Sadducees.

Synagogue: A Jewish place of worship and especially of teaching in various cities, towns, and villages, not only throughout Israel, but also in the diaspora, that is, locales throughout the world where the Jews had fled or had been taken in bondage after the time of the Babylonian Exile.

Temple: There is only one temple, in Jerusalem. The original temple was built by Solomon and was destroyed along with Jerusalem at the beginning of the Babylonian Captivity. When the people returned after fifty years of exile, they undertook the rebuilding of the temple, but they were unable to replicate the scale of Solomon's temple. Herod the Great hoped to win the approval of the Jewish people by restoring the grandeur of the temple, which he planned to be double the size of Solomon's. He began its reconstruction around 14 BC, and work continued after his death in 7–6 BC. Work on the temple was still incomplete when it was destroyed by the Romans in AD 70.

"Word": *Logos* in Greek; Jesus is described as the "Word" of God, a concept rich in meaning, including the wisdom, life, and breath of God. John says that Jesus was sent by the Father to dwell with us: "The Word became flesh and lived among us" (1:14).

Matthew

Years ago I was privileged to be part of an excavation team working on a site in Israel along the coast of the Sea of Galilee. Unfortunately for me, I had broken my wrist the day before leaving home for that memorable experience. With my wrist in a cast, I was assigned the relatively more sedentary task of washing the pottery my colleagues had discovered in their digging. Fortunately for me, my partner most of the time was a self-made, financially successful Texan in less than perfect health who really knew and loved the Bible. As we worked tranquilly side-by-side, taking in the same views of the lake that Jesus had, this humble man recited many biblical stories that stirred us both. He knew a lot about biblical history and could cite long passages, chapter and verse, from memory. Better still, he lived what he believed. He made me think of the scribe Jesus refers to in the Gospel of Matthew who "has been trained for the kingdom of heaven" and "brings out of his treasure what is new and what is old" (13:52).

Matthew reminds me of some classmates I have had—the really organized types who became great teachers because they could present things in a systematic, comprehensive way. Matthew had at least two sources, the Gospel of Mark and a source of Jesus' sayings called *Quelle* or simply "Q." According to Matthew, Jesus fulfilled the Scriptures and taught us the way of righteousness; he was and is the teacher, the true interpreter of the Law and the prophets. Matthew emphasized ethical behavior as well as faith in Jesus, who is the Messiah, the Son of David, the Son of Man. Matthew presented a kind of catechism, offering direction for the faith and behavior of believers who are members of one community, the church. Matthew was especially concerned that the leaders of the church give true guidance to people by exemplifying faith, forgiveness, and vigilance in expectation of the *parousia* as they do the will of God, our heavenly Father.

More than any of the other Gospels, Matthew emphasized leadership in the early church. For instance, Matthew's Gospel has three scenarios in which Peter's unique role among Jesus' apostles is highlighted: Peter's walking on water (14:28-31); the blessing of Peter after his confession of faith in Jesus as the Messiah (16:17-19); and Peter's paying the temple tax for himself and for Jesus from a coin found in the mouth of a fish (17:24-27). Matthew's special treatment of Peter as representative and spokesperson for the apostles and the "rock" upon which the church has been built has prompted many interpreters to connect Matthew with the church at Antioch, where Peter's authority and following were dominant. Others argue that his emphasis on Peter might be an indication that Matthew originated in Rome, where Peter met his death under Nero around AD 64 and where St. Peter has been especially revered ever since.

At a Glance

Who: Matthew the Evangelist composed his gospel in the eighth decade of the first century.

What: The Gospel is narrative theology; Matthew incorporated sources that were part of Christian tradition to recount some of the events of Jesus' life and the early church's belief that Jesus was the Messiah.

When: The events Matthew recorded took place in the first half of the first century AD.

Where: Various locations throughout Palestine, ending in Jerusalem. Possibly written in Antioch or Rome.

Why: To encourage a predominantly Jewish-Christian audience who needed reassurance in light of the increasing hostility between believers in Jesus and the Jews of the synagogues, who were making it difficult or impossible for Christians to stay connected to them.

Structure and Content

1–2: Infancy narrative. Matthew develops the story of Jesus' birth around the Scriptures, showing how Jesus' identity and mission are rooted in the Law and the prophets.

3–10: The beginning of Jesus' ministry in Galilee and the Sermon on the Mount. The gospel is preached through Jesus' deeds of healing and through the mission discourse addressed to Jesus' disciples, commissioning them to do and preach as Jesus has.

11–18: Jesus' teaching divides his listeners into believers and those who reject him. Jesus focuses more and more on teaching his disciples and delivers a discourse on the church, stressing the leadership role of the apostles.

19–25: Jesus makes his way to Jerusalem, warning of the judgment to come and finally delivering the apocalyptic discourse.

26–28: These last chapters recount the passion narrative, Jesus' resurrection appearances, and his commission to the disciples to preach the gospel to the ends of the earth.

Major Themes

- **Jesus the teacher offers the true interpretation of the Law and the prophets.** Jesus teaches that righteousness means doing the will of our heavenly Father. This is the basis of God's judgment.
- **Jesus is our model as God's Son;** he is the Messiah who fulfills the promises of the Scriptures.
- **The church is entrusted with the care of the community** of "little ones" who believe and follow Jesus' teachings on discipleship.

Authorship

Called the "Gospel of Matthew" by the early Fathers of the Church, this is not to be mistaken as the work of the apostle named Matthew who was a contemporary of Jesus. The connection with the apostle Matthew is probably the result of the appearance of the name "Matthew" as the tax collector whom Jesus calls according to Matthew 9:9, a person referred to as "Levi" in Mark and Luke (Mark 2:14; Luke 5:27). Matthew the Evangelist composed this Gospel in the mid-eighties of the first century AD.

Literary Form

Narrative Theology: Responding to the needs of the church, Matthew developed the concept of a "gospel" from Mark and adapted it for his particular audience of Jewish Christians. He conveyed his beliefs about Jesus as the Messiah through stories about Jesus' life, death, and resurrection.

Key Passages

5–7: On a mountaintop, with his disciples gathered around him, Jesus teaches the crowds. The Beatitudes and the Lord's Prayer are incorporated within Jesus' Sermon on the Mount.

10: Jesus sends out his disciples to preach the good news that the kingdom of God is near.

13:1-53: Jesus preaches a series of parables that attracts many but is met with rejection as well. From this point on, Jesus focuses more and more on his disciples, while the leaders of the people mount their effort to put him to death.

18: In response to a question by the disciples about who is the greatest in the kingdom of heaven, Jesus describes the role of the church in seeking the lost sheep and in extending forgiveness.

Food for Thought

The Gospel of Matthew stresses faith in action. Following Jesus imposes moral imperatives. We will be judged on whether we have fed the hungry, given clothes to the needy, cared for the sick, and visited the imprisoned (see 25:31-46). In our precarious world, we learn from Matthew the value of trust in our heavenly Father. Trust banishes fear and doubt. We can ask ourselves, "What more can I do in my own life to show that I have understood the message of Matthew's Gospel?"

Mark

We have all probably thought at one time or another that we live in a very challenging period of history. We might even have wondered if things could get any worse. But our troubles have nothing on the early church. Take the era when Mark was writing, for example. There was a crisis of leadership caused by the deaths of Peter and Paul, who were executed under Nero probably in the early sixties, a little before the time that Mark was writing. There was the threat of apostasy from believers who were disappointed that the promised return of Jesus was delayed and that the church was suffering persecution. There was also the very real possibility that the church would continue to endure persecution from Rome and would have difficulty surviving. Mark was writing for a church facing such challenges.

Mark was probably the first Gospel to be written. Relatively brief at 661 verses, Mark is the shortest of the four Gospels. Mark created a story line or narrative that presents Jesus' ministry as a series of miracles and sayings, set first in Galilee and then on a journey to Jerusalem, where he is put to death only a few days after his arrival. The name "Mark" attached to this Gospel comes from the same patristic tradition that gave us the sequence of the four Gospels. It seems that the anonymous writer himself actually meant the first verse, a mere six words in Greek, to be the title of the gospel: "The beginning of the good news of Jesus Christ, the Son of God." With his Gospel, Mark created a new literary genre, that is, Christology in narrative form. A Gospel is much more than a biography or history; it is a story that unpacks the belief that Jesus is the Messiah in word and deed, the one promised through the Law and the prophets.

At a Glance

Who: The Gospel itself suggests that Mark was not an eyewitness to the events he recorded but that he probably had oral sources among the early followers of Jesus. The author could be a second-generation disciple of Peter, perhaps the son of Mary of Jerusalem, herself known to us as a leader of the early church according to Acts 12:12-19.

What: An account of some of the deeds and words of Jesus, starting with his Baptism and ending with the empty tomb after his death, but without much indication of the time period when those events occurred.

When: The first half of the first century AD.
Where: The events took place at various locations throughout Palestine; many think that Mark was writing in Rome.
Why: To encourage believers of his time; the church was experiencing a number of challenges from within, like apostasy and doubt and fear about its future, and from outside, especially from Rome.

Structure and Content

1:1–8:21: Jesus' ministry in Galilee. Jesus is baptized in the Jordan River by John the Baptist and tempted in the desert before he even begins preaching. He announces the coming of the kingdom of God and calls his apostles. Jesus performs miracles and teaches in parables, which serve to separate those who believe from those who reject him. Many believe and are cured, although many leaders do not believe Jesus' teachings and conspire to have him put to death very early in his ministry (see 3:6).

8:22–10:52: Jesus proceeds to Jerusalem, teaching his disciples along the way. Many follow Jesus, although the leaders become increasingly hostile to him. Jesus predicts his passion and death when at last they arrive in Jerusalem. His disciples are confused and express their fears and reservations but continue to follow Jesus.

11–16: Jesus' ministry in Jerusalem. Jesus arrives in Jerusalem, where he teaches for three days in the temple before he is betrayed by one of his own apostles near the time of the Passover. He is confronted by the religious leaders who have been conspiring against him from the beginning, and is then delivered to the Romans and put to death. The women who go to anoint Jesus find the tomb empty and flee in fear. Additional endings to Mark tell of Jesus' appearances and the commissioning of the disciples to preach.

Major Themes

- **Jesus is the Messiah, the Son of God, the Son of Man.** He calls his disciples as witnesses to his deeds and words and then proceeds to take them on a journey to Jerusalem, where he will be put to death.

- **Jesus' true identity is hidden and mysterious,** not known or confessed by any human being until his death on the cross, when a centurion expresses faith in him (15:39).

- **Jesus' suffering on the cross** reveals the power of God.

Authorship

Tradition from the second century links this Gospel to a man called John Mark or simply Mark, a cousin of Barnabas who accompanied Paul and Barnabas on their first missionary journey but left them midway and returned to Jerusalem (Acts 12:12, 25; 13:5, 13). Paul's later letters seem to indicate that he and Mark had reconciled and that Mark became an important leader in the early church. Mark wrote his Gospel around AD 65, probably in Rome.

Literary Form

Gospel: Mark was the first to create this literary form, which is a faith account, based in history, of Jesus' ministry and of the early Christians' belief that Jesus was the Messiah.

Key Passages

1:1: The title of Mark's Gospel.

15:39: A Roman centurion, witnessing Jesus' death, becomes the first person in Mark's Gospel to recognize his identity as God's Son.

16:8: The women flee the tomb and say "nothing to anyone, for they were afraid." This is the original ending of Mark's Gospel, appropriate to a major theme for Mark that even Jesus' disciples did not truly know who he was without resurrection faith.

Food for Thought

Mark consistently referred to the Old Testament to show how Jesus is a fulfillment of the Scriptures. The Gospel of Mark, the first Gospel, emphasizes Jesus' humanity and relates Jesus' experiences to the church, which is suffering persecution, doubt, fear, and severe threats to its existence from Rome. Jesus is the Messiah who took on these same afflictions.

In the course of our lives, we all may face serious challenges to our faith and even wonder if God has abandoned us. Although Mark tells us in this title verse that Jesus is "the Son of God" (1:1), only when Jesus dies on the cross does a human being, the centurion, identify Jesus this way (15:39). Mark seems to be saying that we cannot truly recognize who Jesus is until we have followed him to the cross. Later, even the women who had followed him from Galilee, who had seen all the miracles and heard his teachings, were still mystified and ran from the tomb, afraid (16:8). When we are suffering, when we experience illness, loss, or death, our faith is shaken. We may not see or understand that God is still watching over us. We need to experience the resurrection before we can understand the full implications of our faith.

LUKE

Our contemporary novels often feature a hero with exceptional gifts who overcomes many obstacles and solves many troubling problems, often leaving us with the impression that everyone involved lives "happily ever after." In Luke's time, there was an emerging literary genre of a similar sort, a kind of biography featuring a certain hero who is blessed by fate and makes the world better through his contributions. But Luke devised a different model for the main character: he depicted Jesus as the one who brings universal peace and healing to a broken world through suffering and persecution, without cursing either God or human beings. He must suffer and so enter into glory, and witnesses are called to observe and follow him.

Luke's is the longest Gospel. In fact, this Gospel is part of a larger work, complemented by a second volume known as the Acts of the Apostles. Acts takes up where Luke's Gospel leaves off, that is, with the Ascension of Jesus. Luke is the only one of the Gospels with a prologue that tells what the author plans to do and acknowledges that he is writing an "orderly account" (1:3). Luke embellished Mark's story line of Jesus' journey to Jerusalem with sayings taken from Q and other sources to emphasize certain themes that Luke found essential for his audience. Among these are perseverance in faith, acceptance of suffering as part of following Jesus, and the importance of being a witness to what Jesus has done and said. Jesus is portrayed by Luke as the prophet, preaching to everyone and especially embracing the poor and the needy.

At a Glance

Who: A traditional view identifies Luke as a physician and a companion of Paul. From the Gospel itself, it is clear that the author was highly educated, knew Greek very well, and was a skilled writer and storyteller. He was not an eyewitness of Jesus' ministry and was probably a Gentile.

What: Luke addressed churches influenced by Pauline missions. Luke elongated Jesus' travel narrative from Mark and, like Matthew, drew also on Q, a collection of sayings attributed to Jesus, and on a variety of other sources, both oral and written.

When: The events recorded are during Jesus' lifetime, in the first half of the first century AD.

Where: The events depicted took place at various locations throughout Palestine. With its predominantly Gentile audience, Luke's Gospel seems to have been composed for church communities in Greece, probably ones familiar with Paul's preaching.

Why: To encourage perseverance in faith through long-term persecution. Luke appeared to have realized that the *parousia* of Christ would be delayed and that Christians would have to learn to live in the midst of a generally hostile world, represented by Rome.

Structure and Content

1:1-4: Prologue. Luke addresses "Theophilus," a name meaning "one who loves God," which could refer to a patron or could be a generalized greeting to believers in Christ. He expresses his desire to present an "orderly account" of Jesus' life.

1–2: Jesus' infancy and youth. Like Matthew, Luke attaches two chapters of introduction to Jesus' public ministry, including the Annunciation and the birth stories of both Jesus and John the Baptist. Luke highlights the roles of women such as Elizabeth, Mary, and Anna and also tells of Jesus' presentation in the temple in fulfillment of Jewish law.

3:1–4:13: As preparation for Jesus' public ministry, Luke tells of the preaching of John in the desert, Jesus' Baptism, his genealogy, and his temptations in the desert.

4:14–9:50: Jesus' ministry in Galilee. Jesus is rejected by his own townspeople and goes to Capernaum, where he is engaged in controversies with the Pharisees. He chooses the Twelve, works many miracles among the people, and teaches in parables, many of which are elaborate and dramatic, to show the priority that the poor and disadvantaged have in the kingdom of God.

9:51–19:27: Journey to Jerusalem. Here Luke elaborates on Jesus' teaching his disciples about the high cost of following him. The road to Jerusalem gets increasingly steeper and harder as the disciples learn that their own future is tied to that of their leader, who will soon be crucified.

19:28–21:38: Jesus' ministry in Jerusalem. Jesus enters Jerusalem and teaches in the temple there, provoking even greater hostility from the Pharisees, Sadducees, and scribes because of some of the parables he tells. Jesus also gives an eschatological discourse.

22–23: The Last Supper, passion, death, and burial of Jesus. Accounts are given here of the conspiracy against Jesus, the Last Supper, and Jesus and his disciples on the Mount of Olives. The Jewish and Roman trials, the crucifixion, and burial all follow.

24: Resurrection appearances in and around Jerusalem. Two men appear at the empty tomb to the women who were going to anoint Jesus' body; Jesus walks with two disciples on the road to Emmaus, only revealing himself to them when they break bread together; and finally, he appears to the disciples in Jerusalem.

Major Themes

- **Perseverance in faith** is required of all of Jesus' followers; he explains this through many parables on his journey to Jerusalem.
- **Witnessing to the gospel** is essential to being one of Jesus' disciples.
- **Jesus is the rejected and innocent prophet,** fulfilling what the psalmist wrote: "The stone that the builders rejected / has become the chief cornerstone" (118:22; cf. Luke 20:17).

Authorship

Traditionally, Luke is described as a well-educated Greek, perhaps a convert from one of the Pauline churches. Luke's Greek is among the best of the New Testament, and he was almost certainly a second-generation convert to Christianity who wrote not only this Gospel but also the Acts of the Apostles.

Literary Form

Narrative theology: Luke expands the gospel form originated by Mark, elongating the narrative of Jesus' journey from Galilee to Jerusalem, emphasizing Jesus' roles as teacher of the disciples and prophet to the people.

Key Passages

1–2: Luke's infancy narrative is composed as a comparison between John the Baptist and Jesus, showing how Jesus is the long-awaited Messiah.

9:51–19:28: The journey narrative depicts Jesus leading his disciples to Jerusalem, teaching them about the high cost of discipleship and the purpose of the journey, which would end in his death. Finally, he reaches Jerusalem and weeps over the city.

23:47: The centurion who witnesses Jesus' death proclaims his innocence.

Food for Thought

It might be said that the very idea of "salvation history" originated with Luke who, in his two-volume work, presents three distinct periods of the history of salvation. John the Baptist represents the end of the first period, that of the prophets who prophesied about a Messiah who was to bring salvation to all the world. Jesus and his ministry represent the second period, the time of fulfillment of the prophecies. Acts of the Apostles inaugurates the third and final period, the time of the Spirit at work in the church, preaching the gospel for all the world to hear.

Luke's Gospel often pictures Jesus eating with his disciples, feeding not only their bodies but their hearts, minds, and souls as well. The world is still hungry for the nourishment Jesus offers. With great compassion, Jesus invites us to come and share his bountiful table. When we eat with him, we integrate his teachings in our lives. Can others see in us how well fed we are by the gospel of Jesus?

John

It was that middle-of-the-night call that every parent dreads. Her teenage son was very seriously hurt in an automobile accident more than a hundred miles away. One friend in the car was killed and another was arrested for drunk driving. Six parents who had previously never met now found themselves united in their shared sorrow and concern. They remained together—physically for several days and nights and emotionally for much longer—sensing perhaps that they would all fall apart if they separated. My friend Mary said she kept remembering the words of Jesus from the cross to his mother and to his "beloved disciple": "Woman, here is your son. . . . Here is your mother" (John 19:26, 27). From then on, she added, "We knew we were *given* to one another."

That story seems to capture the spirit of John's Gospel, devoted as it is to addressing the needs, the problems, and the aspirations of the community the beloved disciple left behind. This mysterious figure, whom we can describe but not identify with certainty, is the source of the tradition and the founder of the community that is the basis of the fourth Gospel. In drawing on the legacy of the beloved disciple, John seems to be at once reconciling and supplementing traditions we find in the synoptic Gospels. At the same time, we find in John some unique characteristics.

We can trace in John a different chronological and geographic framework than in the synoptics. There were three Passovers in the course of Jesus' ministry, according to John, who depicted Jesus traveling back and forth to Jerusalem. Jesus performed some of his most dramatic "signs" (John's term for Jesus' extraordinary works) in Jerusalem. These signs were the occasions for Jesus' grand discourses. John emphasized Jesus' miracles but saw them as revelations of Jesus' identity as God's Son and as the Messiah.

John also includes events and people not found in the synoptics. For example, only John's Gospel tells of Jesus changing water into wine at Cana and curing a man born blind in Jerusalem. John alone introduces us to characters like Nicodemus, the Samaritan woman, and the woman accused of adultery. Only John hints at tensions between Peter and other leaders such as the beloved disciple. Only John tries to resolve these tensions with post-resurrection stories that include references to Peter's rehabilitation with his threefold confession of love for Jesus (21:15-17).

John uses extensive symbolism to show that Jesus is the Messiah, the Son of God. Jesus says that he is "the way, and the truth, and the life" (14:6), the "bread of life" (6:35), and "living water" (4:10). This Gospel also uses a number of literary techniques, such as irony and misunderstanding, to encourage readers to move deeper into the reality of the life of the Spirit given through faith in Jesus.

At a Glance

Who: Although traditionally linked to the apostle John, son of Zebedee and brother of James, the composition of this Gospel has a complicated history. The apparent source of this gospel is the "beloved disciple," someone possibly named John. This source may then have been developed by an editor and finally written down by the Evangelist we call John. Three New Testament letters are also ascribed to this same source.

What: An account of the miracles (called "signs" in John) and teachings of Jesus as the revealer or Word of God. John may have known the other Gospels; his Gospel developed a Christology well beyond the thinking of the synoptics.

When: The events recorded here took place in the first half of the first century AD. This Gospel may have been written between AD 90 and AD 110.

Where: The events recorded took place at various locations throughout Palestine. It was probably written in Ephesus, which is traditionally connected with the apostle John.

Why: To encourage members of the community to persevere in faith with one another and with the greater church.

Structure and Content

1:1-18: Prologue. An introduction to the terms and themes of the Gospel, which presents Jesus as the Word of God made flesh.

1:19–12:50: "Signs," or miracles, reveal God's glory and Jesus' identity as God's Son. Among these are turning water into wine at the wedding at Cana, healing a crippled man at the pool at Bethsaida, feeding the five thousand, and walking on water.

13–20: Jesus lays down his life for God's beloved. After long discourses about the meaning of his impending death, Jesus proceeds to freely offer himself, with his death described as glorifying his Father.

21: Epilogue. Jesus appears to his disciples in Galilee, and there is a second conclusion to the Gospel, in which Peter is reconciled with Jesus and Jesus foretells Peter's martyrdom. The editor indicates that the choice of events recorded in the Gospel is selective and that Jesus performed many other signs and said many other things that are not included.

Major Themes

- **Jesus came to bring light to the world** and life to the fullest.
- **Faith in Jesus** is the beginning of eternal life.

Authorship

The account of one known to us from the Gospel itself as the "beloved disciple" was edited and revised so that it would be accepted by the larger church late in the first century or early in the second century. The beloved disciple is only referenced towards the end of the Gospel, beginning with Jesus' discourses during the Last Supper. In most of the passages referring to him, this unnamed disciple appears with Peter and is contrasted with him.

Literary Form

Narrative Theology: John used symbolism, irony, and misunderstanding in his account of Jesus' ministry to convey his belief that Jesus is the Messiah, the only begotten Son of God.

Key Passages

1:1-18: John's prologue introduces themes that will be developed in the Gospel: Jesus is the incarnate Word of God who existed before the creation of the world, light and life for all who believe.

3:16: "God so loved the world" that he gave his only Son so that we may have eternal life.

19:25-27: Jesus' mother and some other women stand near the cross when Jesus entrusts his mother to the care of the beloved disciple.

Food for Thought

John's Gospel shows some development of Christology and ecclesiology in comparison with the synoptic Gospels. In John, Jesus' identity as God's Son and the long-awaited Messiah is well established. The Sacraments of Baptism (see Jesus' discussion with Nicodemus in chapter 3) and the Eucharist (see the "bread of life" discourse in chapter 6) are also included through John's use of symbolism.

John's emphasis that our first responsibility is to other members of the community shows the importance of his incarnational Christology. God takes on human form and life in Jesus. This implies, at the least, that our special allegiance is to those within our own homegrown communities—our families, neighborhoods, and worshipping communities. It is an awesome thought that we are entrusted to one another as part of our resurrection faith. 1 John says it best: "The commandment we have from him is this: those who love God must love their brothers and sisters also" (4:21). This is not exclusive of wider circles meant to encompass all people, but it does indicate that we learn love and manifest love with those closest to us. We are *given* to one another. From that realization, we can reach beyond our individual lives, empowered by God's Spirit, which is given to us through Jesus. How do I show that the Spirit lives in me?

Acts of the Apostles

With the Acts of the Apostles, Luke complemented his Gospel with "the rest of the story." We are fascinated with the unfinished business Jesus left behind: the project of the church, a worldwide mission, and the experiences that turned the timid and fearful disciples into courageous missionaries willing to take the gospel to the ends of the earth. Acts is their story.

Acts of the Apostles is essentially the acts of two apostles, Peter and Paul. Peter, the spokesman for the Twelve on many occasions, dominates the first part of Acts and represents the mission to predominantly Jewish Christian communities in and around Jerusalem and in Syrian Antioch. Paul and his mission are the focus of the second part of Acts; his mission extended to ever-widening circles of Gentile Christians and even "to the ends of the earth" (1:8), as represented by Rome. Both were flawed and reluctant disciples at first, Peter having denied Jesus and Paul having gone out of his way to persecute the church. But the power of the Spirit led both of them to greatness as apostles. Peter and Paul were both martyred under Nero in the early sixties, about twenty years before Luke and Acts were written. The death of these apostles left a crisis of leadership in the early church. Luke appealed to the inspiration of Peter and Paul to help encourage the church of his day to resolve their internal tensions and live courageously and faithfully amidst the dangers of the present world. It may also have encouraged the early Christians to resist the temptation to despair because of suffering and to avoid the pitfalls of worldly wealth and power.

At a Glance

Who: Written by Luke, the same author who composed the third Gospel.

What: An early history of the transformation of the disciples as they became leaders of the universal Christian mission. Acts recapitulates the Ascension and shows how the community of believers began to preach the gospel in Jerusalem and then expanded the mission to the ends of the earth in obedience to Jesus' mandate.

When: Recounts events from the middle of the first century AD; written around AD 85.

Where: The events described here began in Palestine and spread throughout the known world; Acts was probably written in Greece.

Why: To encourage believers to persevere despite the threat of renewed persecution, especially from Rome. Luke was beginning to understand that faith was required over the long haul and that Christians would have to learn to survive in a hostile environment; they would be required to show that they were responsible citizens in a pagan empire.

Structure and Content

1:1-5: The prologue continues the thought of the prologue of Luke's Gospel. Luke recalls that the "first book," the Gospel, tells what Jesus said and did during his ministry from his Baptism until the Ascension and then leads into the events surrounding Pentecost.

1:6–2:13: Preparation for the church's mission. Luke describes again Jesus' Ascension and his commission of the disciples and then tells of the death of Judas and the coming of the Holy Spirit. Jesus' mandate for the disciples to be his witnesses "in Jerusalem, in all Judea and Samaria, and to the ends of the earth" (1:8) becomes programmatic of the whole of the Book of Acts as the mission of the church expands.

2:14–8:40: The church grows, beginning with its mission in and around Jerusalem. The focus here is on Peter, sometimes accompanied by John, while he fearlessly preaches the gospel; although he encounters obstacles and opposition, the number of the faithful increases daily.

9:1–15:35: The church's mission expands to include Gentiles, as both Peter and Paul begin preaching to them. After we read an account of Paul's conversion experience in Acts 9, we learn that Peter has taken the gospel message to the Gentiles, represented by a centurion named Cornelius, whom Peter baptized along with his whole household. Peter's last words in Acts are spoken in defense of the Gentile mission, free of any restrictions regarding the Jewish Law (15:7-11). This section concludes with a delegation commissioned to return to Antioch with the authority to spread the gospel to Jews and Gentiles alike.

15:36–28:31: Paul extends the mission to the ends of the earth in fulfillment of Jesus' mandate and under the guidance of the Holy Spirit. Despite all kinds of persecution, opposition, and even several imprisonments, Paul preaches the gospel, and the number of converts grows. Even house arrest in Rome as he awaits trial cannot silence Paul or prevent the gospel from spreading.

Major Themes

- **The number of converts to Christ grew despite all kinds of obstacles,** including persecution and the daily threat of death.

- **The Holy Spirit and witnessing to faith in Christ** guided the early rapidly growing Christian community.

Authorship

Acts has the same author as the third Gospel, a Gentile convert who was very sympathetic to the perspective and mission of Paul. Known as "Luke," this author is identified by tradition as a companion of Paul (see 2 Timothy 4:11; Philemon 1:24), referred to in the Letter to the Colossians as "the beloved physician" (4:14).

Literary Form

Faith-history: Just as Luke adapted the literary genre of biography to shape his Gospel, he wrote Acts with the distinctive twist of emphasizing the opposition the fledgling church had met, showing how its power to thrive must come from God and not some human source.

Key Passages

1:8: Jesus commissions his disciples to be his witnesses, starting in Jerusalem and going out to the ends of the earth.

9:1-30 (cf. 22:1-21; 26:12-18): Accounts of Paul's conversion to faith in Jesus as the Messiah.

15:7-8: Peter's last words in Acts are addressed to his brothers and sisters at a meeting in Jerusalem; Peter confirms that the church's mission is extended to the Gentiles, to whom God gave the Holy Spirit "just as he did to us."

28:23-31: Under house arrest in Rome, Paul is pictured as fulfilling Jesus' command that the gospel be preached to all, even to the ends of the earth, despite all kinds of opposition.

Food for Thought

Acts describes the final age of salvation, the age of the church, a community of believers awaiting the return of Jesus and guided by the Holy Spirit. The church was spreading to the ends of the earth, represented by Rome, because of people preaching the gospel as Jesus had commanded the disciples to do. The story of the church depicted in Acts remains unfinished even today. No less than Peter and Paul, we are called and mandated to preach the gospel despite obstacles, hardships, and opposition. We are challenged to allow the Holy Spirit to transform us from timid, hesitant, and fearful followers to leaders who are driven by the Spirit of God, fearless, trusting, and generous in the service of God and the church. Do we honestly think of ourselves as successors of Peter and Paul? How do I hear the challenge of Acts and carry on its legacy? How do I demonstrate that I have taken on the mission to preach the gospel without reservation or boundary to restrict my efforts?

Introduction to the Pauline Letters

My mother's last letter to me arrived the day she died—suddenly and without warning. We had not known about her heart troubles when we had celebrated her birthday a few days previously. We found out that she had written to many people that final week of her life. And she told all of us in those letters that she felt peaceful and happy to have made it to seventy-two years of age and fifty years of marriage. Her cache of letters to various friends and family members in her beautiful handwriting forms a collage of a life of generous self-giving. These letters remain precious keepsakes in this world of instant messaging, quick tweets, and forgotten and deleted emails.

St. Paul is similarly memorialized in his letters, which are cherished by Christians because they reveal the man, his feelings, and his thinking in a way no other medium could have done. We know more about Paul than about any other New Testament person, including Jesus, because we have Paul's own words and reactions, not just what others say about him. In fact, he included many autobiographical notes and often appealed to his own experience in his writings, especially to the Corinthians, the Galatians, the Philippians, and Philemon. In his letter to the Galatians, for example, he referred to a time when he was very ill and suffering from some physical infirmity he described as a trial for them. Nevertheless, they did not "scorn or despise" him but welcomed him as "an angel of God" and took care of him (4:13-14). In turn, Paul said they were his "little children" and that he endured the "pain of childbirth" for them (4:19).

We may take this development for granted, but at the time it was novel as well as effective and extremely influential. Jesus preached only in Palestine, to relatively small groups of people who spoke and understood Aramaic, the dialect of Hebrew that Jesus spoke. Paul wrote in Greek, the language of the empire, and his letters were not only read and reflected upon by local communities but also collected, edited, and published far and wide. Even after he died, Paul was quoted and used as an authority by his wide and varied circle of associates who considered his letter-writing style—engaging, personal, instructional, and exhortative—as a model for carrying on the work of spreading the gospel.

There are thirteen letters attributed to Paul in the New Testament. Only seven of these are indisputably from the apostle himself, which are—in the order of their appearance in the New Testament—Romans, 1 Corinthians, 2 Corinthians, Galatians, Philippians, 1 Thessalonians, and Philemon. The other six letters (Ephesians, Colossians, 2 Thessalonians, 1 Timothy, 2 Timothy, and Titus) are said to be pseudonymous (written in Paul's name, but he was not the real author) or deutero-Pauline letters. Apparently, some disciples of Paul wrote in his name, with the implication that although their beloved leader had already died, he would have written these things if he were still alive.

Today it is a crime to plagiarize another writer; then, it was commonplace to "borrow" the authority of those who had died in order to invoke their memory and draw on their prestige to warn against errors and to encourage people in following the way of truth. After the deaths of Peter and Paul in the early sixties, many problems arose in the church, but there was no definitive authority to settle matters. Some examples are false teachings on such topics as the role of the Jewish Law or parts of it in Christian life, the time and circumstances of the return of Jesus and the end of history, the destruction of the temple (AD 70), the influence of Greek philosophical ideas and the development of Gnostic and Docetist tendencies, and theories about the relative authority or power of spirits, especially with regard to Jesus' humanity. Early Christians depended on the authority and leadership of Paul and the other apostles to help them evaluate the myriad teachings that were circulating in the light of the gospel Jesus preached.

Useful Terms to Know

Body of Christ: This image has four different meanings in 1 Corinthians: first, individual believers as members of the church (see 6:15-20); second, the Lord's Supper as a celebration of Jesus' actions the night before he died (see 11:24); third, the believing community (12:12-27); and finally, the risen Christ (see 15:35-49).

The Collection: The subject of 2 Corinthians 8–9, this was an offering taken up among the Gentiles for those suffering famine in Jerusalem. Paul says that this collection is a "debt" the Gentiles owe because they share in the spiritual blessings that have come to the Jews (Romans 15:26-27). This conception of debt derives from the Greek philosophical idea that spiritual gifts are more valuable than material ones; if one shares the spiritual blessings, one ought to share the less important material blessings as well. This is one example of how Paul meshed Greek and Jewish ideas to develop a theology that derived from Judaism but was made accessible and understandable to the Gentiles.

Freedom: Paul was the only New Testament writer that extolled freedom, which is not taken in the modern sense of "autonomy." Rather, freedom is opposed to slavery to the Law or to sin. Freedom means the power to live according to the Spirit.

Gospel: Paul described the gospel as "the power of God for salvation" (Romans 1:16). Before Mark created the literary form we are familiar with as a narrative about the life, words, works, death, and resurrection of Jesus, Paul used the term "gospel" to mean what Christians preached and believed about Jesus as the Christ.

"Jews as well as Gentiles": In Romans Paul tried to show that the effects of Jesus' death apply to all humankind by repeating the phrase "to the Jew first and also to the Greek" (1:16; cf. 2:9, 10) to show that the Old Testament Scriptures are fulfilled in Christ.

Judaizers: A term coined by commentators and significant for identifying Paul's opponents in Galatia. Paul was not advocating that Jews no longer follow the Law, but he adamantly opposed those who insisted that Gentiles ought to follow such requirements as circumcision, some dietary prescriptions, and perhaps the observance of some special feasts in order to be fully Christian. In his confrontation with Peter, Paul criticized him by saying, "If you, though a Jew, live like a Gentile and not like a Jew, how can you compel the Gentiles to live like Jews?" (Galatians 2:14). That description provided the basis for the new term "Judaizer."

Justification: Justice and its derivatives, such as "justification" and "justify," are attributes of God, out of reach of sinful human beings except through revelation, according to the Old Testament. Justification, or righteousness, is the goal of the Law of Moses, a gift of the covenant. Without the Law, we could not even strive to be just. Jewish commentary on the Law was intended to teach what it means to be justified and how to achieve justification. However, Paul teaches that justification is the gift of God in Jesus Christ that is accessible to all through faith and is one of the principal ways that Jesus' death on the cross affects us. In his efforts to convey its meaning, especially in Galatians and later in Romans, Paul contrasts this notion of justification by grace through faith with trying to attain justification through works of the Law.

The "Lawless One": Paul developed an apocalyptic view in 2 Thessalonians focused on the end-time toward which the church is progressing. Yet, he cautioned, many things, some of them evil and menacing, have to happen before Christ appears. The "mystery of lawlessness" (2:7) is at work, bringing with it increased persecution and suffering for the faithful. Apostasy is increasing along with faithfulness. The "lawless one" (2:3) is not an individual but all the forces that threaten faith and hope. Believers are urged to resist panic and alarm and not to be "shaken in mind" (2:2). Rather, they are exhorted to continue to pray for one another, to work in the world, and to persevere amidst the trials that come from any sources, both external and internal.

Letter versus Epistle: This is a distinction some interpreters make between the occasional "letter," following the Greco-Roman form, and the more formal "epistle," which is a treatise in letter form. The Book of Romans, for example, is categorized as an epistle because of its impersonal and formal tone, objectiveness, and structure.

The Lord's Supper: This is one of the principal ways that the early Christians commemorated the life, death, and resurrection of Jesus. They thought of the "meal" they celebrated together as a memorial of the meal Jesus had shared with his disciples "on the night when he was betrayed" (1 Corinthians 11:23). Paul directed the Corinthians to eat and drink in their own homes (11:22, 34) and to celebrate a commemorative sharing of a loaf of bread and a cup of wine, which probably would also have been a much more manageable and practical way for the whole community of women and men, rich and poor, slave and free, to celebrate in the limited space of the homes of individual Christians or Christian families.

Ministry of Reconciliation: In 2 Corinthians, in the context of his stormy relationships with the Corinthians, Paul described the actions of Christ, who effected reconciliation between humankind and God and now shares with believers the ministry of reconciliation (5:17-21). Paul also wrote in Colossians that all creation is unified and made at peace with God through Christ (1:13-23).

Mystery: The Greek term *mysterion* (meaning "secret" or "something previously unknown that has now been revealed") is used in Ephesians to refer to the inclusion of both Jews and Gentiles in one church (3:5-6), proclaiming one gospel, and thus participating in the saving work of Christ, which reconciles the world to God.

New Covenant: In Paul and Luke, this phrase is used in reference to the Lord's Supper (1 Corinthians 11:25; Luke 22:20). Paul described himself as a minister of the "new covenant" in 2 Corinthians 3:6, contrasting it with Moses' ministry to the "old covenant" (3:14).

New Creation: This phrase first appears in Galatians 6:15 to describe the community of believers in Jesus Christ. It also appears in the Corinthian correspondence (2 Corinthians 5:17), which seems to have been written after Galatians.

Parousia: A Greek word meaning "coming" in everyday speech, Paul may have originated the Christian use of this term in reference to the return or "coming" of Jesus to judge the world. The "time" of Jesus' return is compared to the prophets' description of the "day of the Lord," a moment of judgment and reckoning. According to 2 Thessalonians, the circumstances of Jesus' return were being falsely presented because of a letter purported to have come from Paul. 2 Thessalonians tried to redirect the attention of the early Christians to the fundamentals of the apostle's teaching, such as persevering despite suffering and imitation of Paul in working for a living.

Principalities / Powers: Some teachers of "philosophy and empty deceit" (Colossians 2:8) were disturbing the Colossians, preaching the superiority of some spiritual beings over Christ. The Letter to the Colossians asserted the primacy of Christ over any conceivable realities, physical, spatial, or spiritual. Christ is "the image of the invisible God, . . . for in him all things in heaven and on earth were created" (1:15-16).

Seven Unities: In the context of Paul's prayer for the church, in Ephesians 4:4-6, he wrote that unity is built on the basis of these seven commonly held realities: "One body and one Spirit, . . . one hope . . . , one Lord, one faith, one Baptism, one God and Father of all."

Tongues: One of the gifts of the Spirit that was experienced by many Corinthians. Paul acknowledged that the community had been given every gift, but he reminded them that there are many spiritual gifts that are more important than speaking in tongues (1 Corinthians 14:1-19).

Romans

Most of us have written or received (or both) a circular letter, a missive addressed to friends and family, meant to update us on all of the sender's news. Romans is something like that—a treatise expressed in the more personal tone of a letter. In Romans, sometimes called Paul's *chef-d'oeuvre,* or masterpiece, the apostle laid out the gospel as "the power of God for salvation to everyone who has faith, to the Jew first and also to the Greek" (1:16). Paul wrote this to the Christian community of Rome, saying he intended to go to Rome and there seek aid from them to further his plans to go to Spain as a missionary of the gospel.

As it turned out, Romans is probably one of the last letters Paul wrote, and it includes both his introduction to the Romans before his planned visit to them and also a sort of last will and testament, since he outlined the legacy of the theology he had developed over the course of his missionary career among the Gentiles. When he wrote Romans, Paul probably had no idea that this would be his last great letter. Some interpreters think that Romans was such a satisfactory summary of Paul's theological thought that it could have been used as a circular letter to other churches, appropriate not only for the Roman community but for all Christians. Romans has held a special place as Paul's crowning literary achievement ever since.

Toward the end of his letters, Paul sometimes mentions fellow Christians, at times offering tantalizing tidbits of information in the process of joining their greetings to his or making some request of his addressees. The missionary Phoebe, probably the bearer of this letter to the Romans, is one example. Paul describes her as "our sister Phoebe, a deacon of the church," who ought to be welcomed "as is fitting for the saints" and given all the help and support she needed because she had been "a benefactor of many," including Paul himself (Romans 16:1, 2). Similarly, Paul sends greetings to Priscilla and Aquila, a Christian couple he first met in Corinth, according to Acts 18. We can glean a lot from the mix of people that Paul mentions in his letters—about their diversity, their various roles, and their authority as examples for others as leaders and as participants in the task of building the early Christian communities of believers. These personal greetings help underscore the idea that Paul had collaborators in his mission, personal contacts that meant that he was not an unknown entity to the community in Rome, even though he had not yet visited them.

At a Glance

Who: Written by Paul near the end of his missionary career.
What: A treatise in letter form.
When: Around AD 58, only a few years before Paul was put to death.
Where: Written from Corinth and addressed to the community of believers in Rome.
Why: To set the record straight on what Paul taught as well as to elicit help from the Roman community for his intended trip, first to Jerusalem, where he faced great danger, and then for his projected journey to Spain via Rome.

Structure and Content

1:1-17: The address consists of a greeting and thanksgiving, setting the tone for the rest of the letter. The theme of the letter states that the gospel is God's power to save all who believe (1:16).

1:18–11:36: In summary, Paul's teaching, or the doctrinal section of the letter, insists that all people have access to salvation through Jesus Christ, and all people, as sinners, are in need of this salvation. All since Adam have been under sin and now have access to faith through Baptism into Jesus Christ. The example of Abraham, father of Judaism, shows that salvation is available to all through faith. Nevertheless, Paul struggles with Israel's disbelief. He initially claims that Israel is a spiritual and religious concept and finally affirms that "all Israel will be saved" as part of the "mystery" of God's plan of universal salvation (11:25, 26).

12–15: Paul's exhortations about moral behavior are presented as practical consequences of his teaching on salvation. Paul advocates that Christians living within the Roman Empire act as good citizens, avoiding crime and paying taxes, thereby attracting attention to their belief in Christ by the beauty of their lives and the power of their love. Paul also presents his travel plans, which include a journey to Rome. He asks for prayers for his mission and concludes with a doxology praising God.

16: Cover letter. The main part of Paul's arguments concludes in chapter 15, adding to the impression that chapter 16 was a separate cover letter including greetings to many Christians, including Prisca and Aquila (16:3), the believing couple Paul had met in Corinth who were influential in helping Paul there and also in Ephesus, where he continued his missionary work.

Major Themes

- **Universal sin** was brought into the world through one individual, Adam; likewise, **universal salvation** was brought into the world by one man, Jesus Christ.
- **Eventually, all of Israel will be saved,** after the Gentiles have been given access to salvation in Jesus.
- **Living out one's faith,** even in a hostile environment such as Rome, is possible by imitating Jesus' actions and living according to his teachings.

Authorship

Here at the height of his career, around AD 58, Paul was at his letter-writing best. Interestingly, Paul sent these thoughts to Christians struggling under the hostile Roman regime of Nero some five or six years before Peter and Paul himself would be put to death in Rome.

Literary Form

Epistle: Romans is a well-organized treatise in the form of a letter written to the very important community in the capital of the Roman Empire during Nero's reign.

Key Passages

1:16: Here we have the earliest description of the gospel as "the power of God for salvation to everyone who has faith, to the Jew first and also to the Greek."

5:1-2: Paul asserts that we are justified by faith, and "we have peace with God through our Lord Jesus Christ, through whom we have obtained access to this grace in which we stand."

8:31, 38-39: Paul challenges his believers through use of the rhetorical question "If God is for us, who is against us?" (8:31). Paul goes on to profess his conviction that nothing "will be able to separate us from the love of God in Christ Jesus our Lord" (8:39).

12:14-21: Using proverbs, Paul teaches believers how to live out their faith even in a hostile environment such as Rome. Paraphrasing Jesus' teaching in the Sermon on the Mount, Paul says, "Bless those who persecute you; bless and do not curse them. . . . Do not be overcome by evil, but overcome evil with good" (12:14, 21).

Food for Thought

As the first Christian writer, Paul is a model for us in his total commitment to preaching the gospel. Paul fashioned his theology in contemporary terms and adapted it to the needs of his mixed audience of Jews and Gentiles. Paul founded and formed communities of faith and then continued to minister to these communities through his letters. As one of the last letters he wrote, Romans articulates Paul's legacy to the believers he left behind. In view of his death soon after the letter's composition, Romans was especially cherished by the early church. Here we learn of the apostle's particular affection for this influential community, as Paul wrote in his introduction, "I am longing to see you so that I may share with you some spiritual gift to strengthen you—or rather so that we may be mutually encouraged by each other's faith, both yours and mine" (1:11-12). Here we are challenged to integrate morality with liturgy, as Paul invites us "to present [our] bodies as a living sacrifice, holy and acceptable to God, which is [our] spiritual worship" (12:1). In Romans we are reminded of the centrality of the Scriptures, as Paul tells us, "Whatever was written in former days was written for our instruction, so that by steadfastness and by the encouragement of the scriptures we might have hope" (15:4). Romans thus has much to teach us about our faith and about ourselves.

1 Corinthians

Some interpersonal relationships endure despite deep tensions and huge problems, and if the parties are willing to work things out, many benefits can result. An example is the relationship that Paul had with the Corinthians more than two thousand years ago, a relationship that is still bearing fruit for us as we reflect on Paul's letters to them. The Corinthians themselves seem to have experienced many divisions and conflicts, as they were a diverse group of Jews and non-Jews, men and women, free and slave, rich and poor. One such difficult relationship that Paul alluded to in 1 Corinthians was his own relationship with Apollos, who was a popular Christian preacher first described in Acts of the Apostles as "a native of Alexandria, . . . an eloquent man, well-versed in the scriptures" (18:24). Paul reminded the Corinthians that neither he nor Apollos died for them as Christ did (1 Corinthians 1:11-14).

Paul spent over a year and a half in Corinth living among converts to Christ, and he wrote this series of letters to them after he had gone on to other missions. His letters to the Corinthians adopt different tones—sometimes he acted as friend and adviser, sometimes as a stern teacher and lecturer. But he was always a pastor and fellow believer, conveying the truth that Baptism involves deep commitment and results in unassailable moral standards.

In this letter, Paul also cited the contributions of other leaders who had been influential in the formation of the Corinthian communities of faith. Sosthenes, for example, is identified as the co-author of 1 Corinthians. Finally, 1 Corinthians contains the earliest allusion to the gathering of believers "on the first day of every week" (16:2), as if to suggest that such gatherings were already customary. As early as the fifth decade, when Paul wrote 1 Corinthians, Christians were designating Sunday, the day after the Jewish Sabbath and the day commemorating the resurrection of Jesus, for worship services as part of their regular way of life.

At a Glance

Who: Written by Paul at the height of his missionary career, with a few verses some interpret as additions by other writers.

What: A letter that includes many indications of ongoing communication with and about this fledgling group of small communities of believers who lived in Corinth, a town that was renowned for its competitiveness and significant because of its strategic location on an isthmus.

When: Sometime between AD 52 and 57, probably around 54.

Where: Paul wrote "on the road," perhaps from Ephesus, where he went upon leaving Corinth; he had resided with the community at Corinth longer than any other to this point, for a total of eighteen months (Acts 18:11).

Why: To address issues among the Corinthians, including divisions among them about who had baptized them, about a member in their midst who was practicing incest and going uncensored, about taking one another to court, about divisions among them apparent at liturgy, and about their views of the Eucharist and of the resurrection of Christ.

Structure and Content

1:1-9: The introduction reveals Paul's great love for the church of Corinth, believed to be composed of many smaller communities rather than a single large one.

1:10–6:20: Initially, Paul responds to situations within the community he is concerned about, such as divisions within the community, moral disorders, including a case of incest, lawsuits among members, and sexual immorality.

7:1–11:1: Paul responds to some questions from the Corinthians, first concerning virginity and marriage and then regarding offerings to idols, relationships between the "weak" and the "strong," and forming a Christian conscience.

11:2–15:58: Paul addresses matters of appearance and behavior at liturgical assemblies and then turns to divisions apparent at the Lord's Supper that must be corrected. Paul refers to divisions based on spiritual gifts and insists these can be healed by love. Finally, we read Paul's teaching on the resurrection. Jesus is the "first fruits" and guarantee of our resurrection (15:20-24).

16: The letter concludes with instructions about the collection, Paul's travel plans, an exhortation, and greetings to church members.

Major Themes

- **The cross** is the wisdom and power of God.
- **The community of believers** is described as the "body of Christ" (12:27).
- **Jesus' resurrection** is the foundation of our faith.

Authorship

Paul is the indisputable author of this letter, addressed to a community very well-known to him.

Literary Form

Letter: 1 Corinthians follows the typical form of the ancient Greco-Roman style: it begins with an address, identifying the sender and recipients. This is followed by the longest part, the body of the letter, and finally, there is a fairly elaborate closing that includes Paul's more personal information, such as greetings from mutual acquaintances.

Key Passages

1:11: Paul is advised about problems in the community by people traveling on business; implicit is the idea that Paul wishes to and in fact does keep up with the progress of the community by means of a network of communications.

11:23-26: In this, the oldest account of the institution of the Lord's Supper on "the night when [Jesus] was betrayed" (11:23), Paul presents the blessing of the bread and wine after supper as a memorial in remembrance of Jesus.

12–14: The hymn of charity in chapter 13 is inserted within the context of Paul's discussion about the diverse spiritual gifts of members of the one community of faith, hope, and love.

Food for Thought

As one of Paul's most significant letters, 1 Corinthians portrays a community of believers composed of diverse groups struggling to become the body of Christ. In fact, the Corinthians represented a predominantly Gentile community of an important city in the Roman Empire that tested Paul's gifts as missionary, preacher, and unifier. The existence of the Corinthian correspondence attests to the community's ultimate cooperation with Paul and his authority as their apostle and spiritual leader.

It is in 1 Corinthians that Paul gives his earliest description of the church as the body of Christ and shows how the community of faith differs from any other group of Paul's time. The community of Corinth was made up of Jew and Gentile, slave and free, rich and poor, man and woman, made equal and saved by the death and resurrection of Jesus. This is a unity celebrated in the Sacraments of Baptism and the Eucharist, called in 1 Corinthians the "Lord's Supper" (11:20). How do the sacraments help strengthen our unity as a family, as a parish, as a diocese, and as Catholics living out our faith in a divided world?

2 Corinthians

I have a friend, a monk, who has a letter-writing ministry. He is a teacher, so his letters are full of motivation and encouragement, consolation and challenges. Often he will reveal something about himself and his own experience. He is much more apt to share stories in which other people shine than to brag about himself, despite his impressive education and his considerable gifts. He often shares his own limitations and failings with surprising and inspiring openness, a good example of how such disclosures can result in deeper trust and more open communication. My friend takes a page from Paul's writings to the Corinthians, realizing that we are all companions trudging the road of happy destiny and that we are wounded healers, holding the treasure of God's immeasurable grace in the earthen vessels of our often ordinary but oh-so-precious lives.

One of the fruits of the unusually nettlesome relationship between Paul and the Corinthians is this priceless letter or, rather, collection of letters in the form of a single letter in which Paul portrays himself as vulnerable, eager to be reconciled with the Corinthians, concerned about their welfare, completely dependent on his faith in God, and committed to his mission as apostle to the Gentiles, including the Corinthians. Paul also refers to the extent of his suffering for the sake of the gospel, from torments of self-doubt and anxiety to persecution from outsiders. All told, this is one of the most personal and also one of the most eloquent of Paul's letters.

Timothy, whom Paul called "our brother," is named co-author of 2 Corinthians (1:1). In this letter, we also learn a little about Titus, a companion of Paul on his missionary journeys in Greece and one of his most trusted emissaries. Concerned about the Corinthians, Paul sends Titus to Corinth to help settle some dispute there and restore the Corinthians' confidence in Paul; the longer that Titus is away, the more Paul worries that Titus has not been successful (2:12-13). Finally, Paul meets Titus in Macedonia and receives reassuring news about the Corinthians (7:5-8). Eventually, Titus would be the head of a church in Crete. A pastoral letter in Paul's name is addressed to Titus there.

At a Glance

Who: Paul, the apostle to the Gentiles, is the author.
What: A composite letter, originally at least two letters, with references to yet other correspondence between Paul and the Corinthians.
When: Between AD 54 and 57.
Where: Written in Macedonia and sent to the Christians at Corinth in Achaia.
Why: To address a series of events and negative reports about Corinth and about the accusations some Corinthians were making against Paul.

Structure and Content

1–9: Crisis and reconciliation. After the address, Paul reviews the history of his relationship and communications with the Corinthians. He gives a defense of his ministry and cites his conciliatory actions. Chapters 8 and 9 deal with the collection for Jerusalem.

10–13: In an angry, exasperated defense of his ministry, Paul passionately urges the Corinthians to recognize his apostolic authority. Paul includes biographical material, listing the forms of persecution and suffering he has endured, referring to his visions and revelations, and including a reference to a "thorn . . . in the flesh" given to him to prevent him from becoming too proud (12:7-9).

Major Themes

- **Paul defends his apostleship** to the Corinthians, especially since he has founded and formed and stayed in contact with this community.

- **Paul speaks personally about his own sufferings,** suggesting that they are his "credentials," evidence of his love for and devotion to the Corinthians.

Authorship

The letter was written by Paul at the height of his missionary career.

Literary Form

Letter: 2 Corinthians follows the form of a letter, with a single introduction and conclusion; however, it is probably a composite of several letters written to this community. Chapters 8 and 9 may originally have been separate letters encouraging the Corinthians to give generously to support the church in Jerusalem, while chapters 10–13 may represent another distinct letter, perhaps the letter referred to in 2:4 as written "out of much distress and anguish of heart and with many tears."

Key Passages

4:7: Speaking of his own vocation to minister to the Gentiles, Paul says that we hold a "treasure in clay jars, so that it may be made clear that this extraordinary power belongs to God and does not come from us."

5:18-20: Paul's ministry of reconciliation comes from God who, in Christ, "was reconciling the world to himself." He continues, "We are ambassadors for Christ, since God is making his appeal through us" (5:19, 20). Paul entreats the Corinthians, "On behalf of Christ, be reconciled to God" (5:20).

12:7-9: Paul says that in order for him to be prevented from becoming too proud, he was given "a thorn in the flesh," a messenger of Satan. Three times he appealed to the Lord to take it away from him. But God answered, saying, "My grace is sufficient for you, for power is made perfect in weakness." Paul therefore "boast[s] all the more gladly of [his] weaknesses, so that the power of Christ may dwell in [him]" (12:9).

Food for Thought

In 2 Corinthians, Paul defended his authority as an apostle by reviewing his limitations. In the culture of his time, when honor was the highest commodity, this is an astonishing reversal of values. Our own experience may resonate with Paul's wisdom. We may learn as much from difficulties as from advantages, from sorrow as from joy, from handicaps as from talents—perhaps more. We may learn to trust God and to let the light of God's grace shine through our example. Paul's self-revelations are extraordinary, as much for what they say about his shortcomings as about his strengths and successes. Paul believed that "we have this treasure in clay jars" (4:7). What meaning does this image have in my life?

Galatians

We have probably all heard the advice that if we are angry, we may get some benefit from writing down all our thoughts in a letter. But then we ought to rip it up so as not to damage our relationships by actually sending it! Paul did not heed this advice but instead sent this passionate and angry letter to the Galatians, challenging their willingness to heed the missionaries from Jewish communities that urged them to supplement their Baptism with some aspects of the Jewish Law.

The Galatians must have seen the wisdom of Paul's words, since this letter is preserved among the most important of Paul's letters. Here we encounter the first time that Paul describes what he means by "justification." Here Paul records his prior heated confrontation with Peter at Antioch. Here Paul articulates his teaching that we are justified "by faith in Christ, and not by doing the works of the law" (2:16), insisting that this is the gospel he has been authorized by God to preach, the same one that the Jewish leaders in Jerusalem and Antioch have confirmed.

Some interpreters suggest that Galatians could serve as a "rough draft" of Romans. In Galatians, Paul's writing is adamant and passionate. Romans deals with many of the same ideas, but represents a much more reasoned, objective approach to the meaning and implications of justification in Christ.

At a Glance

Who: Written by the apostle Paul.

What: A letter, a written dialogue with a community that seems to be straying from Paul's teaching, considered one of Paul's four main letters, along with Romans and 1 and 2 Corinthians.

When: Around AD 54–55.

Where: To communities in the large province of Galatia in Asia Minor (modern-day Turkey), either churches in the rural North (a rarity, since Paul usually wrote to Christian communities in large and important urban areas) or in the more urbanized South.

Why: To address issues in the church of Galatia. Some Galatians believed the charges of some Jewish-Christian missionaries, who accused Paul of shortchanging his converts by not telling them that they must complement faith by performing at least some of the requirements of the Law—for example, circumcision and some of the dietary restrictions.

Structure and Content

1–2: Paul defends his authority and the gospel he has preached to the Galatians. His address lacks the customary thanksgiving normally found there. Some autobiographical material is found in this section that helps us fix a timetable for Paul's missionary career.

3–4: Paul states the fundamental effects of the gospel for the community, notably faith and freedom. Faith is understood as belief that Jesus is the Christ. Paul excoriates his enemies in Galatia who preach that the Gentiles should go backwards and return to slavery under the Law; this will not bring them justification.

5:1–6:10: Based on these fundamentals, Paul gives his ethical instruction, exhorting the Galatians to live according to the freedom of the gospel that they have received.

6:11-18: Paul concludes with a few more admonitions and a final benediction.

Major Themes

- **"Doing the works of the Law" is contrasted with "justification through faith in Jesus Christ."** This is Paul's first articulation of this dichotomy.

- **The fruits of the Spirit are enumerated;** they are "love, joy, peace, patience, kindness, generosity, faithfulness, gentleness, and self-control" (5:22-23).

Authorship

This letter was written by Paul and is considered one of his major letters. Paul usually named a co-sender of his letters, but this is not the case for Galatians and Romans, both written to assert Paul's apostolic authority.

Literary Form

Letter: Paul passionately defended the gospel he had preached to the Galatians in this letter he sent to them.

Key Passages

1:11-12: Paul asserts that the gospel he preaches is of divine origin: "I did not receive it from a human source," but "through a revelation of Jesus Christ" (1:12). He passes on through his preaching what he has received to the Galatians and to all the churches.

2:11-14: Paul reviews his confrontation with Peter in Antioch when he accused Peter of hypocrisy for eating with Gentiles but then backed down from the freedom of the gospel when some Jewish-Christians protested that the Gentiles were not following the Law of Moses.

3:28: Paul states that in Christ "there is no longer Jew or Greek, there is no longer slave or free, there is no longer male and female; for all of you are one in Christ Jesus."

6:15: Paul closes the letter by saying, "Neither circumcision nor uncircumcision is anything; but a new creation is everything!"

Food for Thought

Were it not for the writing of Galatians, we might not understand the pain of the transformation of the church from a predominantly Jewish community into a "new creation." Perhaps the early church leaders, James and Peter, for example, had not realized the implications of Baptism as the sign of faith and entrance into the church. In Galatians 3:28, Paul states that all the former divisions that humankind has recognized have lost all significance because of faith—there is neither Jew nor Gentile, slave nor free, male nor female. Paul rejects the existence of two ways or two gospels. There is only the salvation made accessible to all through Jesus.

Christ came for all and showed us that we are no longer under the law but under faith. Gentiles as well as Jews are the children of Abraham and "heirs according to the promise" (3:29). Especially since the Reformation,

Christians have wrestled with the meaning of "justification," particularly as Paul articulated it in Galatians and Romans. Protestants and Catholics alike believe that justification is a result of God's action in Christ bringing salvation to humankind. Catholics tend to emphasize the ethical, communal, and enduring dimensions of faith; that is, Catholics say that while we have been justified, salvation may only be achieved through a life well lived. Catholics stress that the church is a sure guide in helping individuals accept salvation in faith.

Divisions separate and polarize people today in much the same way as when Galatians was written. Perhaps we can find a new identity and mission in Paul's insistence that all that matters is that we are created anew. Paul promises that if we live by that conviction, we will experience peace and mercy. What does it mean to you that you have been made a "new creation" through Baptism?

EPHESIANS

In John Steinbeck's classic story *Of Mice and Men,* Lennie continually asks George to "tell me how it's gonna be." Complying, George describes a time and place that makes Lennie feel secure and happy. Ephesians is like that—a constant reminder of how life in the Lord promises new vistas of hope for all manner of human aspirations: unity overcoming our divisions, the transformation of our relationships, and victory over sin and all the demons that afflict us. We already live this reality because "Christ . . . dwell[s] in [our] hearts through faith" (Ephesians 3:17).

Paul's name is affixed to Ephesians, but there are several significant reasons for wondering whether a later writer claimed Paul's authority in order to give his message more weight. It is remarkable that there is little personal exchange and that this letter seems more like a treatise, especially in view of the fact that according to Acts, Paul spent even more time at Ephesus (two years) than he did at Corinth (eighteen months). The author of Ephesians envisioned a universal rather than a local church, as Paul did in his letters, and the ecclesiology and Christology seem to go beyond what Paul could have articulated by the early sixties.

Consequently, many scholars believe that Ephesians was composed sometime in the nineties as a further development of the ideas contained in Colossians. Both Colossians and Ephesians differ from the undisputed Pauline letters in style and vocabulary. Further, Ephesians' original salutation, addressing the letter to "the saints," lacks the phrase "in Ephesus" (see 1:1), which suggests that the message was intended for a wider audience than that single community. The image and example of Paul as a "prisoner for Christ Jesus for the sake of you Gentiles" (3:1) seems designed to encourage obedience. Nevertheless, for practical reasons, the author of Ephesians is referred to as "Paul."

At a Glance

Who: The author was probably a disciple or disciples of Paul with access to the Letter to the Colossians.

What: An epistle, or more formal letter. The absence of the phrase "in Ephesus" in 1:1 of some manuscripts and the impersonal tone towards this community where Paul had lived for two years prompt some to claim that this was intended as a circular letter sent to more than one community.

When: Sometime in the later part of the first century, between AD 80 and 100.

Where: Apparently sent to Ephesus, a significant Christian community in Greece. It is unclear where the letter was written.

Why: To encourage unity of thought and practice in the church, which is conceived of as a cosmic reality participating in the saving work of Christ.

Structure and Content

1:1-14: The address includes an identification of Paul as author, the customary greeting "grace and peace," and an extended doxology praising God for the many blessings we have received in Christ.

1:15–3:21: The teaching section stresses the unity of all things in Christ and the universal mission of the church. God's plan began in Christ and has continued through the church.

4:1–6:20: The author draws out practical applications from his teachings, showing how they lead to moral imperatives. He then exhorts believers to conduct themselves in ways worthy of the gospel. He draws a contrast between former ways of acting and life in the church. The members of the church, as belonging to the "household of God" (2:19), take on new relationships with one another.

6:21-24: The conclusion includes personal news, greetings, and a final blessing.

Major Themes

- **The church is not only a local but also a universal reality** that participates in the work of Christ.

- **Peace is a characteristic of Christian life,** proceeding from the unity of all things in Christ (1:2; 2:14, 15, 17; 4:3; 6:15, 23). The relationship between Jews and Gentiles is depicted symbolically as the "peace" won by the cross of Christ.

- **Eschatology focuses on the participation of the present church in the ongoing work of Christ** to bring about the reconciliation of the whole world with God. This is the work of members of the church, who exemplify in their relationships with one another a new creation, a new society.
- **The intimate relationship between Christ and the church** is symbolically depicted through marriage imagery (5:21-33).

Authorship

This letter was probably written by a disciple or disciples of Paul toward the end of the first century AD. The letter's Christology, ecclesiology, and eschatology built on Paul's ideas but were developed far beyond what we can expect from the first Christian author whose writing career was confined to a ten-year span; this suggests that these disciples used decades of Christian catechetical and liturgical tradition as the basis of their ideas.

Literary Form

Treatise: Ephesians is a theological discourse with only the basics of the letter form.

Key Passages

2:19-20: The author refers to believers as "citizens with the saints" and "members of the household of God." The church is "built upon the foundation of the apostles and prophets, with Christ Jesus himself as the cornerstone."

3:14-21: Known as "Paul's prayer," this section uses Trinitarian language referring to the Father, Son, and Spirit. The love of Christ "surpasses knowledge" (3:19). God will finish the work begun in us through Christ.

4:1, 17-24: The image of Paul as a "prisoner in the Lord" is used to urge believers "to lead a life worthy of [their] calling" (4:1). All are called to truth and light, renouncing all works of corruption, delusion, and darkness.

Food for Thought

The Christology, ecclesiology, and eschatology of Ephesians seem to go beyond what Paul himself would have developed in the decade in which he wrote. In Ephesians, Christology is closely linked with ecclesiology and soteriology, that is, Paul's teaching about justification and salvation. In Christ there is unity, as all are members of one body, and so the mission of the church is universal. No longer does the author refer to the local church but to the whole church as one body, its members at peace and brought "near by the blood of Christ" (2:13).

Ephesians' author described believers as "citizens with the saints and also members of the household of God" (2:19). Believers' relationships with one another are reflected in the composition of a household. As husbands and wives, children and parents, slaves and masters, we are transformed because of our relationship with Christ in Baptism. Ephesians does not set out to change the world but to change the way believers perceive their relationships to one another by helping them see that we are all justified through Christ. How would our world today change if we were all motivated by "speaking the truth in love" (4:15)?

The prayer known as the "Breastplate of St. Patrick" must have been inspired by Ephesians. It begins and ends by invoking the Trinity. It continues, "Christ be with me, Christ within me, Christ behind me, Christ before me, Christ beside me, . . . Christ beneath me, Christ above me." This parallels the prayer in Ephesians, which expresse the hope that "Christ may dwell in your hearts through faith, as you are being rooted and grounded in love, . . . that you may have the power to comprehend, with all the saints, what is the breadth and length and height and depth, . . . so that you may be filled with all the fullness of God" (3:17-19).

PHILIPPIANS

Perhaps no image of Paul is more poignant than that of him as a prisoner, frustrated in his plans to take the gospel "to the ends of the earth" (Acts 1:8), but neither silenced nor self-pitying. In fact, Paul's serenity and joy are notable in one of his most eloquent letters, this one to the Philippians, written from prison. Philippians exudes affection, joy, and confidence in God. Paul's love for the community is palpable. Paul told the Philippians that he thanked God for them every time he thought of them, which he "constantly" did in prayer (1:3-4). He repeatedly told them to "rejoice" and "not worry about anything. . . . And the peace of God . . . will guard your hearts and your minds in Christ Jesus" (4:4, 6, 7).

The tone in Philippians is so joyful that one can imagine Paul at the peak of his career, successful, on top of the world, feeling no pain. So it might come as a surprise to realize that Paul wrote Philippians while he was languishing in prison, unsure whether he would live or die. Paul was confident that what mattered was that in all things, "Christ is proclaimed" (1:18). Paul was transformed by the death and resurrection of Christ, and so he looked at everything in a new light. Previously, he might have gloried in his religious credentials and boasted of being "blameless" under the law (3:4-6). Now, through his sufferings, which have made him more like Christ, he regards everything in a new way, that is, in light of knowing "Christ and the power of his resurrection" (3:10).

In this short letter, we hear about some of Paul's closest companions, which tells us of the diverse makeup of this important Christian community. Take, for example, Timothy, Paul's co-author. Paul said that Timothy was "like a son" to him (2:22). He was well-known to the Philippians, and Paul encouraged them by saying that soon he would send Timothy to them. Euodia and Syntyche are the names of two women leaders of the church of Philippi who were in some dispute (see 4:2-3); Paul urged them to take on the same mind of Christ that he had exhorted the whole community to adopt in 2:1-5. It should be noted that Acts 16:14 tells us that the host of the house church in Philippi was also a woman, Lydia, a businesswoman. The church in this cosmopolitan European city on the well-used Roman road called the *Via Egnatia* was accustomed, it seems, to women's leadership very early in its history.

At a Glance

Who: Paul is indisputably the author of this letter.
What: A letter Paul sent from prison to the church in Philippi.
When: **AD** 54–56 if it was written in Ephesus or a little later if it was written in Caesarea; as late as AD 62–64 and one of the last letters Paul wrote if it originated in Rome.
Where: Scholars debate the location of Paul's imprisonment, arguing for Caesarea, Ephesus, or Rome.
Why: To encourage the church in Philippi; Paul was concerned about the effect of divisions within the community, persecution, the influence of "Judaizers" who sought to add circumcision to the requirements for being Christian, and the effect of the Philippians' concern for Paul himself and his imprisonment.

Structure and Content

1: After the address, Paul expresses his love for the Philippians in thanksgiving. Writing from prison, Paul says he does not know whether he will live or die and is torn between which of the two possibilities he would prefer. Paul is aware of some of the ways the Philippians are suffering because of his imprisonment, and he feels the tug of their need for him since they are a very young and vulnerable community.

2:1-18: There are divisions in the community (2:2-3), perhaps fueled by disputes between some leaders. Paul urges the Philippians to "let the same mind be in you that was in Christ Jesus" (2:5). This "mind" will empower them to be healed, to persevere, and, ultimately, to be saved.

2:19–3:1: Plans regarding Paul's co-workers (Timothy and Epaphroditus) and Paul's hope of returning to them.

3:2–4:9: Exhortations and warnings about Judaizers—in startlingly severe language—and about divisions within the community. After reevaluating his beliefs, he says that justification comes "through faith in Christ, the righteousness from God based in faith" (3:9).

4:10-20: Paul thanks the Philippians for their partnership with him and for their generous gifts to him. He adds that he knows how to do without, but that their generosity will be rewarded by Christ.

4:21-23: Concluding greeting and blessing. Paul refers to the believers in Philippi and those with him as "saints" (4:22). Another reference in 4:22 to the "emperor's household" has been taken to mean that Paul wrote from Rome, although it is not definitive evidence.

Major Themes

- **Philippians' Christology includes Christ's preexistence** of creation and his equality with God.

- **Joy cannot be taken away** by suffering, imprisonment, or even the threat of death.

- **Partnership in the gospel is essential,** whether that happens by actively preaching it or by suffering for it as a witness.

Authorship

Ascribed to "Paul and Timothy" as co-authors, Philippians has never been seriously disputed as one of Paul's authentic letters. The time and place of his imprisonment, however, are subject to debate, and Philippians is a good example of why these aspects of Paul's letters are so important. If the imprisonment was early, say around AD 53–54, then Philippians would be among Paul's first letters, perhaps after 1 Thessalonians, and Paul would have fashioned his "theology of the cross," usually connected with the Corinthian correspondence and articulated there, on the basis of his own experience of suffering and the threat of imminent death. If the imprisonment was in Rome, leading to Paul's execution, Philippians would be considered one of the last of Paul's letters, dated after the writing of Romans.

Literary Form

Letter: Philippians is a good example of how Paul meant his letters to serve as a substitute for his presence when he was unable to be with the community. Maintaining contact with the community of believers as an apostolic authority was a major concern for Paul.

Key Passages

1:20-26: Paul says that he is torn between wanting to live for the sake of the gospel mission and desiring to die to be with Christ. If given the choice, he does not know which he would choose. He appears unsure of the outcome of his present imprisonment.

2:5-11: In a poem, Paul describes what it means to "let the same mind be in you that was in Christ Jesus" (2:5). This poem may be one of the earliest expressions of belief in the existence of Christ prior to creation and of Christ's "equality with God" (2:6).

Food for Thought

Philippians shows a development in Paul's eschatological thinking from 1 Thessalonians, when he believed the resurrection would happen soon and that the living and the dead would be caught up instantaneously with Jesus. In Philippians, Paul says that after death, Jesus "will transform the body of our humiliation that it may be conformed to the body of his glory" (3:21). Also, the Christological hymn of Philippians 2:5-11 is the clearest statement in Paul's writings of belief in the humanity and the divinity of Jesus: "And being found in human form, / he . . . became obedient to the point of death— / even death on a cross," but God also "gave him the name / that is above every name."

Paul is a model of confidence in God and of joy, even in the face of the most severe suffering, both for the Philippians and for us. Paul urged his readers to "live your life in a manner worthy of the gospel of Christ" (1:27) and to take on the mind of Christ (2:5), who emptied himself to take on our humanity. He was completely selfless in his hopes and prayers for the Philippians. His own experience of suffering and of the cross had shown him that all that matters is that at all times, "Christ is proclaimed in every way" (1:18). How can I make this priority more evident in my life?

Colossians

The wisdom that my parents shared with family members seems to continue to bear fruit even after their deaths. In raising our own children, my siblings and I appeal more and more to sayings of our parents, even when we at times are voicing our own ideas. It seems that arguments from authority continue to have an impact on us even after—or especially after—the death of these loved ones. So it was with Paul and Peter, early giants of the Christian faith, whose reputation and authority increased in the latter part of the first century, perhaps enhanced by their martyrdom under Nero in the early sixties. In fact, some Christians in the early church wrote letters in Paul's name so that their teachings would take on greater authority. The authorship of the letter to the Colossians, for example, is disputed, but some scholars attribute it to a disciple of Paul writing after his death.

Near the end of Colossians, we learn some tantalizing tidbits about other leaders in the early church who had been companions of Paul and who continued his legacy in working to strengthen the foundation of the believing community. Paul included the greetings of some of these other leaders near the end of this letter to the Colossians. Mark, identified as the cousin of Barnabas (4:10), is known to us through Acts, where he was called John Mark (see Acts 12:12, 25; 15:37). It seems that his mother, Mary of Jerusalem, was known to the church through her hospitality to many disciples. If Luke was correct in noting that Mark was estranged from Paul because he wanted to return home after embarking on a mission with Paul and Barnabas (see Acts 15:35-40), Colossians suggests that there was a reconciliation between them and that Mark was well-known and commended to the Colossians. Another companion, also known to us from Acts, is Luke, a Gentile, called in Colossians "the beloved physician" (4:14). Others mentioned in the final greeting are also mentioned in Philemon, including Tychicus, bearer of this letter to the Colossians (4:7); Onesimus (4:9), perhaps the same person who was the subject of Paul's letter to Philemon; Aristarchus (4:10); and Epaphras, apparently the founder of the community at Colossae (4:12).

At a Glance

Who: It is possible that the author was a disciple of Paul writing after the apostle's death, but connections with people mentioned in Philemon are grounds for many to believe that Colossians was written by Paul himself through a secretary.

What: A formal epistle addressing some false teachings, especially about the role of Christ in the universe.

When: Either sometime between AD 80 and 100 or possibly shortly before the death of Paul in the early sixties.

Where: Sent to Colossae, located about one hundred miles east of Ephesus; Paul had spent about two years in the region at the height of his missionary career (Acts 19:10).

Why: To address some of the concerns perhaps laid out by Epaphras or one of his disciples about how false teachers were undermining the singular role of Christ with notions of angels and other beings presented as intermediaries between humans and God and superior to Christ.

Structure and Content

1:1-14: The address includes a greeting, thanksgiving, and prayer. The authors are identified as "Paul" and "Timothy our brother" and the recipients as "saints and faithful brothers and sisters in Christ in Colossae."

1:15–2:5: A Christological hymn and consequences for the community. All have been reconciled through Christ, whose work is still continuing through the work of the apostle and the church. The suffering of Christ and of Paul is held up as a model and as testimony of the divine "mystery" (1:27, 2:2) at work among the Gentiles, such as the Colossians.

2:6-23: Life in Christ and warnings against false teachers. Paul begins and ends this section with warnings about the seduction of false teachings. Carried over from the Christological hymn is the idea that in Christ is the "fullness of God" (1:19; cf. 2:9). Paul then applies the consequences of this Christology to believers, who have been transformed in Christ: we are filled with Christ, circumcised in him, and have died, been buried, and raised to life again with Christ (2:7-13; cf. Romans 6:3-5).

3:1–4:6: Practical consequences of life "in Christ" (1:2). Those who are in Christ reveal their union with him in their relationships and in their actions toward one another and toward the rest of the world. The normal divisions among people such as "Greek and Jew, circumcised and uncircumcised" exist no longer in the unity of all who are "in Christ," but "Christ is all and in all" (3:11).

4:7-18: Final greetings and a benediction. Here we learn more about some New Testament personalities, also mentioned in other letters, notably in Philemon and Acts.

Major Themes

- **Christ is preeminent** above all.
- **Christ's role in creation, redemption, and salvation** is explained and exalted.
- **The consequences for the morality of a believer's life "in Christ"** (1:2) are spelled out: all of one's relationships change when one is in Christ.

Authorship

When it comes to the question of Pauline authorship, one of the most disputed letters is Colossians. Some interpreters note the identification of the same members of the communities mentioned in Colossians, Philippians, and Philemon as the basis for their claim that Paul himself also wrote Colossians. At the end of Colossians, Paul noted that he had signed it "with [his] own hand" (4:18), a suggestion that the rest of the letter might have been written by a secretary at Paul's direction. If this secretary was given license to use his own words and style to convey Paul's thoughts and concerns, that would account for the variance in style and vocabulary that many find in Colossians.

Literary Form

Epistle: The community at Colossae was apparently founded by Epaphras (1:7), who appealed to the Colossians on the basis of Paul's authority to address some of the problems that had arisen. Colossians lacks the personal tone of many of Paul's own letters.

Key Passages

1:15-20: Hymn of Christ's preeminence. Christ is "the image of the invisible God" (1:15), and all things were created through him. Christ reconciled the world to his Father through his sacrifice on the cross.

3:18-24: A section known as "household rules" envisions going around the table of a typical household, addressing the duties of its respective members. Wives and husbands, children and parents, slaves and masters—all form new relationships with one another in love and respect as a result of being "in Christ." Here Paul does not call into question the roles of dominance of husbands over wives or masters over slaves accepted in his society, but in saying that women, like men, and slaves, like their masters, are "in Christ" as a result of their Baptism, he lays the groundwork for the church of the future to challenge that dominance.

Food for Thought

The hymn of Colossians 1:15-20 illustrates the increasingly "high" Christology that developed from the church's years of reflection on the identity, mission, and consequences of Jesus' death and resurrection for the salvation of humankind. As God's gift to us in Jesus was celebrated in the liturgy and as passages from the Scriptures were used to explain the ways that Jesus had brought salvation to the world, the church came to understand that he had been part of God's plan from the beginning. Later councils would clearly state that Jesus is both human and divine. Colossians shows a movement in the direction of emphasizing Jesus' divinity. If written by Paul himself, who appeared to be quoting a hymn already existing and in use by the church, the assertion of Jesus' divinity came very early indeed.

Colossians clearly shows the relationship between being "in Christ" and the morality that flows from that reality. It was typical of Paul in his authentic letters to state the new reality that exists in faith and then to give instruction about how to live accordingly. Colossians is a good example of this structure in action.

1 Thessalonians

A visit to good friends sometimes results in a letter-writing spree, an attempt to continue the camaraderie and good feeling of the visit. This is especially true if the friends visited were experiencing some problems or worries. We want to reconnect as much as possible and help to assuage our friends' pain or concerns with words of hope and comfort. A comparable situation seems to have motivated Paul to write to the Thessalonians, a community that was very receptive to the gospel he had preached to them in person. After his visit, he heard of some concerns they had, and so he decided to write to them, putting their issues into a theological context and then encouraging them to keep the faith.

Silvanus and Timothy are listed as co-authors, perhaps to reinforce Paul's authority, implying that this is a letter written not by one person but is the product of the collective teaching of well-beloved missionaries. Silvanus is perhaps identified with Silas, whom Paul chose as his travel companion for his second missionary journey after splitting up with Barnabas and Mark, according to Acts 15:40. Acts also tells us that shortly thereafter, Paul requested that Timothy join that mission. Paul then had Timothy circumcised so that he would be more acceptable to the Jews and their leaders as an authentic missionary of the gospel (16:1-5). Timothy was a charismatic, popular, and indispensable associate of Paul, someone who contributed much to the Gentile mission.

At a Glance

Who: Paul wrote this to one of his successful communities after he had heard about some questions they were raising among themselves.

What: Paul adapted the Greco-Roman letter form, starting by identifying himself, Silvanus, and Timothy as co-writers and expressing thanks for the Thessalonians' faith, hope, and love.

When: Around AD 48–49, making this the earliest extant letter of Paul; in fact, 1 Thessalonians is the earliest written document of the New Testament.

Where: Thessalonica, situated on the *Via Egnatia,* an East-West travel corridor across Greece from the Aegean to the Adriatic Seas, was one of the first communities Paul founded on his first missionary journey, undertaken because of the revelation from God that he should go to the Gentiles.

Why: To address some concerns in the community at Thessalonica; namely, some members of the community had become skeptical about Paul's claims that Jesus would soon return to judge the world. Paul had also heard rumors about some members of the community who were using Jesus' imminent return as an excuse for their own idle and lazy behavior.

Structure and Content

1: The letter begins with the address, greetings, and thanksgiving. In the greeting, Paul identifies himself and his co-authors. Rather than thanking God for benefits given to himself, his thanksgivings center on the blessings given to the recipients that reinforce their faith and strengthen them.

2–3: Paul's reminders of what he has taught them by word and example are simple and pragmatic: he has given the Thessalonians an example by working with his hands while he was among them, by his willingness to suffer persecution in pursuit of the gospel, and even by writing this letter, which is a form of apostolic "presence" with them. He will continue to care for them and to assert his authority over them.

4:1–5:22: Moral principles for living a Christian life in the light of the gospel. Paul tells them to conduct themselves as "children of light" rather than as children of darkness (5:5) and offers some guiding principles for sexual conduct, for charity among members of the community, and for demonstrating faith in the resurrection of the dead and in the *parousia.*

5:23-28: Concluding prayer and final greeting. This section gives us the sense that Paul's letters were meant to be read—and were, in fact, read—at the liturgies of the believers. Paul concludes the letter with a short prayer that the Thessalonians will become holy and "blameless at the coming of our Lord Jesus Christ" (5:23).

Major Themes

- **Paul shores up the Thessalonians' faith** with frequent allusions to their common experience and reminders about what they "know" and what he has previously told them, after establishing his authority with the Thessalonians as the one who had brought them the gospel.

- **Paul cites his example** from when he was with them and his preaching to them, telling the Thessalonians that they should imitate him.

- **Paul repeatedly refers to Jesus as "our Lord"** and to his coming as the time when he will judge the world.

Authorship

This is the first of Paul's extant letters and is very important for that reason. Paul set out here a pattern of teaching followed by moral exhortations, which he would use in subsequent letters.

Literary Form

Letter: Paul used the Greco-Roman letter form with some signature changes that would recur in other Pauline letters. The greeting "Grace to you and peace," for example, is a combination of the usual Greek *chaire* and the Hebrew *shalom* (1:1). This greeting is embellished with a description of Paul's addressees as "the church" (1:1) or "brothers and sisters beloved by God" (1:4). Paul also presented elaborate "thanksgiving" passages, thanking God for the blessings he had witnessed in the community or for the success of his mission. The first section of the letter lays out fundamental beliefs of Christians, while the second part draws out some practical conclusions of these beliefs as they affect life in the community; this becomes a standard format for Paul's letters.

Key Passages

1:1: In blessing the Thessalonians, Paul invokes "God the Father and the Lord Jesus Christ." This may be an early articulation of Paul's belief in Jesus' divinity.

1:3: The triad of faith, love, and hope appear together for the first time.

Food for Thought

In this first letter to the Thessalonians, Paul indicates his belief that the *parousia* of Jesus is imminent. Paul portrays Jesus as the judge of the world who is merciful to the faithful. Christians must maintain vigilance and hope. 1 Thessalonians provides a good example of the fundamental relationship between faith and moral conduct: Christian beliefs must be reflected in action. The Thessalonians wonder about the meaning of the death of loved ones in view of their eager expectation of Jesus' return. Paul encourages them to translate their faith into trust that they will be reunited by the resurrection. Some Thessalonians have become lazy, idly awaiting Jesus' *parousia* but refusing to work in the world and in the church to contribute to the welfare of others. Paul shows the meaning of charity and compassion, citing his own example as a model. How do I practice faith, hope, and charity in my own world and church—great and small—today? Could I cite my own example as a model for others? In what way?

2 Thessalonians

It is doubtful that Paul himself actually wrote 2 Thessalonians, but he could have. The thoughts surely seem to be similar to his. The author speaks in Paul's name and develops the same ideas that Paul proposed in 1 Thessalonians. The problem for most interpreters is that in 1 Thessalonians, Paul seemed to think that the *parousia* of Jesus Christ would happen sometime very soon. However, in 2 Thessalonians the writer, identified as Paul, warns that many things will happen before the *parousia*. The dawning realization that there would be some extension of time before the return of Christ probably was a slow process. Of course, people can change their minds, but Paul, whose writing career spanned only about a decade, from AD 48–58, might not have been able to conceive a lengthy period of time between the first and the final comings of Jesus.

At A Glance

Who: Probably written by a disciple of Paul, imitating his style and vocabulary.

What: A letter to this early successful community at Thessalonica.

When: Perhaps as late as the end of the first century AD.

Where: Written to the church in Thessalonica, one of the first communities Paul established.

Why: To respond to some misinterpretations of the gospel Paul had preached. In light of the coming judgment, believers must remain vigilant, maintain unity, resist divisions and false teaching, and work hard and avoid idleness.

Structure and Content

1: The address includes a greeting and thanksgiving, all very similar to the address in 1 Thessalonians.

2: This section teaches about the coming judgment, warning against the "lawless one" (2:3, 8, 9) and about the events that must happen before the end. The author reminds the church of the gift of salvation won for believers by Jesus Christ.

3:1-15: Exhortations about ethics. Thessalonians are urged to pray for the writer and for one another, to work as an expression of charity, to remain active and productive so as not to meddle in others' affairs, and to remain obedient to authority.

3:16-18: Final greetings and blessing; the author's final words are "The grace of our Lord Jesus Christ be with all of you," similar to the ending of 1 Thessalonians.

Major Themes

- **The author exhorts the Thessalonians to not be alarmed** by false teachings about the *parousia* or by letters purported to be from Paul that incorrectly state that the *parousia* has already taken place or is imminent.

- **Apostasy and the reign of the "lawless one"** must happen before Christ's return. There will be a clash between the "lawless one" and Christ, a confrontation that will separate the unjust from the just. Such a "holy war" will be finally won by Christ.

Authorship

The author's style imitates Paul's and even copies phrases of 1 Thessalonians, but the tone and the view of the end-time are very different and seem to indicate an intervening time span between the writing of 1 and 2 Thessalonians.

Literary Form

Letter: Using the letter format employed by Paul and relying on his name and authority with the Thessalonians, the author wrote about the coming *parousia* and exhorted the Thessalonians to be faithful to the message Paul had preached.

Key Passages

2:1-4: The *parousia* of our Lord Jesus Christ will not occur until the "lawless one" is revealed. In the end, the wicked will be destroyed. The Thessalonians are not to be swayed or shaken by false alarms purporting to be from Paul announcing "that the day of the Lord is already here" (2:2).

3:10: A reminder of Paul's instruction that "anyone unwilling to work should not eat." This means that those not contributing to the general welfare of the community ought not to expect to share in its benefits. This admonition reflects the common life of the early Christian community as described in Acts.

Food for Thought

In 2 Thessalonians, we see a rudimentary Christian apocalypticism that affirms the coming of Christ as judge while also urging continued faith, hope, and love among the believers. 2 Thessalonians thus builds on the prophets' descriptions of the "day of the Lord" and relates them to the belief that Jesus, who is the Lord, is coming. Jesus is known as "our Lord *(kyrios)* Jesus Christ." He is the Son of the Father. He will come to bring judgment to the world. But before his return, believers are to live calmly and peacefully with one another even in the midst of persecution, regardless of its source. By definition, apocalyptic literature is cryptic, and so the sources of the oppression of the believers are not identified. They could range from the Roman Empire to apostasy within the church and the threat of betrayal.

Believers today would do well to observe the teachings of 2 Thessalonians, especially in view of many contemporary threats to peace of mind. The author tells the Thessalonians to continue to practice faith, hope, and charity even as they confront persecution, to work to better the world and contribute to their own livelihood, and to pray for those in authority and for one another.

Introduction to the Pastoral Epistles

One of my dear friends who was battling terminal cancer at a young age decided to write an open letter to her teenage daughters, articulating her spiritual legacy to them. Perhaps unwittingly, she was echoing the action of biblical figures such as Jacob, Moses, Joshua, Paul, and Jesus, who are each featured giving a "farewell address" near the end of their lives. The tradition usually follows a clear pattern: a leader calls together his heirs and predicts his imminent death. He warns them about future threats or hardships and encourages them to take inspiration from his life, including the motivations for his actions. He admonishes them to remain faithful to this legacy. Finally, amid tears and heavy hearts, they hug and kiss, promising to keep faith with one another. Establishing and passing on the legacy of a beloved leader is one of the ways the faithful express their longing for life to continue eternally.

The next three New Testament books, known since the eighteenth century as the "pastoral letters," picture Paul as an older man in prison. He is writing to his spiritual descendants Timothy and Titus, passing on to his younger colleagues wisdom and encouragement they will not only personally treasure but, in turn, will pass on to the next generation. These letters, although probably not written by Paul himself, carried apostolic authority. All three, but especially 2 Timothy, could serve as a model of a "farewell address" in writing.

Christian communities were battered by doctrinal and leadership disputes in the waning years of the first century after the death of the first and second generations of Christians. Pummeled also by the persecution under Domitian (AD 91–94), these communities were still searching for their own identity, distinct from their Jewish roots or their pagan backgrounds. The stress of persecution gave the doctrines of Gnosticism, with its world-hating tendencies, more credibility. Religion seemed like a refuge from the doubt, anxiety, and depression of the human condition. Paul, the martyr who suffered from internal conflict and external persecution, became the perfect authority to address the contemporary threats to the stability of the Christian church.

The relationship among the three pastoral letters provides an interesting study. 1 Timothy and Titus, with their impersonal tone and emphasis on the practical virtues that ought to be exhibited by church leaders, are more like each other than either one is to 2 Timothy. 2 Timothy is much more personal and pictures Paul as an old man, lonely, facing the prospect of dying in prison. This letter fits in well with Philippians and Philemon, both authentic letters from Paul counted among the "prison letters." If 2 Timothy was written by Paul himself, it would date from the early sixties. If 2 Timothy was composed after 1 Timothy and Titus, it belongs near the end of the first century, when the church was facing persecution from Domitian, the Roman emperor, much like it had been near the end of Paul's life under Nero.

Useful Terms to Know

Bishop: From the Greek word *episcopos,* which means "overseer," the term referred initially to fiscal responsibility. 1 Timothy gives qualifications of bishops in 3:1-7, noting that he must "manage his own household well," for if he cannot do this, "how can he take care of God's church?" (3:4, 5). According to Titus, bishops and elders often had similar roles and responsibilities, as the early Christian community in Crete developed new styles of leadership different from such roles as apostle, prophet, and missionary that Paul himself was concerned about.

Deacons: Based on passages from Acts and 1 Timothy, deacons were ordained by the laying on of hands to administer the goods of the church to those in need (see Acts 6:1-7; 1 Timothy 3:8-13).

Elder: From the Greek word *presbyteros,* the term appears in 1 Timothy with the implication that this is an office of the church recognized by ordination through the laying on of hands (see 5:22). Elders have the role of teaching and preaching and ought to be supported by the community. The Book of Titus blurs any evident distinction between the offices of presbyter and bishop.

"Real Widows": 1 Timothy seems to indicate that "real widows" meant those who had no husband, children, or grandchildren; in other words, these were older women who relied exclusively on the church and ought to be supported by the community. Such women would be significant role models and able to teach younger believing women the values advocated by the church. Note that this is the only gender-specific role in the church that Paul describes (see 5:3-16).

1 Timothy

The image of Paul in this and the other two pastoral letters is probably a fiction of an author writing near the end of the first century to invoke a devoted and beloved apostle speaking to his younger dedicated follower. In times of trouble, we like to reach for inspiration and strength from heroes who have endured similar hardships. Faced with challenges and uncertainty, we look for stability, reassurance of the goodness and meaning of life, and encouragement to persevere. Paul and Timothy were probably dead by the time this letter was written, but the church was in need of creative and courageous leadership within the continuing gospel tradition, and so the author invoked their memory and authority to encourage the church to persevere.

At a Glance

Who: Most likely written by a disciple or disciples of Paul, invoking his example as a leader giving advice to a younger colleague.

What: A letter giving encouragement to church leaders encountering unforeseen problems of discipline and the threat of false teachers leading people astray.

When: Proposed dates range from Paul's own time (early sixties) to as late as the middle of the second century AD. The most likely date is near the end of the first century, around 90, based on the advanced church order that describes the roles of bishops, deacons, and elders.

Where: Paul, depicted as writing from Macedonia, addressed Timothy as leader of the church at Ephesus where he had left him.

Why: To inspire courageous and faithful leadership as the church faced an uncertain future.

Structure and Content

1: The address, in the style and language of Paul's own letters, is followed by a warning against false teachers. "Paul" refers to his own experience and his previous instruction to Timothy. Paul is depicted as the true teacher as he contrasts reliable doctrine with false, misleading guides.

2–3: Worship and leadership roles, including requirements for certain church offices such as bishops and deacons, and proper conduct for members of the church are explained. 1 Timothy 3:16 contains an early Christological creed cited as fundamental and unifying for factions in the church that were formed on false teachings.

4:1–6:10: The author writes about the goodness of creation and teachings on various leadership roles such as widows and elders. He warns Timothy against excessive ascetics and admonishes slaves to be obedient.

6:11-21: A summation of advice to Timothy regarding personal conduct, the traditions of faith, and the promise of immortality. He gives a final warning against wealth in this world and a closing exhortation to Timothy and the community.

Major Themes

- **Leaders need to be teachers** and to counteract false teaching
- **The church needs role models** who are supporting instruction with exemplary living.

Authorship

This letter was probably written by a disciple of Paul from a later generation of leaders, citing Paul and Timothy's relationship as exemplary and authoritative.

Literary Form

Epistle: A formal, impersonal letter meant to inspire good church leadership at a time when the community needed to survive in the Greco-Roman world.

Key Passages

1:1-2: The address echoes those of Paul's authentic letters, referring to his authority as an apostle and his close relationship with Timothy, who is addressed as "my loyal child in the faith" (1:2).

3:15-16: The Pauline author links behavior in "the household of God" with faith that Jesus "was revealed in flesh, / vindicated in spirit, / seen by angels, / proclaimed among Gentiles, / believed in throughout the world, / taken up in glory."

Food for Thought

1 Timothy shows some progression in the church toward internal order and the recognition of ecclesial offices, designated by gestures such as enrollment and the laying on of hands. The beginnings of a Christian creed might be seen in 3:16 in reference to Jesus' Incarnation and his exaltation after death. Jesus will come on the day of judgment as the "King of kings and Lord of lords" (6:15). 1 Timothy reminds us that we live in the "household of God" (3:15) and that our riches are not of this world but of the next.

In this book, we see the church adapting to life in its own times, focusing on good leadership and on keeping true to the traditions that had come from the apostles as they waited for the coming of our Lord Jesus Christ. Leaders and offices emerged from the church's changing needs. Regardless of their specific duties, all designated leadership roles reflect faithfulness to the mission of the church established by Jesus. Pastors show by the power of their example what it means to be a disciple of Christ.

2 TIMOTHY

I keep an old and tattered letter from my mother in the top drawer of my dresser. I have it memorized. But there are times since her death when I have taken it out to read, as if by unfolding the paper and looking again at the words, I can bring her nearer. Sometimes we need to be reinspired and reinvigorated with the encouragement that comes from those who have gone before us. That's what my mother's letter—one of the last she wrote—does for me.

And so it was with Paul and Timothy, apparently, as 2 Timothy testifies. It is presented as a letter of encouragement to Timothy, Paul's companion on his second and third missions. But it may actually have been written to inspire believers at least a generation after the death of Paul. The contemporary position of most interpreters with regard to this letter is that Paul actually was not the author; by the time this letter was written, both he and Timothy had died. Yet this opinion does little to lessen the value and the relevance today of its message. The author implies that based on what we do know about Paul's relationship with Timothy, even if Paul himself did not write this letter, he could have. What the letter communicates to us is the strength and depth of their affection and mutual respect as well as their devotion to the future of the church.

We learn of some significant people in Timothy's life who appear to have given encouragement to him as well as to Paul himself. Among them are Lois and Eunice, respectively Timothy's grandmother and mother. Acts indicates that Timothy was the child of a Jewish mother and Gentile father (16:1). Paul says in 2 Timothy that Timothy had been taught the Scriptures from infancy, suggesting that his grandmother and mother raised him as a Jew. We also have a tantalizing note in this letter about Luke and Mark. In the final greetings of this letter, Paul is pictured lonely and longing for some of his disciples. Luke is with him; he asks Timothy to come and to bring Mark with him (cf. Colossians 4:10-14).

At a Glance

Who: Probably written by a disciple of Paul, invoking the apostle's image and authority for the encouragement of the community. If Paul himself wrote this letter, he did so very late in his career, not long before he was killed under Nero.

What: A farewell address in the form of a letter.

When: Written either at the end of Paul's life in the sixties or sometime in the nineties when the church was suffering a persecution similar to the one Paul had endured.

Where: Paul is pictured as writing from prison, supposedly from Rome. It is addressed to Timothy, who was entrusted with the care of the Christian communities in Ephesus.

Why: To encourage Timothy to persevere in leading the church, in teaching and correcting heresy, and in maintaining his authority and influence through his example.

Structure and Content

1:1-2:13: The letter begins with a greeting and thanksgiving. This letter envisions an elderly and benevolent Paul, a contemporary of Timothy's grandmother, giving the young leader Timothy his prayerful advice. Paul's encouragement to Timothy is meant to stir up the courage and confidence that God has worked through Paul, whose legacy is still ongoing and reliable.

2:14–4:18: The author gives advice on correcting false teaching.

4:19-22: Final greetings, personal requests, and blessings.

Major Themes

- **Paul is described in very human terms,** as preparing to be put to death, lonely and abandoned by all but the most loyal of disciples, Luke and Onesiphorus. Yet Paul is hopeful and faithful.

- **Christians must accept whatever happens to them** and, like Paul, faithfully look for the *parousia* of Jesus.

Authorship

It is difficult to determine whether Paul actually wrote 2 Timothy or if it is a letter written in Paul's name after he had died. 2 Timothy is very personal, in the style of Paul and different from the other two pastoral letters (i.e., 1 Timothy and Titus), which were more likely composed later.

Literary Form

Farewell Address: Common elements of the farewell address found in 2 Timothy include the image of a leader who, sensing that he will die soon, gathers his sons or heirs to give them final instructions. He predicts his imminent death and outlines the legacy he leaves with his successors. He charges them with a mission, warns about hardships they will encounter in his absence, and concludes with embraces and gestures of affection.

Key Passages

1:5; 3:15: Paul recalls the image of Lois and Eunice, who brought up Timothy in the faith through their example and by teaching him the Scriptures from childhood. This helps Timothy understand that salvation comes through faith in Jesus Christ.

3:16: The first Christian statement of belief about the authority of Scripture: "All scripture is inspired by God and is useful for teaching, for reproof, for correction, and for training in righteousness."

4:6-7: In an allusion to his impending death, Paul says that he is "poured out as a libation." Then using sports imagery, he compares himself to a boxer and a runner, saying, "I have fought the good fight, I have finished the race, I have kept the faith."

Food for Thought

2 Timothy 3:16 asserts the Christian belief that "all Scripture is inspired by God" and significant for its guidance in truth and righteousness. That is true, not only of what was written before 2 Timothy, but also of 2 Timothy itself. We think of tradition as what is the old, tried, and true ways

of doing things. But these pastoral letters show that the apostle thought of tradition as not only what was passed on but the way it was adapted to the needs of different communities as they grew and came to terms with evangelizing, with church order, and with relating to and growing in the world. Both letters to Timothy warn the younger pastor about the dangers and futility of participating in philosophical discussions that distract from the truth and jeopardize one's focus on the important priorities facing the Christian community. We might substitute for "philosophy" the kinds of debates over politics and religion today that threaten to destroy relationships and undermine the essentials of our own communities—our families, parishes, and nation. We can turn to the Scriptures for inspiration on how to heal our divisions, how to prioritize our common values, and how to be a good example to others so that the whole community is strengthened in practicing faith, hope, and love.

Titus

This letter is addressed to Titus, a Gentile Christian who was Paul's representative with the unruly Corinthians and his trusted companion on several missions, including one to the authorities of the Jerusalem church. Titus is known to us from Paul's own letters, but he is not named in Acts. In Galatians, Paul wrote that the Jerusalem authorities did not demand that Titus become circumcised, indicating that he was a Gentile before joining Paul's missionary entourage (2:1, 3). In 2 Corinthians, Paul recounted that he had sent Titus to Corinth and then anxiously awaited his return to Macedonia with a report about the community (2:13; 7:6, 13-14). When Titus finally arrived with a positive report, Paul was immensely relieved. Paul also sent Titus to take up the collection in Corinth and then to take the proceeds to Jerusalem for the relief of the poor who were suffering from a famine there (see 2 Corinthians 8:6, 16-24).

Yet there are several reasons for questioning whether this is really a letter between Paul and Titus. Several factors undermine the idea that this letter was actually written by Paul before his death in the early sixties AD. The tone of this letter is impersonal, like that of 1 Timothy. The author describes a church order and criteria for recognizing church offices that seem to be later developments, aspects of a church well established in its world. The letter thus seems to be a product of a later time, written in Paul's name to a younger well-known co-worker and dealing with the kinds of problems that arose as the church tried to settle into its Greco-Roman environment and faced many struggles, both internally and externally.

At a Glance

Who: Written in Paul's name, but the author was likely a disciple from a later time.

What: Instruction emphasizing church order and avoiding religious controversy.

When: Probably near the end of the first century AD.

Where: To Titus in Crete, a Gentile Christian who was a disciple of Paul and emissary to the Corinthians, now pictured as the trusted head of the church in Crete, a large island in the Mediterranean.

Why: To advocate for strong Christian leadership with designated roles, recognizing virtues that all Christians should imitate; written because philosophical issues were threatening the unity of the church.

Structure and Content

1: Following the address, the apostle advises Titus to appoint other local leaders in the church at Crete. He addresses the qualifications required for the offices of elder and bishop. Titus faces many problems with unruly members who have not changed from their former way of life, and so Paul advises him that they need strong and good leaders who will set an example for them.

2: Instruction on Christian life. Leaders must confront heresy. The behavior of Christian men and women distinguishes them as believers awaiting the appearance of "the glory of our great God and Savior, Jesus Christ" (2:13). Titus' role is to constantly remind believers of these things.

3: Further instructions for Titus. He should instruct the community to be obedient to civil authorities, avoid philosophical debates and quarrels, and issue up to two warnings to heretics and then cut off communication with them. Finally, the author urges the members of the community to provide hospitality for missionaries. He ends with final greetings.

Major Themes

- **Exemplary Christian living** is more important than participating in theological arguments.

- **Leaders are trusted servants** of the community and must lead by example.

Authorship

One of the deutero-Pauline letters, Titus is often linked to 1 Timothy, which also stresses the need for recognized Christian offices in the church and the importance of leaders as models for others to imitate.

Literary Form

Letter: This book is ostensibly a letter written by Paul to Titus but is actually a kind of reflection on Christian leadership that suggests a more organized and settled community than any known in Paul's time, modeled on the household with a structure of authority and leadership.

Key Passages

1:12: A poet from Crete is quoted in a scathing indictment of his own countrymen as "liars, vicious brutes, lazy gluttons." The point seems to be that Titus has greater responsibility to teach sound doctrine because the people of Crete have an established reputation for stubborn resistance to the truth.

2:1-16: Titus is admonished to exert his authority to "teach what is consistent with sound doctrine" (2:1). Titus should be motivated by the realization that "the grace of God has appeared, bringing salvation to all" (2:11).

Food for Thought

The office of bishop that later on became very important in the church has its roots in the pastoral letters of Titus and 1 Timothy. Titus especially stresses the teaching role of the bishop. That role has been underscored in many church documents, especially since Vatican II. Good teachers know that actions speak louder than words and that we teach best by example. The pastoral letters also indicate that the early church depended upon a harmony achieved by the leadership of many people filling diverse roles. Today we need all the gifts and talents, dedication, and commitment to the gospel we can muster. Thus, we will, despite our individual limitations, continue to aspire to become a worthy community of faith.

PHILEMON

Philemon is at once a personal letter written by Paul to an individual, unlike any of the other Pauline letters still in existence, and also a public letter with important Christian ethical implications. Paul wrote to a slave owner, Philemon, in the community at Colossae and entrusted the delivery of this letter to Onesimus, a runaway slave. Paul requested that Onesimus be permitted to return to Paul, adding that there was a new relationship among the three, now "brothers" in the Lord Jesus since Paul had baptized Philemon and later Onesimus (see 12-16).

Significantly, other believers were brought into the discussion about Onesimus' future, either because they were also members of the church at Colossae or because they were present with Paul and apparently known to the Colossian community. Mention of them provides a glimpse into the diversity of the community and the surprisingly democratic form of deciding appropriate Christian behavior that Paul had advocated. The salutation of the letter includes Apphia and Archippus, perhaps Paul's wife and son, respectively, as well as "the church in your house" (2), reflecting the practice of celebrating the Lord's Supper and other prayers in the homes of believers. People from various backgrounds are included in the conclusion of the letter. For example, one named Epaphras is identified as Paul's "fellow prisoner in Christ Jesus" (23). According to Colossians, Epaphras was from Colossae and the founder of the church there (7).

At a Glance

Who: Paul is the indisputable author of this letter.
What: A letter to Philemon, whom Paul had previously baptized, regarding Onesimus, a runaway slave.
When: Between AD 58 and 61.
Where: Paul was writing from prison, probably in Ephesus or Caesarea.
Why: To attain Philemon's permission for Onesimus to return to Paul.

Structure and Content

1-6: Salutation and thanksgiving. Paul and Timothy are identified as co-authors, but the letter is written in the first person singular, as if by Paul alone. The thanksgiving follows the style Paul had adapted from the typical Greek letter; he thanks God for Philemon's faith and for his partnership with Paul in spreading the gospel.

7-22: Paul asks Philemon to accept Onesimus back without retribution for Onesimus' theft or running away. Paul approaches him as "your partner" (17) and as a brother, just as Onesimus now is. Paul cleverly asks that Onesimus' debt be charged to himself, adding that Philemon owes Paul "even your own self" (19). Paul says that he trusts in Philemon's compliance and hopes that he will be able to visit soon.

23-25: The final greetings include a liturgical conclusion. Paul greets by name many of the other leaders of the church of Colossae, underscoring the public nature of this letter. It is reasonable to assume that additional pressure from the community was brought to bear on Philemon to free Onesimus and send him back to Paul, who states that he would like to have him nearby.

Major Themes

- **The relationship established by Baptism** takes precedence over all other previous relationships.
- **Entrance into the new life of faith** has ethical implications for all of our lives.

Authorship

This letter was written by Paul, probably late in his missionary career.

Literary Form

Letter: This letter was meant to be both personal and public; although it was addressed to Philemon, the fact that Paul also named and greeted so many other leaders of the church at Colossae underscores the public nature of this letter.

Key Passages

8-9: Paul appeals to Philemon to treat Onesimus as a brother rather than to punish him for running away. Paul portrays himself as "an old man" and a "prisoner" for Jesus Christ who has the authority to command obedience from Philemon, but instead Paul prefers to appeal to him on the basis of love.

22: Paul announces his intent to visit Philemon, asking that a guest room be prepared for him. This could have significance for dating the letter and ascertaining where Paul was imprisoned as he wrote it. It appears that Philemon was written during the same imprisonment as Philippians was.

Food for Thought

Even though there are no great implications here for salvation history or Christology, Philemon illustrates the practical consequences of conversion to Christ. Indeed, the cost of discipleship is high. Christian life often involves choices that end up transforming our whole lives. Paul confronts Philemon with a dilemma. If Philemon does not punish Onesimus for running away, he will put his own authority in jeopardy with everyone, especially with other slaves. But Paul insinuates that Philemon cannot punish Onesimus, who has now become his brother in Christ, even implying that he ought to free Onesimus so that Onesimus could be "useful" (the meaning of the name "Onesimus") to Paul and to the church. This letter thus illustrates that it is and perhaps should be "inconvenient" to be a Christian in a pagan world. What hard choices do we as believers today face because we are committed to values foreign to our world?

Hebrews

During the liturgy, when there is a selection from this work, the reader might introduce it by saying "A reading from Paul's Epistle to the Hebrews." It might therefore be surprising to learn that Paul was probably not the author, that this is not an epistle, and that it was not addressed to the Hebrews. Rather, this is a treatise of encouragement to Christians that has only the most rudimentary elements of a letter, that is, the closing greetings to members of the community. The designation "Hebrews," a reference to the Israelites when they were enslaved in Egypt, was probably meant to describe a community of the diaspora, believers in Christ who now understood themselves to be sojourners in a world that in many ways was not their lasting home. This message of encouragement was presumed to be from Paul for many years, probably because of its place in the New Testament. But since the nineteenth century, most interpreters have disputed the assertion that Paul was the author. And there is no claim in the work itself to be from the apostle, although some of the language, such as "new covenant" and "body of Christ," may have been borrowed from Paul's letters.

Hebrews is the only New Testament writing that speaks of a Christian priesthood. The only priest of the new covenant is Jesus, a unique high priest whose sacrifice was also unique; it was offered once for all people and all time. The language, particularly of the middle part of Hebrews in 4:14–10:39, is liturgical and focuses on the contrast between the high priesthood of the old covenant and the old sanctuary in the wilderness and the sacrifice of Jesus on the cross in perfect obedience to God, a sacrifice that atones for the sin of all humankind and renders all other sacrifices unnecessary.

At a Glance

Who: The writer is anonymous.
What: A message of encouragement in sermon form with greetings at the end that are more typical of epistles.
When: Probably in the nineties AD.
Where: The origin of the writing and the addressees are unknown.
Why: To encourage Christians to renew their fervor and commitment when they were beginning to grow weary of the demands of faith

Structure and Content

1:1–4:13: God has definitively spoken in Jesus, who is superior to the prophets and Moses and even to angels, but who is fully human and faithful.

4:14–10:39: Jesus is our high priest, mediating our offering to God through his sacrifice. Jesus is our representative before God, offering hope to humanity. His sacrifice is one, not many, once and for all. The sermon focuses here on Jesus' identity and all that he has accomplished for those who follow him.

11–12: Exhortation to live by faith. The emphasis here is on living by faith. The author reviews the whole story of Scripture, focusing on "so great a cloud of witnesses" (12:1) from Adam's son Abel, through Abraham, David, Samuel, and many others who were "commended for their faith" yet still "did not receive what was promised" (11:39). The author urges believers to "run with perseverance the race that is set before us" while keeping their eyes on "Jesus the pioneer and perfecter of our faith" (12:1, s2).

13: The conclusion includes final instructions, a blessing, and greetings. The author exhorts us to mutual love, hospitality, and care for the poor and imprisoned. Believers are to avoid false teaching and continually offer praise to God.

Major Themes

- **Jesus is superior to all other beings** as the only begotten Son of God and perfect mediator between God and humans.
- **Jesus' sacrifice for humanity** is perfect and unique.
- **Our confidence in Jesus as mediator and high priest** motivates us to act more faithfully as God's people.

Authorship

Although almost no one still holds that Paul wrote Hebrews, there is no agreement about other suggested authors. Most scholars place the writing of Hebrews after the destruction of the temple in AD 70 and before the beginning of the second century.

Literary Form

Sermon: While Hebrews is sometimes referred to and categorized as a letter, it is actually a sermon, intended to encourage and strengthen Christians in their faith.

Key Passages

1:1-2: Previously God spoke to us through various prophets. We are now in the last days, and God has spoken to us definitively through the Son, through whom he created the world.

4:15-16: Jesus, our high priest, has taken on our humanity in every respect except sin. Because of Jesus, we are able to "approach the throne of grace with boldness" (4:16), knowing that we can find there mercy, grace, and help in our time of need.

13:2: An exhortation to practice hospitality, "for by doing that some have entertained angels without knowing it."

Food for Thought

Hebrews uses Scripture to support the contrast between the old and new covenants and the old and new priesthood. Hebrews implies that all the promises of the covenant since Abraham have been fulfilled in Jesus. Celebration of the Christian liturgy helped develop this Christology, sometimes called "high" Christology because it increasingly emphasized Jesus' divinity (in contrast to "low" Christology, which stressed his humanity). While the terminology can be problematic, it is meant to focus on the idea that over time, the Christian faith moved toward an understanding of Jesus as God, as God's Son, and as the fullness of God's Word in creating, recreating, and saving the world. Such ideas were not instantly accessible to Christians but became part of Christological teaching over a period of time. The continuous celebration of the liturgy with its reflection on the meaning of the sacraments, especially Baptism and the Eucharist, helped the church arrive at this understanding.

Hebrews is meant to stir Christians wavering in faith to more fervor and commitment. Reading it slowly will impress us with its beauty and truth. Hebrews explores the meaning of the Sacraments of Baptism and the Eucharist that we celebrate today, as the church has continually for over more than two thousand years.

Introduction to the Catholic Epistles

The catholic epistles are a group of seven letters ascribed to certain important early Christian leaders and named for them rather than for the communities to which they are addressed. Eusebius, writing in the early part of the fourth century AD, first referred to these seven writings as "catholic," meaning "general" or "universal"; this is usually the sense in which this category is understood. Although some of these letters, namely, 1 Peter, 2 John, and 3 John, are addressed to specific churches, perhaps the best meaning of "catholic" here is thus understood in reference to the canon of the New Testament, since the message of these letters has been understood from earliest times to apply to all the churches. The seven books that comprise this category are the Letters of James, 1 and 2 Peter, 1, 2, and 3 John, and Jude.

From their placement in the New Testament after Paul's letters, they have traditionally been understood as somehow responding to Pauline thinking, either by agreeing with him and reinforcing his theology, by cautioning believers about some of Paul's writings, or by directly confronting and even disagreeing with Paul. Nearly every aspect of these catholic epistles is debated by scholars: the genre (i.e., is one or another truly a letter, or is it a sermon with a letter format); their addressees (some are addressed to specific churches, and others are not); the identity of the actual writer; and the date of writing.

Useful Terms to Know

Antichrist: This term appears only in the letters of John (see 1 John 2:18, 22; 4:3; 2 John 1:7). The author wrote of the struggle between good and evil and related this struggle to the suffering of the community. The drama in the final times of the church was experienced in the opposition between the true Johannine Christians and the false teachers and false believers who had quit the community; these latter were referred to as "the antichrist" or "antichrists." They were opposed to God and to Christ. Believing in Jesus Christ means "abiding in" and remaining with the community, especially in hard and dangerous times (see 1 John 2:3-6).

Composite Scripture Quotation: In describing Christ, 1 Peter uses a combination of quotes from Isaiah 8:14 and 28:16; this is the same combination that appears in Paul's Letter to the Romans (Romans 9:33; cf. 11:11). The appearance of the same combination in two works suggests that there might have been "testimony books," that is, written or oral sources containing Scriptural quotes that could be used for catechetical (instructional) or apologetic (defensive) purposes. Rather than seeing an interdependence between Paul and 1 Peter, interpreters suggest that they could have used the common source of testimony books for such quotations.

Faith: Generally in the New Testament, this term means "trust." In Jude, faith already has the sense of the content of Christian belief or the authoritative teachings of the church community. This developed meaning is one of the reasons that most scholars give a late first century or early second century date for Jude.

Friends: A Johannine term for the disciples of Jesus, derived from Jesus' words the night before he died: "No one has greater love than this, to lay down one's life for one's friends. You are my friends if you do what I command you. I do not call you servants any longer, . . . but I have called you friends, because I have made known to you everything that I have heard from my Father" (John 15:13-15). In the spirit of this tradition from the beloved disciple, the Johannine letters address the community members as "children" (e.g. 1 John 2:1, 18; 3:18) and as "beloved" (e.g. 1 John 2:7; 4:1; 3 John 2).

Gnosticism: A heresy that was popular during the first few centuries of Christianity, Gnosticism focused on a kind of secret special knowledge that was required in order to be saved. It also downplayed Jesus' humanity and even denied his death on the cross.

Scriptural Prophecy: Not a prediction but an interpretation under the guidance of the Holy Spirit. 2 Peter 1:20-21 gives us an early description of the divine inspiration of Scripture.

Trinitarian Teaching: Jude 20-21 uses language that was foundational for the formulation of the doctrine of the Trinity. While today we are used to such ways of speaking about God, this is language probably much too sophisticated for a writer who was supposed to be a contemporary of Jesus. This language is one of the reasons that scholars ascribe a later date to Jude.

"Walk in the truth": This phrase from 3 John 1:3 means to act with integrity to the gospel. The false teachers that were threatening the community tended toward Gnosticism, stressing knowledge based on revelation rather than ethics or behavior. The author of 3 John insists that the "truth" involves acting according to Jesus' teaching.

JAMES

A rower in a boat has a unique perspective of time. For the most part, we probably think of the past as something that is behind us and the future as something that is in front of us. But a rower is looking at the past, and based on where she has already been (as well as other information, of course), she continues to navigate the waters. In a sense, the past is before her and the future behind. That perspective could apply to the Epistle of James, which puts before our eyes the experiences of our ancestors, such as Abraham, Rahab, and Elijah, and encourages us to identify with them. Based on past experience, both theirs and ours, we can be confident, despite the turbulence we feel in the present, that the same God who brought us this far will continue to be with us. The past is before us, showing us the way of trust. We can go into the future, not knowing its twists and turns, with confidence in God.

James urges us to pray for wisdom that will dispel out doubts and fear, showing that faith without action is useless. Trust in God will empower us to forget about ourselves and instead help and comfort others. We should draw near to God, be tolerant and at peace with one another, and patiently and eagerly await the coming of our Lord Jesus Christ.

Confusion about the author of James may stem from the fact that the New Testament identifies more than one follower of Jesus with that name. Two are listed among the apostles (see Matthew 10:2-3; Mark 3:17-18; Luke 6:14-15). One is called "the son of Alphaeus," about whom we know nothing further. The other is called one of the "sons of Zebedee," nicknamed "sons of thunder," who witnessed Jesus' Transfiguration and his agony in the Garden of Gethsemane. Around AD 44, Herod Agrippa had this "James, the brother of John, killed with the sword" (Acts 12:2).

Another person named James is referred to as a brother of Jesus by the Evangelist Mark (6:3) and "the Lord's brother" by Paul (Galatians 1:19). The designation "brother" is extended to relatives of Jesus and does not conflict with the Catholic teaching of the virginity of Mary. This James appears not to have been a follower of Jesus during his earthly ministry but became a follower after Jesus' death and resurrection and was the head of the church in Jerusalem (see Acts 15:12-21). The letter of James, although not actually written by this leader, who was a contemporary of Jesus, seems to have been inspired by the tradition linked to this James.

At a Glance

Who: Attributed to "James, a servant of God and of the Lord Jesus Christ" (1:1); it was probably written by a disciple of James, "the Lord's brother" (Galatians 1:19), who became the head of the church in Jerusalem.

What: Although it begins with elements of a letter format, James is more like a sermon. Addressed to "the twelve tribes in the Dispersion" (1:1), James was probably intended for believers loyal to the Law of Moses.

When: Written near the end of the first century, between AD 80 and 100.

Where: Written from some very important, predominantly Jewish-Christian church, perhaps Jerusalem or Antioch.

Why: To address problems of practice and belief that were developing in churches, such as partiality toward the rich, the neglect of "works" of faith, especially toward the needy, and disillusionment with the delay in Christ's return.

Structure and Content

1: After a short opening address, James extols the value of trials and temptation in proving virtue. James encourages the faithful to persevere.

2–3: In a diatribe echoing themes from traditional Jewish wisdom literature, James cautions against partiality toward the rich, faith without works, and speech without wisdom.

4–5: The letter ends with exhortations about right living and right behavior of the members of the Christian community, vigilance for the coming of Christ, and the power of prayer.

Major Themes

- **Faith must be expressed** in good works.

- **We must care for the poor, the needy, and the ill among us,** rather than the rich.

- **We must be vigilant** as we await the return of Christ.

Authorship

This letter is linked to the tradition of James, "the Lord's brother" (Galatians 1:19) and the leader of the church of Jerusalem, who represented the early church's concern for the preservation of Jewish laws and practices, especially social justice and its priority for the poor and suffering.

Literary Form

Sermon: This "letter" has only the rudiments of a letter format, such as a greeting that addresses a very general audience, but it lacks other properties of a letter. Rather, it is a diatribe against bad practices and beliefs that James saw developing in the church.

Key Passages

2:15-17: "Faith by itself, if it has no works, is dead" (2:17). The church has a responsibility to help the needy. Wishing a brother or sister well but not giving assistance for their needs is not enough.

5:14-15: As representatives of the church, elders should be called to pray over and anoint members who are ill.

Food for Thought

James has frequently been linked to Matthew's account of the Sermon on the Mount as part of the Christian concern for social justice as a required corollary to faith. Scholars point out the many parallels between Matthew and James, including their emphasis on mercy toward the poor and suffering (James 2:13; Matthew 5:7); the importance of peacemaking (James 3:18; Matthew 5:9); the benefits of trials (James 1:2; 5:10; Matthew 5:11-12): the necessity of action rather than mere lip service (James 1:22; Matthew 7:24); and other themes. Both James and Matthew were intent on preserving the important Jewish ideas of obedience as action that stems from faith and on performing deeds of loving kindness in celebration of the covenant. Because of this emphasis, James figured prominently in the discussions and conflicts of the Reformation, especially over the necessity of works accompanying faith.

James is light on Christology per se but accents the importance of living according to the gospel as people awaiting the coming of Christ. James demonstrates the link between faith and social justice, which seems especially relevant in today's world when the cries of the needy are sometimes muted by a jaded, individualistic society. James reminds us that the poor, the suffering, and the ill among us are an invitation to live the gospel, and he cautions against pride, which tempts us to think we are self-sufficient. James calls us to become a peaceful presence in a high-anxiety world, models of trust in God rather than in self, and nonjudgmental, compassionate caretakers of others rather than selfish consumers of our world's limited resources.

1 Peter

St. Francis is famously quoted as saying, "Preach the gospel at all times; use words if necessary." This could be a delightful and memorable paraphrase of the advice given to wives of pagan husbands in this first letter of Peter, which says that even if these husbands are not obedient to the gospel, they will be won over by the beauty of their wives' lives (3:1-2, 5). Once again we have the Scriptures urging us to live the gospel so that others can see in our conduct, our words, our choices, and our example the power of God working for the salvation of our world.

As a well-loved apostle of Jesus, chosen by him for many special revelations, including the Transfiguration and Jesus' prayer in the Garden of Gethsemane the night before he died, Peter held a special place of honor in the church. His eventual death in Rome as a martyr under Nero only added to the esteem that the whole church felt for this flawed but faithful apostle. It is therefore no surprise that written works would appear in Peter's name. A combination of moral encouragement and reminders about Christian instruction, 1 Peter appears to be addressed to believers in the five provinces of Asia Minor from Peter himself. But there are some questions about whether the Galilean fisherman who was Jesus' close companion actually penned this message to Christians of a predominantly Gentile background. The excellent Greek, for example, could hardly have been written by one who, like Peter, spoke Aramaic, a dialect of Hebrew; additionally, we have no reason to believe that Peter was literate. The use of the Septuagint translation of the Old Testament, the familiarity with many of Paul's ideas, and the warnings about keeping faith despite persecution all suggest that this letter was written well after Peter's martyrdom in the sixties. 1 Peter may have been composed as late as the nineties, when the Emperor Domitian led a brutal persecution of Christians, not unlike what Nero had done in the sixties.

At a Glance

Who: A disciple of Peter, writing in Peter's name.
What: A sermon on the effects of Baptism in the form of a letter addressed to communities in Asia Minor.
When: The nineties AD.

Where: From Rome to five communities in Asia Minor.

Why: To encourage faith and to remind believers about basic Christian instruction.

Structure and Content

1:1–2:10: The address identifies Peter as the sender and names five churches of Asia Minor. The author sums up the themes of this letter by saying that believers have been given "a new birth into a living hope through the resurrection of Jesus Christ" (1:3). Christ is described as the precious "cornerstone" of the church, but as a stumbling block to many, using Old Testament passages to support such claims.

2:11–4:11: Christian life in the midst of a hostile world. Believers are called to be an example for others and to be responsible citizens, even in the empire, as "aliens and exiles" (2:11). Even if they are slaves, they can identify with the sufferings of Christ. Rather than adorning themselves with outer accessories, Christian women married to pagan spouses are advised to convert them with the beauty of their lives. Believers live by a different standard than pagans do, formed by the sufferings of Christ and awaiting his return, knowing that "the end of all things is near" (4:7).

4:12–5:11: Encouragement for the persecuted. Suffering and persecution are trials that may tempt the faithful to abandon their beliefs. They must remain innocent and steadfast and "glorify God because [they] bear [God's] name" (4:16).

5:12-14: The writer concludes by joining greetings to the churches from "your sister church in Babylon" (5:13), a reference to the church at Rome, the presumed origin of this writing.

Major Themes

- **Believers are encouraged to persevere** and maintain their faith even in times of trial and suffering.

- **Believers are stewards of God's grace** and ought to act in a way that honors their faith, even in the face of persecution and hostility.

Authorship

This book was probably written in the eighties or nineties in Rome by a disciple of Peter who invoked his blessed memory.

Literary Form

Homily: 1 Peter is based on the model of the Pauline letters, but it is actually more of a baptismal homily on the meaning of belonging to the Christian community and on suffering for the faith.

Key Passages

1:3-5: Believers are given "a new birth into a living hope" through Jesus' resurrection (1:3). Believers are "protected by the power of God" (1:5).

3:15-16: Always be ready, regardless of circumstances, to give "an accounting for the hope that is in you . . . with gentleness and reverence."

4:8-11: Believers are called to be "good stewards of the manifold grace of God" (4:10) in all that they say and do.

5:6-11: The author exhorts the believers to "cast all your anxiety on [God], because he cares for you" (5:7).

Food for Thought

Works like 1 Peter depict the church showing signs of coming to terms with living in the world for an indefinite period of time. Believers were realizing that the *parousia* would be delayed, and they would have to live their faith in the midst of oppression, suffering, and uncertainty. 1 Peter acknowledges that structures in our world affect us and may oppress us, but they do not have to threaten or limit us. The author's advice to wives of pagan husbands is a good example. At a time when women were expected to follow the religion of their spouses, 1 Peter tells wives to convert their husbands with the beauty of their lives (see 3:1-2, 5). This advice would have actually undermined the absolute authority of the husband in favor of attracting him to the faith of his wife.

In a hostile world, it is not only possible but probable that faith will be challenged during times of suffering and that believers will have to choose to persevere. For the author, the various roles of subordination, such as women to men and slaves to masters, provide examples of redemptive suffering that can sabotage the status quo and change structures from within. Thus, for example, suffering without retaliation can change the oppressors (see 1 Peter 4:1-6). Such ideas can, of course, be abused. But 1 Peter is dealing with a church struggling in the hostile environment of the Roman Empire.

1 Peter reminds us that in all we do and say, we are giving "an accounting for the hope that is in [us]" (3:15), attempting to attract others to the gospel, and acting as a sign in the world of God's power and grace. What challenges to this fidelity do we face as Christians today? We may be free from persecution for our faith; have we considered how that makes us freer to live it? Or do we take faith and freedom for granted?

2 PETER

The many differences between 1 and 2 Peter indicate that they were written by two different authors. Like Paul, Peter was larger than life in the early church, especially after his death as a martyr. It makes sense, then, that in honoring the memory of Peter and Paul, others would write in their names, asserting their authority to confront false teaching and to encourage believers to stay on course with the teachings that came from them—which is exactly what the church needed around the time that 2 Peter was written.

However, for a long time there was resistance to including 2 Peter in the canon of the Scriptures, precisely because its authenticity as one of Peter's works was questionable. On the one hand, the author claims to be "Simeon Peter" in the very first verse. He also says this was the second letter he wrote (see 3:1). He further acknowledges that he was present at the Transfiguration (1:17-18), which the Gospels corroborate (see Matthew 17:1-9; Mark 9:2-8; Luke 9:28-36). On the other hand, the author appears to have written from the perspective of a later time in the history of the church, well after the first generation of Jesus' own disciples had died. He says that false teachers were denying the *parousia,* a charge that would hardly have surfaced while Peter was still alive. The author writes that he wants to confirm the teachings of "your apostles" (2 Peter 3:2), as if the apostles preceded him. And he refers to the writings of Paul as Scriptures (3:16), a characterization that would hardly have been accepted in Peter and Paul's own time. Lastly, 2 Peter incorporates much of the Letter of Jude, suggesting it was after Jude. The preponderance of the evidence thus indicates that 2 Peter was written well after 1 Peter, after Jude, and even after the nineties, when the church suffered persecution from Rome.

At a Glance

Who: A pseudonymous writer, using the name of Peter the apostle.
What: A farewell address (1:12-15) to the church.
When: Written around the beginning of the second century AD and, as such, one of the last writings of the Bible to be composed.
Where: Perhaps written to the church in Asia Minor but applicable to the universal church; it is unclear where the letter originated.

Why: To warn against false teachings, including Gnosticism, and to reaffirm the basics of Christian teaching, especially the *parousia,* the reliability of the teachings based on Jesus' ministry, and the mission of the apostles.

Structure and Content

1: The opening verses imitate a letter's address, as the author claims to be Peter, "a servant and apostle of Jesus Christ" (1:1). He writes to reinforce belief in the divine authority that is the basis of our call and to defend belief in the *parousia* despite its delay.

2: Denunciation of false teachers. This section offers encouragement to believers, who face challenges from insiders in the church in the form of false and dangerous teachings and from outsiders who mock their beliefs, especially about the *parousia,* which has not yet happened.

3: The author advises preparedness for the *parousia*. He refers to the letters of Paul, which many find "hard to understand" (3:16), and insinuates that they have the authority of Scripture. He offers final encouragement.

Major Themes

- **The *parousia* will come as promised,** despite its delay, and believers need to be prepared for Jesus' return.
- **Be on guard against false teachers;** instead, hold on to the teachings of the apostles.

Authorship

This letter was written by a pseudonymous writer in the very late first century or the first quarter of the second century AD. It was written in Peter's name, but not by Peter and not by the author of 1 Peter. One section seems to be an edited form of Jude, which suggests that it was written after Jude's composition around AD 80.

Literary Form

Farewell Address: Meant to evoke the memory and authority of Peter to combat false teachings, this book is only nominally a letter.

Key Passages

1:1: In the tradition started by Paul, the author is identified as "Simeon Peter, a servant and apostle of Jesus Christ" and is addressed to a general audience of all those who have received the faith.

3:3-4: False teachers, called "scoffers," are condemned as licentious when they challenge, "Where is the promise of his coming?" They are portrayed as denying God's just judgment.

3:15-16: The author warns that the letters of Paul contain things "hard to understand" (3:16), which some are inclined to twist and misinterpret.

Food for Thought

2 Peter, drawing on a number of themes also found in Jude, refers to former times of trial when God rescued the righteous, such as Lot, but punished the wicked, such as Sodom and Gomorrah (see 2:4-10). These biblical references may indicate the beginning of a sense of Christian interpretation of the Scriptures written with the authority of the apostles, represented by Jude and Peter. It is in Christ that God's judgment of the world will take place. This is both a warning for the wicked, such as the "scoffers," and vindication for the just who suffer just as Noah and Lot did.

2 Peter reminds us that Jesus will come at the *parousia* and will judge the world. Evil will be condemned and faithfulness rewarded. Some in the early church struggled with the temptation to give up faith in light of the delay of the *parousia*. False teachings of all sorts challenged believers who awaited Jesus' return but faced persecution and disappointment in the interim. Does suffering put a strain on my faith that God is constant in love and mercy and that my life counts in God's eyes?

1 John

Of the three letters that bear the name "John," 1 John is the most similar to the Gospel of John. In reading 1 John, we can picture a community that was very familiar with the Gospel of John, led by a pastor who used certain key ideas to remind his community to hold fast to the traditions found in that Gospel. Both the Gospel and 1 John focus on terms like "life," "light," "love," "commandment," and "abiding in God." 1 John is a rereading of the Gospel, applying its main ideas to the painful situation of a community divided, suffering from the rejection of members who have abandoned them. The schism was both doctrinal and ethical, that is, affecting belief as well as practice. The picture of a pastor reminding his suffering community about the fundamentals of the gospel may have helped form the image of 1 John as a letter, even though it has none of the characteristics that we have come to expect of a letter; there is no address, or greeting, no thanksgiving, and no conclusion.

At a Glance

Who: Attributed to the same tradition as the Gospel of John, stemming from "the beloved disciple" (cf. John 13:23; 19:26; 20:2, 21:7, 20), who was considered the founder of the community and thus provided the inspiration for this tradition.

What: A homiletic reminder of fundamentals for a community suffering schism, with implicit references to the Gospel of John.

When: Sometime after the writing of John's Gospel, around the turn of the first century AD.

Where: John's community is traditionally located in Ephesus.

Why: To comfort a community that was experiencing a schism, with some of the most influential and wealthy members leaving while knowing the needs of the community.

Structure and Content

1–2: After a short prologue, the author describes the way of light, that is, how to follow God who is light. Jesus foretold that divisions would arise;

they are a sign of the end-time when antichrists and false prophets will appear, tempting people to deviate from the path of truth.

3:1–5:12: God loved us in Christ, and so we must love one another. God abides with those who keep these truths. There are many false prophets, so spirits should be tested to make sure they are from God. Readers are instructed to reject the antichrists and believe in the Son. Those who believe that Jesus is the Christ are born of God, and God abides in them.

5:13-21: The epilogue encourages believers to have confidence that they may have eternal life.

Major Themes

- **Love one another;** this is how others will recognize the ones who belong to God and in whom God dwells.

- **Act as children of God,** who is light and life.

Authorship

This letter is linked to the Johannine community rooted in the tradition of the Gospel of John. This community came to be linked to "the beloved disciple" mentioned in the latter part of John's Gospel and traditionally linked also to John, the son of Zebedee and one of Jesus' closest companions.

Literary Form

Treatise: This is a homiletic rereading of the Gospel of John, applying its key ideas to the contemporary situation of the Johannine community, which was experiencing schism and confusion.

Key Passages

1:1-4: The author declares his purpose for writing: to remind the community of the truths of the gospel, "so that our joy may be complete" (1:4).

2:18-19: Believers are warned that this is the "last hour" (2:18), that is, when the antichrist—anyone opposed to the truth—will cause division. Apostates who are believers but who have left the church never truly belonged to the church.

Food for Thought

The community of John clearly felt betrayed by the departure of some with whom they had shared many things, including their deep belief that Jesus is the Son of God, the Word of life, the Christ. Yet 1 John urges the "little children" to continue to live and love as God has loved them. Christ, our advocate, has given us the commandment to love one another. This is the sign that God lives in us. How central is this commandment to my life, to all my thoughts and actions towards others?

2 John

Sometimes anger, frustration, and fear can cause us to overstate a position and take an "either-or" stance with no apparent room in between. Such an extreme reaction can at least have the advantage of clarifying our views. 2 John draws this kind of mutually exclusive division between believers and those who are disturbing them. But when we think of the stakes of a young church struggling against the false teachings of Gnosticism on the one hand and, on the other hand, the problem of becoming accepted by the greater church represented by the apostles, especially Peter and Paul, we can better understand John's urgency. He encouraged fragile community members to remain together, to resist false teachings, to avoid despair, and to keep the faith. He needed them to take his warnings seriously. The obstacles and dangers were grave.

The author of 2 John is probably the same as that of 1 John, and the author wrote this second work not long after the first, addressing the same believers and emphasizing the same dangers. The author of 2 John used the expression "new commandment" (5), which is vocabulary gleaned from the fourth Gospel and dominant in 1 John. Jesus spoke of the "new commandment" he modeled in his washing of the apostles' feet (see John 13:1-18, 34). This new commandment is both simple and very demanding. We are told to "love one another" (13:34) and to remain in the community that Jesus has founded (1 John 2:7-11; 4:7-21; 2 John 5-11).

At a Glance

Who: Written by "the elder" *(presbyteros)* (1), the same person who wrote 1 John, based on similarity of language and of issues (namely, that of false teaching).

What: A letter to the "elect lady and her children," the church (1).

When: Written sometime around the turn of the first century AD.

Where: Traditionally thought to have been written in Ephesus.

Why: To encourage members of the community to persevere in mutual love and in the truth, especially about Jesus as the Christ, and to warn about the antichrist.

Structure and Content

1-11: After the opening address, greeting, and thanksgiving, the elder issues a warning to avoid deceivers and to persevere in love of one another.

12-13: Final greetings and an expression of hope for an imminent visit.

Major Theme

- **Love one another;** remain in that love, and avoid deception.

Authorship

This letter is attributed to the author of 1 John, who was a member of the community rooted in the traditions of the "beloved disciple" of the fourth Gospel.

Literary Form

Letter: Using the traditional form, 2 John is a letter, in contrast to 1 John, which is more of a treatise than a letter.

Key Passages

1-2: The elder addresses the church as "the elect lady and her children" (1), claiming to know the truth because "the truth . . . abides in us and will be with us for ever."

7: The author warns that the many deceivers who deny "that Jesus Christ has come in the flesh" represent the antichrist.

Food for Thought

2 John reminds us that Christians must not only be baptized but must remain faithful members of the community. The historical Jesus, who came in the flesh, is God's son. All who deny his humanity are antichrists.

Remaining in the community as faithful believers and loving one another are the sum of the Christian life. This is easy to say but difficult to do. The deceivers tried to convince the members of John's community that they had received a revelation that made them superior to others. They believed that possessing that revelation assured them of salvation. John's emphasis on mutual love of the people nearest to us, the people of our same community, shows how constant and demanding the life of faith really is.

3 John

The early church depended upon at least two types of responses to Jesus' mandate to preach the gospel to "all nations" (Matthew 28:19). On the one hand, there needed to be missionaries like Paul and other apostles who fanned out into the world, taking with them "no gold, or silver, or copper . . . , no bag for your journey, or two tunics, or sandals, or a staff" (10:9, 10). On the other hand, these missionaries had to be received by some who would believe and then offer them hospitality and assist in sending them on the next stage of their mission. The radical lifestyle of these missionaries demanded resident sympathizers who would supply them with food and shelter and the daily bread that would sustain them on their way.

3 John tells us about some of these people who offered hospitality to traveling missionaries. For example, Gaius, to whom 3 John is addressed, is commended for his generosity and courage. In contrast, there were others who were less than generous in their hospitality. 3 John introduces us to Diotrephes, the arrogant leader who not only refused hospitality to traveling preachers but tried to keep others from offering it as well. Diotrephes would not acknowledge the authority of the elder who wrote this letter. Acts also tells us about the expansion of the church under the guidance of the Holy Spirit, which called for extreme generosity from both missionaries and local supporters. There were people like Lydia who were anxious to put before Paul all the resources of their houses and business networks (16:11-15, 40). But surely sometimes there were bumps in the road, as in the case of Ananias and Sapphira, who would rather have kept a little for themselves than pledge all of their wealth to the service of the church (5:1-11).

At a Glance

Who: Like 2 John, 3 John was written by "the elder" (*presbyteros)* (1), probably someone from the same community as the author of 1 and 2 John and the fourth Gospel.

What: A letter of complaint about an inhospitable, disruptive fellow Christian called Diotrephes, whose behavior contrasts starkly with that of the addressee, Gaius.

When: Written around AD 100.

Where: Although there is no indication in the letter, the origin may be Ephesus, which may have been the origin of 1 and 2 John as well.
Why: To exhort Gaius to remain faithful and welcome strangers and new members into the community and to warn him about Diotrephes.

Structure and Content

1-12: An address and thanksgiving are followed by complaints about Diotrephes, a commendation for Gaius, and a recommendation for Demetrius, the ambassador of the elder-author.

13-15: Final greetings include the hope of a future visit.

Major Theme

- **The importance of showing hospitality** is stressed, as well as acting according to the truth.

Authorship

This author was probably not the same person as the Evangelist, but he was an authority writing from the same community.

Literary Form

Letter: This letter was written to contrast the behaviors of recognized leaders (Gaius and Demetrius versus Diotrephes) in the church.

Key Passages

1: Address of the elder to the "beloved Gaius."

5-8: The author commends Gaius for his hospitality, saying that all those working to spread the gospel are "co-workers with the truth" (8).

11: An exhortation to the "beloved" to "not imitate what is evil but imitate what is good. Whoever does good is from God; whoever does evil has not seen God."

Food for Thought

Because of its emphasis on knowing the truth, the community of "the beloved disciple" was suspected of Gnosticism, a heresy in the first few centuries of the church. The community seemed to have learned that the demands of following Jesus included "walking," or acting, in the truth, and not just knowing the truth. This letter shows that the balance between contemplation and action has been part of Christian life since the beginning, as it stresses the demands of hospitality for the missionaries in particular. The demands of Christian hospitality are perhaps greater now than ever before. We could use these demands in our world as a basis for a personal and communal examination of conscience. Are we practicing Christian hospitality, in the fullest sense of the term.

Jude

The Gospel of Matthew tells us that the disciples came to Jesus and asked, "Who is the greatest in the kingdom of heaven?" (18:1). In response, Jesus placed a small child in the middle of the circle of his followers and said, "Whoever becomes humble like this child is the greatest in the kingdom of heaven" (18:4). He then went on to add that "it would be better for you if a great millstone were fastened around your neck and you were drowned in the depth of the sea" than that anyone cause scandal to "one of these little ones who believe in me" (18:6). Jude might have been thinking along the same lines when he deplored the damage that "certain intruders" (4) were doing to the community he addressed. They sought personal gain while they flattered some and slandered others. They were following the example of false leaders such as Cain, Balaam, and Korah who, in word and deed, led people astray (11). They defiled the flesh, rejected authority, blasphemed, and slandered the saints (16). Jude's strong language and stark comparisons are meant to drive home the importance of good leadership, good example, and pastoral care worthy of the gospel.

Those who read Jude sometimes evaluate this work as negative and without much inspiration. Perhaps Jude's complaints about ungodly "intruders" who were disturbing the community appear to be too general to be useful. But Jude's advice is really very simple: keep the faith, regardless of the temptations and trials that come one's way. There is nothing more important or more valuable than faithful service to Jesus Christ.

At a Glance

Who: The author purported to be Jude, the "brother of James" (1), but the letter was probably written by someone else under that pseudonym.

What: A diatribe against false teachers, using only the rudiments of a letter: a greeting that includes the identity of the ascribed writer and is addressed to "those who are called" (1), a traditional way of speaking about believers, and a concluding doxology in the tradition of Paul.

When: Sometime around the turn of the first century AD.

Where: Probably written from Palestine, reflecting concerns about orthodoxy and orthopraxy.

Why: To warn against those who had infiltrated the community and were undermining the basis of faith.

Structure and Content

1-2: Opening formula. Using the letter format in the tradition of Paul, Jude opens by identifying himself and his addressees, concluding with a blessing. He professes to be a faithful disciple of Jesus and also an authoritative figure in the early church of Palestine as the brother of James, the leader of the church in Jerusalem.

3-16: The author exhorts the believers to keep the faith, preserving it against all "intruders" (4); this includes a warning against disobedience and a description of the ways in which the intruders undermine community, with examples from the Scriptures and other literature.

17-23: The author then reminds the community of their ethical teaching based on tradition passed on from the apostles. The threefold remedy for all the bad influences of the intruders involves an appeal to the Trinity. Finally, Jude offers pastoral advice along with his reiterated appeal to preserve the faith.

24-25: The letter concludes with a doxology.

Major Themes

- **"Keep the faith" is Jude's key thesis;** it seems to refer to a body of doctrine rather than simply a commitment to Jesus Christ.

- **This faith is to be preserved** against all manner of external threats.

Authorship

There are several men named Jude or Judas in the New Testament. Luke lists "Judas son of James" as one of the apostles chosen by Jesus (6:16; Acts 1:13). But a few scholars takes Jude's self-identification literally and ascribe this letter to a contemporary of Jesus.

Literary Form

Letter: Jude contains the rudiments of a letter, including an introduction and closing in Paul's style, but Jude is actually more of a warning against certain dangers to the community coming from those who purported to be members but who undermined the faith through their bad example, grumbling, and criticism, slandering some while flattering others for personal gain.

Key Passages

20-21: Believers are urged to nurture faith by praying "in the Holy Spirit," preserving themselves in the love of God, and looking "forward to the mercy of our Lord Jesus Christ that leads to eternal life."

Food for Thought

Jude warns us about all sorts of distractions that can prevent us from preserving the faith entrusted to us. Greater dangers to Christian life may come from apathy and a lack of vigilance rather than from major crises or outright persecution. Jude warns about the danger of those who participate in Eucharistic gatherings but fail to understand the spiritual meaning of the Eucharist as participation in one body (see verse 12). These "intruders" use every occasion for self-promotion and aggrandizement. Jude uses strong language and strong threats about judgment and fire to convey the truth that disciples must preserve purity of heart, integrity in action, and simplicity and honesty in speech. How is my heart in this regard?

Revelation

Sometimes it seems like we are scaring ourselves to death. Technology has made it easy to access an endless amount of information, and at times we are tempted to think that the news is all bad. The Book of Revelation has too often been used as one more harbinger of frightening catastrophes, but it was not intended to scare people—just the opposite. The symbolic, cryptic language was meant to speak a message of comfort and encouragement to the hearts of the faithful. It is crisis literature, but it is meant to bring reassurance in the midst of oppression, persecution, and fear. Written in the waning years of the first century AD, Revelation was not supposed to be taken literally with specific or convoluted warnings about political events in our contemporary world. Rather, it was written to support the faithful who were suffering on many fronts, from external oppression to internal division caused by apostasy and fear. Revelation was meant to interpret the present, which was a time of suffering, rather than to predict precise or specific events of the future.

Like poets and songwriters, the author of Revelation uses a variety of symbols to communicate his message: to admonish believers to hold fast to Christ, to give witness to others who are suffering, and to persevere, because evil will perish and the faithful will live forever in peace. The use of symbols such as numbers, colors, and precious metals provides excellent evidence that Revelation is not meant to be taken literally; its meaning is embedded in this powerful symbolism. For instance, the number 666, assigned to the second "beast" (see 13:11-18), probably originally stood for Nero, who died about thirty years before the writing of Revelation. Perhaps the author was alluding to the Emperor Domitian, who was persecuting Christians at the time Revelation was written, or maybe he meant the Roman Empire or evil in general. Whatever the case may be, the number 666 certainly was not intended to be applied to specific people or events in the distant future. Colors are also symbolic in Revelation. For example, red (for blood) refers to the suffering of the Lamb or of the martyrs. Similarly, precious gems have symbolic connotation: heaven's gates are made with pearls (see 21:21), a symbol of its priceless treasure.

Revelation concludes with imagery of water and the tree of life (see 22:1-5), images taken from Genesis, which represent the promise of eternal life and bring the story of salvation full circle, to completion. Revelation affirms that the promise of Genesis is fulfilled in Christ.

At a Glance

Who: The author identified himself as "John" (1:1, 4, 9; 22:8). He was banished to the penal colony on the island of Patmos because of his faith. Based on theological and linguistic similarities with the author of the fourth Gospel, it is probable that the author of Revelation was a disciple of the Evangelist.
What: An encouragement to Christians suffering persecution, written in apocalyptic, symbolic style and language.
When: In the nineties AD.
Where: Written in Greece to Christians suffering persecution under the Roman Emperor Domitian.
Why: To encourage other Christians, to warn the churches, and to promise ultimate divine retribution for those oppressing the faith.

Structure and Content

1:1-8: John begins with an introduction consisting of a prologue and an address to "the seven churches that are in Asia" (1:4).

1:9–11:19: John presents the first cycle of visions, including a vision of the "Son of Man" (1:13-20). He then addresses each of the seven churches, encouraging them and exhorting them in turns (2:1–3:22). He witnesses heavenly worship and sees "the Lion of the tribe of Judah, the Root of David" (5:5), who alone is able to open the scroll of the seven seals. He hears the seven trumpets, heralding great destruction and woes (8:6–11:19).

12–16: This section describes the second cycle of visions. First, "a woman clothed with the sun" (12:1) gives birth to "a male child, who is to rule all the nations with a rod of iron" (12:5). John then describes two beasts, the first of which is a hideous amalgamation of various animals and the second of which has the number 666 assigned to it (13:1-18). Finally, he describes the "Lamb, standing on Mount Zion" (14:1), surrounded by the 144,000 redeemed believers.

17–18: Babylon is depicted as a woman who is "drunk with the blood of the saints and the blood of the witnesses to Jesus" (17:6). The fall of Babylon is heralded by an angel with "great authority" (18:1).

19:1–22:7: This section begins with a hymn celebrating God's victory; then John describes Christ's victory and his visions of the last things, including the thousand-year period between the chaining of Satan and the end of this world (20:1-10). John declares that final judgment is approaching, which is death to evil and life in the New Jerusalem for the community of the just.

22:8-21: The epilogue is a collection of prophetic oracles stressing the end of suffering and the promise of reward for faithfulness. The just are those who live expecting Christ's return.

Major Themes

- **God is victorious over evil, and soon evil will be eliminated once and for all.** Evil is depicted as a beast (chapter 13), menacing people of faith. He is the form of Satan, along with the dragon (12:3-9) and the "whore of Babylon" (17:1-6). Evil in all its forms will be conquered at the final judgment.

- **The faithful are called to witness to the Lamb** whose sacrifice has won salvation for all; those who remain faithful will be vindicated. The just are thus covered in white, in the pure baptismal robe that indicates their faithfulness (7:9-14).

- **Numbers, colors, precious metals, and references to transcendent "super-humans" as well as Scripture pervade Revelation.** For instance, the "woman clothed with the sun" (12:1) is a vehicle of salvation: the child born of a woman is the Messiah. Even before he is born, he will be threatened by the dragon, representing Satan (12:1-6).

Authorship

This book was written by John, an exile in Patmos, an area traditionally linked to the Evangelist of the same name and to the "beloved disciple" of his Gospel. The author, writing in the nineties AD, was probably a second- or third-generation disciple of the Evangelist.

Literary Form

Apocalyptic Literature: Revelation follows a long tradition of using symbols to create a mysterious world understood by insiders (that is, the oppressed faithful), but whose meaning remains mysterious to outsiders.

Key Passages

1:4, 8: John writes to the seven churches of Asia, speaking as a prophet and a seer of the revelation of God, "the Alpha and the Omega," the One "who is and who was and who is to come, the Almighty" (1:8).

12:1-6: A great sign appeared in heaven of "a woman clothed with the sun, with the moon under her feet, and on her head a crown of twelve stars" (12:1).

13:18: The author speaks directly to believers in a code that calls for the wisdom of insiders: "Let anyone with understanding calculate the number of the beast, for it is the number of a person. Its number is six hundred and sixty-six."

21:9-21: John gives a beautiful depiction of the new Jerusalem, heaven; it is filled with precious metals and jewels, symbolic of its priceless treasure: "And the twelve gates are twelve pearls, each of the gates is a single pearl, and the street of the city is pure gold, transparent as glass" (21:21).

Food for Thought

Revelation asserts that all history is fulfilled with the victory of Christ; we are in the last stages of the struggle between evil and good. Evil will be eliminated and good will be rewarded when finally all has taken place, and

God has re-created the world. Under the influence of Christian liturgy, the Christology of Revelation asserts the universal power and invincibility of Christ and his faithful followers.

Revelation is an acknowledgment of the ongoing struggle in this world between good and evil for the hearts and minds of humans. The victory of God through Christ is sure, but we are in the in-between time when it often seems as if the powers of evil are greater than the Lamb and his followers. Our call is to be hopeful, to be faithful, and to bear witness to Jesus regardless of the dangers and afflictions that threaten us.

This book was published by The Word Among Us. Since 1981, The Word Among Us has been answering the call of the Second Vatican Council to help Catholic laypeople encounter Christ in the Scriptures.

The name of our company comes from the prologue to the Gospel of John and reflects the vision and purpose of all of our publications: to be an instrument of the Spirit, whose desire is to manifest Jesus' presence in and to the children of God. In this way, we hope to contribute to the Church's ongoing mission of proclaiming the gospel to the world so that all people will know the love and mercy of our Lord and grow ever more deeply in love with him.

Our monthly devotional magazine, *The Word Among Us*, features meditations on the daily and Sunday Mass readings, and currently reaches more than one million Catholics in North America and another half million Catholics in one hundred countries around the world. Our book division, The Word Among Us Press, publishes numerous books, Bible studies, and pamphlets that help Catholics grow in their faith.

To learn more about who we are and what we publish, log on to our website at www.wau.org. There you will find a variety of Catholic resources that will help you grow in your faith.

Embrace His Word, Listen to God . . .

www.wau.org